# POETS
## IN PERSON

To My Mother

# POETS IN PERSON

## A Listener's Guide

Joseph Parisi

Modern Poetry Association
American Library Association
Chicago   1992

ISBN 0–8389–7575–5
© 1992 by Joseph Parisi
Copyrights and Acknowledgements begin on page 276

"Poets in Person: Reading, Hearing, and Talking About Contemporary Poetry in America's Libraries" has been funded by a grant from National Endowment for the Humanities and is jointly sponsored by the Modern Poetry Association and the American Library Association.

# CONTENTS

# PREFACE

More poetry is being published today and more people are attending poetry readings than in all of U.S. history. In libraries and community centers, on campuses and in coffeehouses, an ever-growing audience is discovering the pleasures of poetry— listening to visiting authors and local practitioners, taking writing workshops, discussing and sharing what they've heard and enjoyed. Still, for many, poetry remains mysterious, something neglected or misunderstood in school and now seemingly out of reach. But confronted with the sheer volume and variety of poetry being produced throughout the country, even the most devoted aficionado must at times feel overwhelmed and confused.

In planning the "Poets in Person" programs, we wanted to help dispel the mystery and untangle the confusion by outlining the primary sources and several strands of contemporary poetry. Within a practical framework, we wished to trace its complex history since World War II through the lives and works of the writers who have shaped it. The most effective way to do so, we believed, was through the voices of those poets themselves.

Thus, from an initial long list, we selected thirteen writers who have been instrumental in launching major movements and represent principal trends in the art today. Allen Ginsberg, Adrienne Rich, W. S. Merwin, John Ashbery, and other authors of their generation who appear on "Poets in Person" were "present at the creation," setting the several new styles, recasting traditions, and even redefining the meaning of poetry in America since the Fifties. In the lives and significant work of the other generations, we sought to examine influences and further innovations that show the vitality and continuing evolution of American poetry to the present. Through the careers of all thirteen authors, we also wanted to indicate how the dramatic social and cultural changes in the U.S. over the last decades have affected the practice of poetry, and how the individuality of these writers reflects the remarkable diversity of the country itself. Finally, we hoped that through their first-person accounts the poets would give unique insights into the creative process itself.

When we first approached the authors with the idea of a

new audio series featuring contemporary poets reading their poems and discussing their work—why they write as they do, the making and the meaning of key texts; how they came to be poets and how their careers have developed—their responses were enthusiastic. In accepting our invitation to appear in the series, A. R. Ammons wrote that the audio format was particularly attractive to him, because "the medium of sound provides the most vivid way to participate in the imaginations and feelings of poetry." In discussing the series with literary critics and broadcasters, we received warm support. They agreed that there was a need for a clear, concise survey, and that the intimacy of audio made it the ideal medium for presenting poetry. Following extensive discussions, we offered a detailed proposal to the Media Division of the National Endowment for the Humanities, which awarded a planning grant. With additional aid from the Prince Charitable Trusts, preparations were finished, and the Endowment offered its support for the several aspects of the project.

"Poets in Person" was produced over a three-year period. In the planning phase, several literary scholars and critics—most of them poets themselves—consulted on topics, questions, and poems to be included on specific programs. With the series host, they later served as interviewers during three-hour recording sessions with individual poets. The readings and interviews were taped in New York City, San Francisco, Chicago, and Ithaca, New York, over an eighteen-month period; transcribing, scripting, editing, and studio production on the final half-hour programs proceeded simultaneously. The series was completed in June and "Poets in Person" was first aired over National Public Radio member stations in the summer of 1991. The programs have since been rebroadcast around the country.

Within their compact timeframes, the programs clearly indicate the major aspects of the lives, techniques, and literary affinities of the authors. In their interviews, the poets speak candidly about their families, friendships, training, and artistic goals—and with a minimum of technical jargon. As expected, each is articulate in explaining the origins, meanings, and methods of his or her work. Several take the opportunity to clear up old misconceptions and misinterpretations. With vivid details and telling anecdotes, all of the authors in the series reveal themselves as warm and engaging personalities, experienced in life, unpretentious, and unpredictable.

Each program presents on average five complete poems (several programs contain more), with generous excerpts from longer works. For several poets of the "older generation," this is particularly important, as the selections trace the development in their styles over long careers. Most of the poets in the series make frequent public appearances, and it is apparent that for them poetry readings are not merely recitations: in their intonations, emphases, and phrasing, they *interpret* their words, guiding listeners toward understanding. Equally important, in the process of oral interpretation, they reveal that poetry, as practiced today, has a human face, as well as several voices, voices that speak to contemporary concerns and convey ideas with immediate relevance in our lives.

On "Poets in Person" they speak directly to our perennial concerns and the central issues that confront us today—the relations between women and men, parents and children; the possibilities of love and the inevitability of loss; nature and the environment; the effects, good and bad, of modern science and technology in a complex society; the challenges to faith and the struggle for meaning in the modern world; the aspirations, disappointments, and joys that make up the human condition. In their poems, they consider these subjects with insight, deep emotion, frequent humor, and the gift of memorable language.

While each of the programs can stand independently as a concise and lively introduction to the individual artist and his or her work, heard in its entirety the "Poets in Person" series presents a compact overview of the principal poetic movements, critical theories, and varieties of writing styles in the United States since World War II. With their interviewers, the thirteen writers reveal historical contexts and a wide range of influences. They relate contemporary poetry to literary traditions and genres, a variety of aesthetic viewpoints, philosophical trends, foreign literatures, and aspects of related art forms (especially painting), as well as modern science and technology, popular culture, and their individual regional and ethnic heritages. In their personal accounts, the poets also chronicle the social and political changes in the American landscape since World War II. Following the arcs of their careers, we can observe how these fundamental cultural transformations have altered not only the composition of poetry but also the very conception of the art.

On his program, W. S. Merwin remarks, "I really think that a poem begins with listening and ends with *hearing* something." On "Poets in Person," all the authors, established and younger talents alike, invite listeners to *hear*, to discover, and "to participate in the imaginations and feelings of poetry." In the course of the series, as they demonstrate its several varieties in America today, they prove that contemporary poetry is not only comprehensible but compelling.

For review and as a resource for reading and discussion groups, this guide prints all the selections read on "Poets in Person," including the complete texts or sections of longer poems which are excerpted on the tapes because of time constraints. As companions to the programs, the essays provide biographical and bibliographical details, with brief commentary; included is information from the full interviews, as well as occasional commentary from several sources. These sketches indicate each writer's primary influences or relations to other artists and to literary traditions, with attention to the characteristic subjects and technical or stylistic elements that distinguish each poet. The Introduction offers a brief summary of the critical and historical contexts for the diverse poetries that arose after World War II.

In outlining the course of each author's life and publishing career, this guide focuses on several of the works on the programs (as well as other significant poems) and tries to complement the tapes by highlighting each writer's distinctive contributions to the development of American poetry. After hearing the programs and reading and discussing the poems, listeners will probably want to explore further. The bibliographies list collected works and individual poetry volumes by the authors, as well as their prose books and selected biographies and critical studies about them. General histories and other reference works on American poetry are included; the audiography provides information on other readings by the poets available on cassette.

In its several phases, from planning and production to distribution, many people contributed to the realization of the "Poets in Person" audio project. We extend our thanks first to the poets, who arranged busy schedules to take part in the series and maintained their good humor through the hours at the microphone (even when conditions sometimes proved less than ideal), and who allowed us to present their poems on tape and in this book. With sensitivity and insight, the consulting scholars offered expert knowledge on program content, conducted the interviews, and reviewed drafts of the scripts, which attempted to distill their lively discussions with the poets. It is difficult to thank any of them properly for their critical commentary and care in the making of the series and this book, but special acknowledgement is due to J. D. McClatchy. As principal consultant to "Poets in Person," he offered his wise counsel at every stage of its development; with characteristic generosity he read virtually all the materials, from proposals and scripts to several essays in this guide, and was available whenever he was called upon for advice, which was often. Elizabeth Carlson, with Jim Rutke, performed the laborious task of transcribing the interviews. She then advised the writer-producer through the several drafts for each script, and her good judgment and long experience in audio production helped make a shapeliness of what first seemed an impossibly unwieldy *embarras de richesses*. Roger Bourland not only agreed to write the theme for the series, but after hearing the first rough-edited segments went on to compose additional incidental music for every program, over seventy original pieces in all. Paul Grigonis displayed admirable professionalism during the long months of meticulous studio production, and schooled a neophyte radio producer in the finer points of the audio engineer's craft, and art.

When we presented the idea of a radio series on living American poets to the Endowment, we received cautious encouragement, followed by valuable suggestions for developing the programs, and then initial support for in-depth planning. We are grateful to Grace Cavalieri and to Candace Katz of the NEH for all their assistance during the preliminary stages of the project. The Prince Charitable Trusts offered additional aid to complete the preparations, as well as the advice and continuing cordial interest of Program Officer Jill Darrow. The Media Division of the NEH then provided major funding to support the actual production of the programs and related print materials. When we approached National Public Radio in late 1990 about broadcasting "Poets in Person," Cultural Programming Director Murray Horwitz and Senior Producer Andy Trudeau immediately accepted the series, after hearing only the few programs completed at that time. Their faith in the project was greatly appreciated and did much to hearten us during the final, often trying phases of production.

Besides publishing *Poetry* Magazine, the Modern Poetry Association has sponsored several educational programs. The American Library Association is well known for its creativity in presenting public programming in the humanities, particularly through its national "Let's Talk About It" and "Voices & Visions" projects. Together we approached the NEH's Division of Public Programs for assistance in developing a cooperative project that would make the "Poets in Person" series available for use in reading-and-discussion programs in public libraries throughout the country. The MPA's proposal was accepted, and work began on the several aspects of the pilot project. With ALA Public Programming, we prepared a number of supplementary written materials, including the "Poets in Person" *Programmer's Guide for Libraries.* With NEH support, we also organized a training seminar for the twenty teams of public librarians, humanities scholars, and state representatives selected from around the nation for the first demonstration programs. The workshops were held in the fall of 1991, launching "Poets in Person: Reading, Hearing, and Talking About Contemporary Poetry in America's Libraries." It was a great pleasure working with the ALA and such skilled, enthusiastic colleagues as Deb Robertson, Sally Mason, Peggy Barber, and Asa App. Alice Fulton, as consulting scholar, and Marilyn Boria, as consulting public librarian, also contributed much to the planning and success of the seminar workshops.

Thomas C. Phelps, Senior Program Officer in the NEH Division of Public Programs, was an invaluable counselor to the "Poets in Person" library project: our sincere thanks to him and to the National Endowment for the Humanities, whose generous support made the audio series and the library project possible. To Patrick Shaw, President, and to all the Board members of the Modern Poetry Association, we are most grateful for warm support and helpful advice from the earliest planning stages of the two "Poets in Person" projects.

However inadequately, I should like to express my gratitude to my colleagues at *Poetry*: to the associate editor, Stephen Young, who assumed extra burdens during the long period the project was underway; and to the managing editor, Helen Lothrop Klaviter, who as Assistant Project Director made everything move smoothly. Her efforts—in helping draft proposals, preparing budgets and reports, arranging complicated schedules and travel arrangements, acting as liaison with poets, scholars, program officers, printers, publishers, librarians, and the many others involved in the programs—were tireless, and she remained ever cheerful, despite the pressures of the additional responsibilities she took on at the Magazine to relieve the editor and producer.

J. P.

# INTRODUCTION

In the late Forties and early Fifties, Allen Ginsberg and his friends sensed the start of "a whole new age" in American poetry, he recalls on "Poets in Person." For these members of the postwar generation, revival of the art meant "looking for a fresh source of inspiration in our own persons, in our own minds, in the spontaneous awareness that we already generated among each other." But this renaissance brought renewal and found inspiration by looking backward, as well: to the Teens and Twenties and the experimental methods of the Modernists— Ezra Pound, T. S. Eliot, and William Carlos Williams especially —and earlier still, to the example of Walt Whitman in the 19th Century. In the author of "Song of Myself" they found a model of democratic idealism, inclusiveness, and openness in subject matter and style. Whitman's principles were reinforced more immediately by Williams, who encouraged many young writers personally and provided appealing examples of poems that were rooted in the particular, local details of American life and were written using our colloquial speech. As Karl Shapiro says on his program, Williams "really made a difference in the possibility of younger poets writing at ease in the American language."

Following "Whitman's suggestions for candor, spontaneity, frankness," as Ginsberg says, was not welcomed in the American Academy when he, Adrienne Rich, Maxine Kumin, and their peers were being educated and started publishing. At mid-century Whitman was acknowledged in the university but still largely neglected, while most writing about contemporary American life was simply ignored. Williams himself, although an important and prolific member of the early Modernist group, was largely disregarded by English departments, who much preferred T. S. Eliot's poetry and criticism, particularly his theory of impersonality in art. By the late Twenties Eliot had established himself as literary arbiter in London; but by then the former radical innovator had become far more conservative, praising Tradition, objectivity, intricate verse structures, and the complex wit and irony of Dryden, Donne, and other 17th-century masters. Eliot's tastes and demanding criteria, as codified in the classroom by the New Criticism, exerted strong influence for decades.

"It was a question of non-political tone, a non-rebellious tone . . . privacy," Ginsberg says of the attitude in "academic" verse, and the instruction of poetry, when he was in the university. The conservative social and political climate after the World War II and through the "tranquilized Fifties" (as Robert Lowell called them) was not receptive to frankness, either. During this "uncandid period," Ginsberg remarks, "there was a kind of homogenization of opinion and a stultification of thought, and a closeting of emotion . . . and total censorship of literature." Given their unorthodox ideas and unconventional behavior, "for trying to write about [their] own lives" Ginsberg, the Beats, and their kindred spirits would have been "drummed out of the Academy."

Rejection of "academic" poetry and New Critical standards, emphasis on candor and the self, and focus on the actualities of contemporary life and language became touchstones for the radical changes in American poetry during the Fifties and after. Today, of course, not only the works of Ginsberg and other once-suspect authors, but all varieties of poetry have been admitted to the Academy. And now, since nearly all serious poets take university writing courses, hold M.F.A. degrees in poetry, or teach in writing programs, the term "academic" hasn't much meaning, certainly not the pejorative sense it once carried. The sophisticated poetry fostered by the New Criticism —allusive, ironic, oblique; marked by intellectual content and patterns of imagery shaped in formal structures of high finish— did fall out of favor during the Sixties and Seventies, but it never vanished. Besides James Merrill, Maxine Kumin, Karl Shapiro, and others featured on "Poets in Person," the list of contemporary poets who began as formalists and have continued to work within the tradition—and to reinvigorate it with their original variations—is very long, and includes Richard Wilbur, Mona Van Duyn, Anthony Hecht, Richard Howard, and John Hollander, to mention only the most prominent. Ginsberg himself began composing in stanzas and rhyme and in recent years has on occasion returned to writing in forms, while many young poets now call themselves formalists without embarrassment. Adrienne Rich, W. S. Merwin, and many others of their generation also wrote in the expected academic modes before they changed styles (often several times) in later the years.

At present, the spectrum of American poetry is very wide, representing the pluralism of our society. Amid this abundance and absent a single "authority" (the kind of arbiters Eliot and the Academy once supplied), it is difficult for any one type of verse to predominate. The range of styles in America poetry today, the several transformations in the art since the Fifties, and the factors influencing those changes—social, political, psychological, philosophical—are highlighted as the "Poets in Person" authors tell their personal histories.

For the young postwar poets, the New Criticism was a central force—whether they accepted its standards or rebelled against them—as they started to develop their individual talents. A decade before "Howl" and the well-publicized anti-establishment activities of the Beats, the older Karl Shapiro (he was 30) initiated opposition to Eliot and the restrictions of the Academy. While serving in the war, he wrote his *Essay on Rime*, which attacked the New Criticism for its over-rationalizing of poetry. Later he castigated Eliot and Pound for returning poetry "to the stacks" in their "museum-like poems," as he says on his program. In several essays he blamed them for "removing the arts from people and returning them to the classroom" and for cutting off their own work from life through "a cult of Intelligence" which likewise "eradicated as best it could any influence by D. H. Lawrence, William Carlos Williams, Blake, Walt Whitman, and all other 'Romantics' and humanists."

But Shapiro, Ginsberg, and the successful poets of their generations were also well-acquainted with library stacks (nearly all attended prestigious schools) and became generally well read, not only in the academic canon, but in "unauthorized" literature, as well. As most of the poets indicate on their programs, both sanctioned and "outside" readings shaped their development. In part, the new generation's rebellion was a revolution in the primary sense of the word; returning to the original innovators, they renewed the "Romantic" tradition of Whitman and revived the early experimental methods of the Modernists, as their listing of influential forbears indicates.

In his *Autobiography*, Williams wrote that after its publication, in 1922, Eliot's *The Waste Land* had "wiped out our world as if an atom-bomb had been dropped on it." He complained that, following his aesthetic rival's great success, "My contemporaries flocked to Eliot." But after the World War II (and the actual dropping of the bomb), aspiring writers flocked to Williams, many coming literally to his door. And other indigenous Modernists, so long overshadowed by the expatriate Eliot, came to the fore and received increasing critical praise. Most were fortunate to live long enough to accept major prizes, and to evolve their styles, as they continued to be highly productive over their long careers. Not only did poets of widely different tastes "rediscover" and imitate Williams, but many came to appreciate the singular accomplishments of the "other Modernists," as well, Wallace Stevens's in *Harmonium* and Hart Crane's in *The Bridge* particularly. Always a difficult character both as a poet and a person, Ezra Pound remained problematical for critics, and acceptance of his later work was further complicated by political controversy (as Shapiro's comments indicate). However, Pound's poetry and opinions, particularly his imagistic technique and Do's and Don'ts on composition, were and remain pervasive influences on poets of every description. (On his program, Charles Wright acknowledges his debt to the *Pisan Cantos* particularly.) It was often the early work of the Modernists, with its reforming attitude and inventive methods, that especially attracted poets who were coming of age in the postwar era. Dissatisfied with the status quo, the new generation identified with the iconoclastic motives of the older poets.

"Make it new," Pound had commanded, and Eliot, Williams, Marianne Moore, and the other Modernists who heeded the call had also rejected the poetic styles they had grown up with but eventually considered out-moded. While fiction had admitted aspects of the modern world, turn-of-the-century "genteel" verse had remained aloof. To the aspiring poets, its abstract diction and overworked conventions seemed increasingly empty, irrelevant, or incapable of dealing with the present realities of a rapidly changing, technological society. Their original perceptions were reinforced by new aesthetic theories (from the Symbolists, T. E. Hulme, Ford Madox Ford), while their experiments imitated techniques of avant-garde art (Dada, Cubism). These combined and resulted in the radical practices that forever altered poetry. Free verse and imagism, use of collage, ellipsis, disjunction—these, they believed, more accurately expressed complex modern consciousness and the fragmentary character of contemporary life.

After 1945, American life was no less complicated, despite its placid surface, and Ginsberg and the younger poets who felt the dominant academic verse constraining and inadequate turned again to the techniques of the Modernists to depict present-day complexities, not least the conflicts in their personal lives and psychic states. Like the Modernists, they too found additional inspiration in alternative aesthetics, foreign literatures, and avant-garde art. Both in style and content, the new generation's radical experiments to "make it new" provoked controversy, and with Ginsberg's "Howl," a sensational court case. In their different ways, innovative works by John Ashbery, Adrienne Rich, A. R. Ammons, W. S. Merwin, and James Merrill, and others on "Poets in Person" have raised critical hackles, as well. At first, the Modernists' "New Poetry" also had outraged the general public and the literary establishment alike— *vers libre* was most upsetting—but it was scholarship and careful criticism emanating from the Academy which eventually validated it.

Indeed, although the New Criticism was disparaged by latter-day revolutionaries, the New Critics provided the Modernists with their strongest lines of defense against conservative opposition. In *A History of Modern Poetry*, David Perkins points out:

> Essentially the New Criticism was a rationalizing of the Modernist legacy. The New Critics retained basic Modernist values—economy, wit, irony, impersonality, scrupulous handling of form—but abandoned, without saying so, specific technical features of Modernist poetry, such as the extreme ellipsis, fragmentation, and discontinuity of *The Waste Land* and the *Cantos* and the density of symbolism and overlap-

ping myth in *The Waste Land* and *The Bridge*. As a result the New Critical style was cautious and traditional in comparison with the high Modernism it descended from, and, unlike high Modernism, it did not seem in the least disorienting, grand, or revolutionary.

Among the postwar poets, Ginsberg, Ammons, Merwin, Ashbery, and Wright are direct descendants and offer the most obvious examples of "the extreme ellipsis, fragmentation, and discontinuity" of the high Modernists. As they mention, Ginsberg and Ammons had first-hand contact in visits to Dr. Williams. (Wright tracked Pound around Venice, but hesitated to talk to the old master.) Each of them also found other, non-literary inspirations and more recent materials and original methods to shape their individual styles, as they reveal on their programs. But even for them, as for most of the authors featured on "Poets in Person," the New Criticism was an undeniable influence. In fact, from the late Thirties to the mid-Sixties, few literature students could avoid it, especially after Cleanth Brooks and Robert Penn Warren conveyed the New Critical doctrines neatly in *Understanding Poetry* (1938) and it became a standard textbook.

As noted, Merwin, Kumin, and Rich, like Gwendolyn Brooks and so many others, began their careers adhering to the principles of academic poetry. In highly polished pieces, they employed allusion, irony, and an impersonal stance, conveying ideas and images within challenging forms. But eventually they moved to freer and more experimental methods, and as their work evolved they began to use more "open" structures and to speak directly in more personally revealing poems. Others, like James Merrill, who first found expression through mastery of the rich repertoire of standard poetic forms and techniques, remained faithful to this heritage and to their own temperaments, but adapted the received methods. They also found new ways to accommodate contemporary matters and autobiography within the tradition, Merrill most remarkably in his epic, *The Changing Light at Sandover*.

Autobiography figures prominently in the work of all the "Poets in Person" authors, and their ways of treating the self offer useful reminders of the variety of approaches, and some of the difficulties, in presenting private matters through this public medium. From the start, Ginsberg made his personal life the central topic of his work. In "Howl" he depicts himself and his friends as social outcasts, rejected but also heroic; in their suffering and madness, people in the poem are portrayed as saintly victims of an unjust, materialistic society. The poem is both personal and political, as details of his life form the basis (particularly in the "Moloch" section) for an indictment of the oppression Ginsberg views in America's "hyper-technological," "hyper-destructive" postwar civilization. In its open forms and prophetic tone, the style of the poem is reminiscent of Whitman, but Ginsberg is much more explicit. For its theme of alienation, its use of loose structure and the uncensored vernacular, and the obscenity trial it provoked, "Howl" attracted wide attention. On all levels, it violated New Critical dogma, and it encouraged others to freer expression. In Ginsberg and those who have followed his example, self-revelation has been taken to extreme degrees, and the term "confessional" has been given to what has become a subgenre. (The word was coined by the poet and critic M. L. Rosenthal in a review of Robert Lowell's *Life Studies* [1959], and has since been applied, liberally and sometimes inaccurately, to many poets, including W. D. Snodgrass, Theodore Roethke, John Berryman, Sylvia Plath, and Anne Sexton. On her program, Maxine Kumin notes Sexton's influence in breaking taboos concerning "proper" topics in poetry.)

Using the self as subject has now become so prevalent in American poetry that it is taken for granted. But for many of the poets trained in the New Criticism, learning to speak in the true first-person singular was a complicated matter. Eliot had promoted the classical ideals of emotional restraint and "impersonality" in poetry, frequently using irony as a distancing device. Elaborating on Eliot's ideas, I. A. Richards, William Empson, John Crowe Ransom (whose 1941 book *The New Criticism* fixed the name), as well as Brooks and Warren, were careful to distinguish between the author of a poem and the *persona* or speaker in the poem; thus the "I" was understood to be, not the poet (as naive belief would have it), but another invented character. This distinction was part of the larger project of the New Critics, to differentiate imaginative writing from ordinary prose; they valued, and their methods treated, literary texts not merely as historical or biographical documents but as independent works of art.

As the postwar generation passed into the Fifties and Sixties, departing from the persona to speak in their own voices was not simply a matter of violating aesthetic decorum. The example of the confessional poets, but more, the social and political changes taking place, caused a reassessment of the impersonal stance of the poet and the use of the gender-neutral "I." For women poets particularly, this reevaluation meant confronting a complex of social, psychological, and sexual issues. For Ginsberg, Rich, and other non-conformists who found American society repressive, self-revelation also meant exposing social ills and questioning the status quo. On his program, Ginsberg speaks further about the question of self-censorship, and the need for poets to "trap" themselves in the "original mind,"

> before we begin doctoring it up to make it more acceptable socially; to get the raw perception, which sometimes may seem . . . embarrassing, or socially inconvenient. However, in the long run, it turns out to be the most convenient socially, because the most truthful. That's the area which is most precious and most interesting and most personal and most intimate, and it's the hardest area to show other people. And yet it's the very stuff of truth and poetry and imagination.

Schooled in the poetic tradition of reticence and emotional restraint, Maxine Kumin and Adrienne Rich long found it difficult to reveal the "most personal and most intimate" sides of their lives. Recalling her friendship with Anne Sexton, Kumin acknowledges her literary confidante for encouraging her "to put aside academic concerns and be more open, to confront my own being, confront the world around me." Sexton's willingness to discuss the sexual details of her life and her distressing psychological problems offered a powerful precedent for many other women poets, notably Sharon Olds.

Adrienne Rich underwent a protracted and painful process of self-analysis before she found the means to express her deepest conflicts as a woman and a poet. When he chose her for the Yale Younger Poets award in 1951, W. H. Auden praised the 21-year-old Rich for her "capacity for detachment from the self and its emotions." Following her marriage, she confronted her own life and then the cultural traditions that shaped it, reappraising her roles as daughter, wife, mother, and lover. Her involvement in the social causes of the Sixties and Seventies, interaction with minority students, and engagement in the feminist movement made her realize that the personal is political. ("Did you think I was talking about my life," she states in a poem. "I was trying to drive a tradition up against the wall.") As her personal and social critiques developed, Rich shifted from the impersonal pronouns of early poems to direct address. Through her intellectual and spiritual search, she disclosed deep and often unpleasant cultural truths. She also found an authentic voice in which to speak of her own life and for the suffering of others.

In her work, Gwendolyn Brooks has always drawn from her experiences in the black community. She also began as a traditionalist, using a variety of forms (especially the sonnet), irony, personas, and other poetic devices in her incisive portraits of ordinary people. But during the Sixties, after her encounters with young and often militant black writers, she too reevaluated her role as a poet. While she did not completely leave old forms and techniques behind her, Brooks became more outspoken and began to experiment more extensively with free verse and looser structures, as she wrote more directly about the lives of black people, particularly the young. Rita Dove has frequently taken autobiography and black history as her subjects. Educated in the Seventies, she was perhaps less directly affected by the academic strictures that influenced older poets; and without the kinds of aesthetic issues they had to resolve, she (like Gary Soto and most others in today's younger generation) did not have to choose sides in the critical debate now ended. In her subtle and carefully crafted poems, she has moved freely among a wide variety of topics, forms, and techniques.

In recent years, Maxine Kumin has treated autobiographical subjects more openly and in a range of poetic styles but never abandoned the formal methods of her earliest work. Nor has she allowed the extremely intimate revelations that identify Sexton and the other confessional poets. As for the matter of impersonal or direct speaker in poetry, she once replied, when asked whether the *I* in a poem referred to a character or to the poet herself: "It can be either and it can be a little of both, because the *I* is the persona that the poet is hiding behind." Equally proficient in formal and free verse, she has preferred structure, especially when dealing with personal matters. She has said, "The tougher the form the easier it is for me to handle the poem, because the form gives permission to be very gut-honest about feelings." On "Poets in Person," Kumin explains that poems

> emotionally painful, difficult, personal for me to write . . . are the poems that I am most likely going to hammer into a really tight metrical pattern, because the form gives you permission to say the hard things. It's exactly like building a building . . . you excavate for the cellar, and then you put up these wooden forms, and then you pour the concrete, and then after it's hardened, you knock the wooden forms away. And that's what the formal pattern does for the poem.

James Merrill speaks of poetic structure in a related metaphor. On his program, he explains: "I always loved the idea of received space. It's never occurred to me to build my own house. But I love to fit myself into existing rooms. And the same way with forms. . . . The idea, it seems to me, is to use the elements of the form that are still viable nowadays." Autobiography has been the central subject of Merrill's poetry; on his program he says, "I'm at home with the idea of telling myself the story of my own life." In doing so, the master craftsman has used traditional poetic tools to shape that story. For him, as for Kumin, forms are not inhibiting, but sophisticated means of sharing confidences with the reader. Working in most of the poetic genres, from the short lyric to the epic, he has subtly refashioned them in his personal style. Merrill's work is self-referential, and as later poems return to earlier ones, individual details and nuances contribute to the continuing account of his life. Avoiding a straightforward "plot," the poet prefers to unfold his autobiography by implication and indirection: "I like the idea of hinting at a story, at a narrative."

"I'd always wanted to write, as they say, but I thought to write meant to write stories and fiction, and I couldn't write stories," Charles Wright recalls on his program. But as a 23-year-old soldier in Italy, he started reading Pound and "now I found something that I thought I could do, which is the lyric poem . . . an associational kind of progression and not a straight Frostian, Dickensian narrative, and I thought, well, I could do that because that's the way my mind seems to work, in fits and starts—it jumps from one thing to another." Later he discovered his major subject, "which was my own wonderful self." (Although he says he has been "doing my autobiography in poems ever since," he also cautions that "most all of the stories that come out in my poems are things that not necessarily happened to me but I would like to have had happen to me.") Like Merrill, Wright has used an incremental method to tell and imaginatively retell the story of his life, returning often to childhood. But he prefers free verse, in which he displays the intensity and spiritual consciousness of Emily Dickinson while adapting the imagistic methods of Pound and Eugenio Montale. The Italian modernist in particular taught him how "to move a line, how to move an image from one stage to the next. How to create imaginary bridges between images and stanzas and then to cross them, making them real, image to image, block to block."

As Wright has forged his own "associational kind of progression," Ginsberg, Ashbery, Ammons, Merwin, Rich and at times others in the series have found their individual ways of using that technique; in this they share a common legacy from the Modernists' experiments. But other influences played their parts, as the series indicates. On their programs, both Wright and Ginsberg indicate specific ways they applied the non-representational painterly techniques of Paul Cézanne in their poetry, to overlay and arrange images (Wright) and to create the sensation of space and motion in metaphors (Ginsberg). John Ashbery notes how the Abstract Expressionists' improvisational attitude toward composition prompted him to try writing "by just plunging in." He adds that their concept that "the work of art is somehow a history of its own making" also influenced his procedures: "I, like Pollock, can be writing for quite a long time without having any idea what I'm writing about. . . . In that sense, writing a poem is a sort of embarking on a voyage toward some unknown point—and perhaps not ever arriving there, either."

This sense of adventure and openness to experience is a characteristic that all the authors on "Poets in Person" share, however different their aesthetics. The series and the essays which follow trace some of the routes on their journeys. As the poets talk of their lives, they mention many inspirations that helped them on their way. This companion will discuss some of the more important influences, from literary forbears and alliances, art and popular culture, philosophical and social movements, theory and criticism. As the eclectic and representative group on the series demonstrations, there is more variety than ever before in American poetry. But the public for poetry today is likewise diverse, and no one poet presumes to speak for everyone. Nor can any one school of criticism dictate to artists now. These programs remind us that poets, not critics, make the rules and that final authority lies with the authors, and with us listeners and readers in the audience.

# ALLEN GINSBERG

Robert Frank

"So there was maybe a whole new age of looking for a fresh source of inspiration in our own persons, in our own minds, in the spontaneous awareness that we already generated among each other. And that does go back in history to Walt Whitman's suggestions for candor, spontaneity, frankness, camaraderie, spiritual tenderness," says Allen Ginsberg at the start of his "Poets in Person" interview, recalling the early years of the "Beat Generation."

From today's vantage point, it may be hard to appreciate the stir they created during the Fifties and Sixties. In the "new age," championing candor, spontaneity, and the maxim "First thought, best thought," the Beats opposed the English and European aesthetic traditions which long dominated American writing. In place of T. S. Eliot's theories and the narrow curriculum of the U.S. academy, they embraced the democratic idealism of Whitman and the practice of William Carlos Williams, making their own experiences of America, its local realities, and its spoken language the essence of their innovative art. By the Seventies and Eighties, their once-radical style—idiosyncratic, loosely structured, frankly autobiographical—had itself become the dominant mode; the old avant-garde became the new orthodoxy. Today, books of the Beats, once scorned and often condemned as indecent, are fixtures on English department syllabi. Some are even considered classics: like Whitman's "barbaric yawp," Ginsberg's "Howl" has entered the canon.

In breaking away from the past and focusing on the actualities of contemporary American life and language, Ginsberg's circle caused not only a literary about-face but helped create a larger social phenomenon, the counterculture of the Sixties and Seventies. Ginsberg has said that he was first drawn to Williams's poetry because its open forms implied an open mind. In the conformist, inhibited atmosphere of postwar America, the Beats, with their ribald humor and unconventional lifestyles, came to symbolize freedom of expression; while Ginsberg, ever at the forefront, became the prophetic voice of the disaffected. His poetry records a personal spiritual quest, but it also expands an older Romantic myth. In Ginsberg, William Blake's Innocence continues to contend with the Experience of the repressive, materialistic, modern world.

Allen Ginsberg was born in Newark, New Jersey, in 1926 but grew up and attended schools in nearby Paterson, where his father was a high school English teacher. His parents could hardly have been more opposite in character. Louis Ginsberg, himself a poet of modest reputation who wrote traditional verse, was a model of middle-class propriety and restraint. Naomi Levy Ginsberg was a Communist and an ardent supporter of labor causes of the radical Left. She suffered from depression and paranoid delusions of persecution by the government, and had to be institutionalized a number of times when the poet was a child; she eventually died in a mental hospital in 1956. Her instability doubtless contributed to Ginsberg's own psychological problems as a youth, particularly conflicts about his sexual identity. But her idealism and pain profoundly influenced his work—above all, "Kaddish," his harrowing elegy for her—and instilled in him a lifelong compassion for the oppressed.

In 1943, at age 17, Ginsberg entered Columbia University with a scholarship. His teachers included the conservative critic Lionel Trilling and the traditional poet Mark Van Doren; despite their aesthetic differences with their student, both men long supported him, even when he got into trouble. As Ginsberg notes on "Poets in Person," the English department at Columbia, like most literature faculties during the Forties, was dominated by the theories and taste of T. S. Eliot and concentrated on English texts. The American tradition was taken far less seriously—Whitman, Ginsberg says in his interview, was given "some distant credence as a forbear; but, on the other hand, he was considered rather an unkempt, ill-mannered, boorish, provincial jerk"—and writings about contemporary life were virtually ignored if not scorned. "It was a question of non-political tone, a non-rebellious tone, and certainly a non-sexual tone, certainly non-homosexual tone, privacy," Ginsberg recalls. During this "uncandid period" stretching to the Sixties, he adds, "there was a kind of homogenization of opinion and a stultification of thought, and a closeting of emotion, I think, and total censorship of literature." Not only were books by Henry Miller, William Burroughs, Jean Genet, and D. H. Lawrence still forbidden, but "salacious passages" in Catullus and Petronius were permitted to be printed only in the original Latin.

Even as a student, Ginsberg himself was disciplined for offending the authorities with his language, and lifestyle. In his third year he was reported for writing rude remarks on his dorm window; when the dean of students entered Ginsberg's room and discovered him sharing his bed with an ex-Columbia undergraduate, Jack Kerouac, he expelled him for a year. As so often in Ginsberg's life, potential disaster proved a fortunate fall, or at last a mixed blessing. He now began his extracurricular education and informal apprenticeship for the poet he would become.

At the time of their first meetings, Ginsberg recounts, "I was writing rigid, formal, classic poetry, and Kerouac saw me as a very intelligent young guy but sort of stuck in a closet of mind. And he encouraged me to be more spontaneous in my writing and just take my notebooks and write them up as they were, the notes, the raw notes, rather than attempting to turn them into poems." The future author of *On the Road* (1957) became the aspiring poet's mentor, along with William Burroughs, the future author of *Naked Lunch* (1959). On the program, Ginsberg acknowledges:

> I always felt like a simple jerk from New Jersey. I didn't really feel that I had much authority intellectually myself, and so I decided that I'd better learn from these guys by listening and not questioning and not arguing with them especially. . . . I was sort of empowered by them . . . they gave me a sense of confidence in my own mind.

Older, vastly wiser about the world, and very widely read, Burroughs opened his protégés to a broad range of contemporary experimental writing and other literature outside the restrictive canons of the American academy. He also introduced them to the New York subculture of crime, sex, and drugs. In 1947 Ginsberg met Kerouac's good friend Neal Cassady, who became the idol and eventually the mythologized image of the "Beat Generation," as Kerouac called the then-small group that met in Burroughs's apartment. Handsome, free-spirited, and largely self-taught, Cassady was a brilliant talker whose ideas about spontaneity of expression—and enthralling examples in his own non-stop monologues—Ginsberg, Kerouac, and others tried to emulate. (Cassady became Dean Moriarty in *On the Road*; *Planet News* is dedicated to him, and he is the subject of many Ginsberg elegies.)

At the same time Ginsberg was also imitating the work of older models, William Blake and William Carlos Williams. As a teenager, Ginsberg had interviewed Dr. Williams for a Paterson newspaper at the poet-physician's home in Rutherford. "When I went to see him, I couldn't understand his poetry because I was trained to expect it would rhyme," he tells Lewis Hyde on the program. But in March of 1950 he heard Williams read "The Pure Products of America Go Crazy" at the Museum of Modern Art,

> and I suddenly realized he was just talking, that his poetry was the same as some earnest, clear, very intelligent person just talking in his kitchen to some-

body also very close. And that was like a great trans-
formative moment in my mind . . . understanding
that this new principle of poetry was identical with
the living language, rather than an archaic language
being imitated.

But before coming under Williams's influence, Ginsberg was attracted to the archaic language of William Blake, and even more
to his mystical vision, which has proved an abiding inspiration.
Writing at the beginning of the industrial revolution in England,
Blake foresaw the destructive force this new power would un-
leash on nature and the mass society it helped create. Like the
later Romantic poets, Blake rejected Enlightenment optimism
and its overemphasis upon Reason, and he denounced the shack-
ling of the human spirit and the increased political oppression,
particularly of the underclasses, made possible by the triumph of
technology. These ideas and especially Blake's prophetic tone
would later contribute to the composition of "Howl," especially
the "Moloch" section, with its indictment of materialism and
America's "hyper-technological," "hyper-destructive" postwar
civilization.

   In the summer of 1948, Ginsberg was living in East Harlem
and studying Blake. He had returned to Columbia and dropped
out again, following an unsuccessful love affair with Neal Cassady. Depressed and lonely, he had the first of several visions
while reading Blake's "The Sick Rose." Ginsberg thought he
heard the voice of Blake himself speaking to him and felt the im-
manence of a benevolent god. (Later visions presented obverse
and frightening images of an alien, consuming presence. For decades, the Blake vision obsessed Ginsberg; in 1986 he called it the
"only genuine experience I feel I've had . . . a complete absorp-
tion of all my senses into something totally authentic as an experience.") The episode led him to write several poems, some of
which he sent to William Carlos Williams in 1949. Williams
wrote back: "In this mode perfection is basic, and these are not
perfect." This was, Ginsberg tells Lewis Hyde, "a very nice way of
letting me off the hook."

   Despite the interruptions and emotional turmoil during

his college years, Ginsberg received his degree in 1948. The following year he moved to the lower East Side and took part-time jobs. He also took in Herbert Huncke, who served Burroughs and the others as a guide to the Manhattan underworld and who first used the term "beat" (or derelict, his usual condition) to describe them. The word suggested not only musical rhythm but the depressed state of this postwar generation, and perhaps its beatitude. No saint himself, Huncke was a petty thief and junkie who sponged off of the overly generous Ginsberg and used his apartment to store loot. When Huncke and his cohorts were arrested for possession of stolen property, Ginsberg was implicated, although innocent. Through the intercession of a Columbia law professor and Lionel Trilling, he was able to escape prison, by entering a plea of mental instability. During his eight months of "rehabilitation" in a psychiatric institute, Ginsberg met Carl Solomon, a fellow inmate who furthered his artistic education. Conversations with this self-described "professional lunatic-saint" convinced Ginsberg of the importance of the irrational unconscious in poetry (particularly as exemplified by the French Surrealists) and of the poet's political role as outsider, prophet, and social critic. Ginsberg acknowledged his debt to Solomon in the dedication to and the third section of "Howl."

Before he could achieve that landmark in American poetry, Ginsberg first had to undergo several personal struggles and stylistic transformations; how far he travelled in his poetic development can be traced in his work to that point. The earliest poems, dating from 1947—collected as *The Gates of Wrath* and published in 1972, after the singer Bob Dylan rediscovered them among his papers—are highly structured (as Kerouac noted) and mostly in rhyme, including imitations of 17th-century English masters (Donne, Marvell, and other favorites of T. S. Eliot), verses to Neal Cassady (though his gender is kept "secret"), and the stanzas prompted by his visions. It is easy to see why Dr. Williams was disappointed with these attempts to "make contemporarily real an old style of lyric machinery." Derivative in form and metrically unsure, these emotional out-

pourings by a heartsick (if very bright) adolescent were replaced, however, by the more ingenious efforts in *Empty Mirror*.

Gathering work up to 1952, the collection was printed in
1961 as Ginsberg's second book, following *Howl*. As he did for
that volume, Williams provided the introduction to *Empty Mirror*, in which he pronounced: "This young Jewish boy . . . has
recognized something that has escaped most of the modern age,
he has found that man is lost in the world of his own head." It is
not surprising that the old Modernist should like the new work,
since the shorter lyrics resemble his own early poems, with their
tight forms and imagistic detail. Other, more ambitious pieces
already show elements of what would be Ginsberg's distinctive
style or anticipate the methods of his mature work. "Hymn," for
example, employs long lines arranged in paragraphs like those
of "Howl"; while "Paterson" evokes the rhythms and tone
characteristic of his long poems of the Sixties and Seventies. But
the young poet is too much absorbed in his own angst, as his
confessional voice ruminates on his romantic difficulties, gro-
tesque visions, and spiritual distress; allusions to his mother's
suffering and his own imprisonment in an asylum add to the
general gloom. Too often sentimentality, murky images, abstractions, and vague diction mar what are still just promising
compositions.

Although he was not very successful getting published
during the early Fifties, these very active years provided Ginsberg with a wealth of ideas and material for the work to come.
His friendships deepened with the Beat group, which now included another young poet, Gregory Corso. Like Kerouac, Ginsberg became interested in Buddhism and continued to write
extensively, keeping a notebook as his friend had recommended
and applying his more open, spontaneous approach. He also
grew closer to Williams and followed his example in using the
American language and natural speech patterns. (In "The
Green Automobile," written in 1953, the poet neatly combines
Kerouac's flowing style with Williams's colloquial diction and
laddered stanzaic form.) In 1952 Ginsberg went to Cuba, then
spent several months with a friend in Mexico, where he ex-

plored the Mayan ruins; "Siesta in Xbalba" (dating from 1954) recalls this happy time. His extensive travels across the country and around the world in the years ahead would provide occasions for a great deal of poetry.

In 1954 Ginsberg finally moved to California, at the urging of Kerouac and Cassady, who preceded him. As he relates on "Poets in Person," they became acquainted with other like-minded, innovative writers, including Gary Snyder, Philip Whalen, Lou Welch, Robert Creeley, and Kenneth Rexroth, a poet of the older generation in whose house they often met: "We all smoked a little pot; we all were interested in Oriental thought or the nature of consciousness . . . we were all interested in this open form of poetry that we'd picked up from Williams or from our own spontaneous ideas, like from Kerouac."

Robert Creeley arrived in San Francisco in 1955, as Ginsberg notes. Creeley had edited *Black Mountain Review*, and he provided a link to the Black Mountain school of poets led by Charles Olson. An unaccredited college in North Carolina (closed in 1956), Black Mountain attracted experimentalists in several fields, the painter Robert Rauschenberg, the composer John Cage, and the dancer-choreographer Merce Cunningham among them. Like Creeley and Robert Duncan, Olson admired Ezra Pound, and inspired by the stylistic methods of the *Cantos*, he developed his theories of "projective verse" and "open-field" or "organic" form. Elaborating on Williams's notions about metrics (as in his somewhat contradictory concept of the "variable foot"), Olson stressed the importance of breath, rather than the iamb, as the basis for rhythm in poetry. While Ginsberg's use of "open" form originates from Kerouac and differs somewhat from Black Mountain theories, many other anti-academic poets were strongly influenced by Olson's ideas, particularly his argument that the poetic line should be determined by the individual writer's natural breathing patterns.

In San Francisco Ginsberg eventually took a job in marketing, but soon became dissatisfied, and with the support of his psychiatrist he decided to drop out and become an "urban hermit." He also met Peter Orlovsky, and the young poet became his lover and lifelong companion. Recalling his friends in those years on the program, Ginsberg says they formed a "committee of correspondence": "There was very little sense of competition. It was more a sense of familial camaraderie, and enthusiasm, and tenderness, actually, toward each other's work and in each other's eyes."

In August of 1955, shortly after meeting Orlovsky, Ginsberg sat down and started to write a poem, beginning: "I saw the best minds of my generation destroyed by madness, starving hysterical naked . . . ." He penciled "Howl for Carl Solomon" on the top of the completed typescript and mailed Kerouac the first part of what was to become the most famous poem of their generation, and probably of the second half of the century. (Barry Miles points out that although Kerouac is usually given credit for the title and Ginsberg himself long believed he suggested it—he even thanked Kerouac for it on the dedication page—it was the author's own; here and elsewhere, this essay is indebted to Miles's fascinating, exhaustively detailed biography.) Part II, as the poet explains on the program, was written after he took peyote. Under the influence of the hallucinogen, he looked at the Sir Francis Drake Hotel in downtown San Francisco and saw in the facade the image of "a real robotic face . . . the night sky had that reddish glare of neon in the smog and mist, so the whole thing looked like the floor of hell, frankly. I just kept saying, 'Moloch, Moloch, where am I? Moloch.'"

Written against the backdrop of the Bomb and the Cold War, the televised hunts for supposed Communists and "un-American activities" by Sen. Joseph McCarthy and Richard Nixon, and the growth of what President Eisenhower termed the military-industrial complex, "Howl" crystallized the fears and alienation of the Beats and many other young people who felt stifled by the conformity and the repressive atmosphere of postwar American society. "And suddenly," Ginsberg remarks before reading from the "Moloch" section, "the whole fate of western hyper-technological, hyper-industrialized, hyper-destructive, hyper-rationalizing—Eurozenic, as Blake would call it—western civilization seemed to be caught up in its own demolition . . . [Moloch, the biblical false god to whom children were sacrificed] seemed like a horrific image; but on the other hand it was a very beautiful image, like a Miltonic image, basically."

Into the poem Ginsberg distilled his life and his friends' experiences—the collage of part I catalogues and celebrates the deeds of Kerouac, Burroughs, Huncke, Solomon, and other "best minds," while lamenting their sufferings—combining ideas from his wide reading—from Milton, Christopher Smart, Blake, and Shelley to Rimbaud, García Lorca, Antonin Artaud, Eliot, and Hart Crane—and the stylistic methods of his more immediate mentors. With Kerouac's spontaneity and Williams's concrete, American language, he expressed his anguished vision in detail-filled, Whitmanesque lines which extended to the length of his own breath. Indeed, the poem was composed to be read aloud. Ginsberg's new prosody in "Howl" was meant to reflect the "natural flow of the mind," with the long, often paragraph-length lines written (or uttered) as "one speech-thought-breath," and unconstrained by conventional metrics. On "Poets in Person," Ginsberg notes that he also tried to apply in the poem the techniques Cézanne used in his paintings, creating a sensation of space by the juxtaposition of different images (e.g., "cannibal dynamo" and "hydrogen jukebox") "which are opposite in intent but which, nevertheless, when placed together . . . make the mind link together very far apart distances."

In October Ginsberg organized a public reading (his first) with Gary Snyder, Philip Whalen, and others (Rexroth was master of ceremonies) at Six Gallery. By the end of Ginsberg's dramatic reading—or incantation—the audience was sobbing and cheering, realizing, Michael McClure later recalled, "that a barrier had been broken, that a human voice and body had been hurled against the harsh wall of America . . . ." Ginsberg had become a bard and the leading spokesman of the Beat "movement." (Not all the West Coast writers wanted to be labelled as members of this "San Francisco school"; Rexroth and others later felt Ginsberg had stolen the spotlight from their scene.) Mimeographed copies of "Howl" were distributed to friends and family (Naomi Ginsberg read the poem shortly before she died), as well as to several famous writers and critics.

Lawrence Ferlinghetti, founder of City Lights Books, published *Howl and Other Poems* in October 1956. The next spring U.S. Customs officials seized copies arriving from the printer in England, then police arrested Ferlinghetti for distributing "obscene" material. During the long trial, several prominent literary figures offered testimonials, and the defendants were found not guilty. Judge W. J. Clayton Horn's remarks provide a neat précis of the work:

> The first part of "Howl" presents a nightmare world; the second part is an indictment of those elements in modern society destructive of the best qualities of human nature; such elements are predominantly identified as materialism, conformity, and mechanization leading toward war. The third part presents a picture of an individual [Carl Solomon] who is a specific representation of what the author conceives as a general condition. "Footnote to Howl" seems to be a declamation that everything in the world is holy, including parts of the body by name. It ends with a plea for holy living .... The theme of "Howl" presents "unorthodox and controversial ideas." Coarse and vulgar language is used in treatment and sex acts are mentioned but unless the book is entirely lacking in "social importance" it cannot be held obscene.

Needless to say, the trial provided abundant, free publicity. Initial critical responses were decidedly mixed, however; Richard Eberhart gave the book a glowing review in the New York *Times*, but generally academicians and the leading literary journals were unfavorably impressed. *Time* and *Life* ran features on Ginsberg, but their interest was not primarily literary. Ginsberg promoted the book tirelessly, and as his fame grew he energetically worked to get his friends' work published and recognized, as well.

From mid-1956 on Ginsberg travelled abroad extensively, to the Arctic, Mexico (to visit Kerouac), Tangier (Burroughs), Spain, Italy, Vienna, Munich, Paris, Chile. In South America he took *yage,* an Indian hallucinogen (and had a bad trip), and he continued to experiment with other drugs, including LSD (with the Harvard professor-turned-guru Timothy Leary). In Paris, in 1957, he wrote a section of what was to become "Kaddish," parts I and II of which were finished in a single two-and-a-half-day session in New York while he was under the influence of amphetamines: speedwriting indeed. Recalling the composition of "Kaddish" on the program, Ginsberg says, "At some point or other I realized that the strongest trauma and influence and drama of my life was my relation with my mother . . . whose chaotic emotion and behavior had a great imprinting on me. . . . At the same time, I loved her a great deal." By the late Fifties he was already famous as a poet of openness; yet, he adds, "I hadn't written about the thing that was closest to my most candid heart. And that was my mother." A Kaddish had not been said after Naomi Ginsberg's funeral, and Ginsberg's late commemoration of her is incomparable, and generally considered the deepest and most moving poem he has ever written.

"Strange now to think of you, gone without corsets & eyes, while I walk on the sunny pavement of Greenwich Village," part I begins. In the proem the poet describes his preparations to write the elegy as memories of his mother start to flood his mind. Following this sometimes surrealistic montage of images, part II is a very detailed but fragmented narrative of their early life together, especially Naomi's paranoia and the boy's fears during her periods of madness, and other autobiographical episodes, ending with her final letter to her son. Philosophical reflections and psychological revelations are intertwined as the story rushes onward with a tragic intensity. In the following "Hymmnn," the poet is reconciled to "the world which He has created according to his will," and blesses his mother in death and also the "Holy One" who has allowed such pain. After a kind of litany in part 5, the poem concludes with a haunting image of crows cawing overhead during the funeral service. On "Poets in Person," Ginsberg describes part 2 as "the release from my unconscious, from my inhibition"; the poem as a whole may be viewed as an emotional and spiritual catharsis.

*Kaddish and Other Poems: 1958–1960* was published in

1961, as one of the most tumultuous periods in American history was about to begin. During the Sixties and Seventies, Ginsberg maintained a frenetic pace, travelling, giving readings, participating in demonstrations for numerous social and political causes; his increasingly high public profile as an activist at times overshadowed his original literary role. Nonetheless, he was prolific, perhaps too much so; even ardent admirers agree the quality of much of his writing after *Kaddish* slipped. A decline is noticeable even in "At Apollinaire's Grave," "Death to Van Gogh's Ear," and other fine elegiac pieces originally printed in the *Kaddish* collection, where looser language and less stirring images fill out the lines. One problem may be that many of the poems were the less fortunate products of writing in a drugged state; titles dating from 1959–60 include "Mescaline," "Lysergic Acid," and "Aether," which is rather gassy. (In 1963 Ginsberg published *The Yage Letters*, his correspondence with Burroughs about their experiments with that hallucinogen in Peru.)

*Reality Sandwiches* (1963) proved something of a disappointment coming after *Kaddish*, though it would be unfair to expect anyone to sustain the level of the earlier masterpiece. The new collection included older poems ("The Green Automobile," "Siesta in Xbalba") but mainly pieces arising from Ginsberg's several trips: "a wind-up book of dream notes," the back cover announced. These have the easy tone of a journal, as the poet chronicles his years from the Fifties in San Francisco and the excursions to the Arctic, Europe, Peru and back to New York. As mellowness replaces the anger of the first poems— Ginsberg and the Beats never lost their irreverent sense of humor, of course—the image of the middle-aged poet-sage begins to emerge.

*Planet News: 1961–1967* (1968) is an engrossing account of Ginsberg's many activities during this eventful period, when he travelled through Asia, India, and Eastern Europe and across the United States. With political commentary, the volume also provides a record of a poet's spiritual pilgrimage and transformation. Ginsberg's opposition to American materialism and militarism had been voiced in his earliest work, but travelling through Asia as the Vietnam war expanded gave him an even greater sense of social crisis. In "Television Was a Baby Crawling Toward That Deathchamber," one of the first poems in the book, he depicts the medium as an insidious force for political and commercial propaganda, distorting history and reality with seductive images. "Describe: The Rain on Dasaswamedh" portrays a simple street in India, offering a sharp contrast to the American scene critiqued in "Television was a Baby."

In India Ginsberg had consulted with gurus, who advised him to seek enlightenment, not in otherworldly visions, but in the physical body and the earthly realities of this life. In Israel Martin Buber had urged him to find meaning in personal relationships, not in an inhuman universe. Then, in Japan, after visiting Gary Snyder (who was studying Zen in a monastery), Ginsberg had a vision which convinced him to abandon drugs and his former way of living. "The Change: *Kyoto-Tokyo Express*" (dated July 1963) announces his liberation and decision to embrace human reality, declaring: "Open the portals to what Is"; released from his long nightmare and "reborn"—"My own Identity now nameless"—he turns outward to others "And the Sun the Sun . . . ."

In 1965 Ginsberg was crowned King of the May in Prague, as noted on the program, but was soon expelled by the authorities for making statements about freedom of expression. Through the Sixties he exercised that right in this country (though he was also put on the FBI's Dangerous Security List in 1965) as he crisscrossed the States in a Volkswagen bus and gave readings and talks on many campuses. The very long "Wichita Vortex Sutra" (a portion of which is read on the program) describes his journeys in 1965–66 through pastoral "Middle America" as U.S. involvement in Vietnam deepened. The poem provides a vivid collage of the times, while castigating the administration's actions (particularly its abuse of language) in pursuing the undeclared war. Ginsberg's readings, speeches, and participation in several "be-ins" made him a leading figure in the anti-war movement. (He directed an "exorcism" of the Pentagon in 1967, for example, and was later arrested with Dr. Benjamin Spock for blocking a military induction center; he also tried to calm the crowds during the "disturbances" at the 1968 Democratic convention in Chicago, by chanting a mantra.) And so the author of "Howl" became the bard to yet another generation of disaffected youth.

The Fall of America (1972) covers some of the same territory as the preceding volume with poems recording Ginsberg's cross-country travels from 1965 to 1971, but it contains fewer extraordinary pieces and is generally much more pessimistic in tone; the poet condemns the war, pollution of the environment, the media in service to the military-industrial complex, and materialism, reprising the critiques of earlier work. The book received the National Book Award in 1974, but critical opinion remains divided. During this period, Neal Cassady and Jack Kerouac died; the original Beat circle had disbanded and the movement, such as it was, had dissipated long before. Their free-wheeling spirit, captured briefly by the "flower-power" generation, was difficult to replicate amid the grim realities of war abroad and social unrest at home.

In 1974 Ginsberg, the perennial academic outsider, co-founded the Jack Kerouac School of Disembodied Poetics at the Naropa Institute, a Buddhist university in Boulder, Colorado. Part of each year the poet is in residence, teaching Tibetan meditation and breathing methods as aids to composition. A guiding principle at the School remains Kerouac's dictum "First thought, best thought." The rationale behind the practice of "spontaneous prosody," Ginsberg explains on "Poets in Person," is

> to trap ourselves in our Ur-mind—natural mind, original mind—before we begin doctoring it up to make it more acceptable socially; to get the raw perception, which sometimes may seem . . . [a] "sore thumb," out of place, embarrassing, or socially inconvenient. However, in the long run, it turns out to be the most convenient socially, because the most truthful. That's the area which is most precious and most interesting and most personal and most intimate, and it's the hardest area to show other people.

And yet it's the very stuff of truth and poetry and imagination.

Still, one need not be a rigid formalist to observe that first thoughts, even "best thoughts," do not of themselves necessarily constitute best writing. Bias against revision allows the pen to ramble, prolixity (and plain carelessness) can result, and self-revelation may become self-indulgence. In Ginsberg's work, early and late, bloated pages betray an oversized ego; readers less fascinated with his autobiography than the author himself may find many stretches of his true confessions (and the loosely fashioned effusions of his kindred spirits) simply tedious.

In *Mind Breaths: Poems, 1972–1977* (1978) and *Plutonian Ode: Poems, 1977–80* (1982), Ginsberg considers familiar topics but treats them in new ways. The strong influence of Buddhist meditation and its breathing methods are evident here, particularly in the first volume's title poem and "Thoughts Sitting Breathing." Other pieces are styled upon American sources like the blues and are accompanied by musical scores; the poet likes to sing these lyrics while accompanying himself on a small pump-organ or harmonium. He has also collected several such pieces in *First Blues: Rags, Ballads & Harmonium Songs, 1971–74* (1975). On "Poets in Person," Ginsberg reads " 'You Might Get in Trouble' " (from *Mind Breaths*) and "After Whitman & Reznikoff" (from *Plutonian Ode*).

In 1984 Ginsberg published his *Collected Poems, 1947–80*, a volume of 837 pages. This edition rearranges the contents of original books "in straight chronological order to compose an autobiography" and reprints material from rare chapbooks by small presses to "fill in gaps in the sequence." The author notes one advantage of the new ordering: "Disparate simultaneous early styles juxtaposed aid recognition of a grounded mode of writing encouraged by Dr. Williams, 'No ideas but in things.' " Ginsberg also provides extensive notes to the poems, the introductions and epigraphs from original editions, dedications, and book-jacket copy. But, aside from correcting typographical and other unintentional errors, the texts have undergone little emendation, as Ginsberg remains true to earliest principles: "'First thought, best thought.' Spontaneous insight—the sequence of thought-forms passing naturally through the ordinary mind—was always motif and method of these compositions."

*White Shroud: Poems, 1980–1985* appeared in 1986, Ginsberg's sixtieth year. The title poem looks back, a quarter-century later, to "Kaddish," conjuring images of "the family together again, first time in decades" in a dream vision filled with regrets but ending in relief. Another figure from the past returns in the poem "Written in My Dream by W. C. Williams." Other pieces in this substantial collection display a very rich variety of subjects and styles: rap and rock-and-roll lyrics on political themes, satires, open-form improvisations, blues and other pieces with musical scores, "American" haiku (seventeen syllables in one line), erotic narratives, didactic pieces, instructions for Buddhist sitting meditation, a rhymeless sonnet, and even an "Old Love Story" in heroic couplets.

In 1986, *Howl (Annotated with Original Mss)* was issued, marking the thirtieth anniversary of that first and most famous work in Ginsberg's expansive publishing career. If the personality of the poet has mellowed since "Howl," his conscience has not, as he remains a strenuous, vocal critic of restrictions on individual liberty and free speech, repressive governmental policies, and other forces of intolerant authority. He continues to receive awards at home and abroad, and the erstwhile radical is now a member of the American Institute of Arts and Letters. When he is not teaching at the Jack Kerouac School or maintaining his usual hectic schedule On the Road, Ginsberg lives in his old apartment on Manhattan's Lower East Side.

# KARL SHAPIRO

Helen Whittemore

Independent, iconoclastic, outspoken, Karl Shapiro has been a controversial figure in American letters. During World War II, and well before the Beats and the counterculture movement, Shapiro boldly voiced his opposition to the high Modernism of T. S. Eliot and the New Criticism that had dominated literature and the Academy since the Thirties. At the same time, he produced two poetry collections containing some of the best war poems ever written by an American, and which established him as one of the outstanding talents of his very gifted generation. Yet over his long career, despite receiving numerous honors and holding prestigious literary positions, the poet-critic has managed, by circumstances, temperament, and his own strong will, to remain an outsider.

Karl Shapiro was born in Baltimore in 1913, just as the Modernist movement whose tenets he would attack so vigorously was getting under way. Shapiro's father and relatives were businessmen and professionals and, as he relates in *The Younger Son*, the first volume of his autobiography, and on his program, there was no literary atmosphere in his early home life. His older brother was the better student, and in an essay the poet has noted that his father encouraged that son "to write and perhaps even to become a writer. My brother won a literary reputation while still in high school."

In the same article, "American Poet?", Shapiro admits "a lack of interest in study (I went to three high schools and two universities and am without a degree)," and suggests several reasons he became a poet:

> a hypersensitivity to my Jewishness, aggravated by complex social distinctions in the South and in Baltimore; self-pity; eroticism; lack of seriousness . . . love of impressions and hallucinations; a tendency to speak in analogies (which perhaps led to a love of rhyme); a love of the obscure and esoteric; and a desire to impress by being witty or profane or irreverent. . . . All I know is that by the age of seventeen I spent most of my time and all of my money in secondhand bookstores. The poetry shelves were the ones I searched most closely.

In his perusals, Shapiro discovered an absence of poets with Jewish names, as he recalls on the program, and considered changing his name. "In those days, believe it or not," he explains in *The Poetry Wreck*, "it was impossible to get a poem published if you did not have an 'Anglo-Saxon' name, but I decided to stick to my name; that decision made me 'Jewish.' " (Eventually he did exchange his original Carl for Karl.)

Shapiro followed his brother to the University of Virginia, in 1932, but stayed only a semester. He felt out of place, rejected not only by the WASPs but also by the Jewish students of German ancestry, who then tended to look down on later Jewish immigrants from Eastern Europe. (Shapiro's family had come from Russia.) The painful experience on campus later provided the basis for one of his best-known poems, "University." Shapiro then worked, not very happily, in the family business. In 1935 he privately printed a book of poems, which went unnoticed but did help him win a scholarship to Johns Hopkins. He lost the scholarship, in the midst of the Depression, when a history professor gave him a low mark, claiming Shapiro was "too bitter against big business." He then entered library school in Baltimore; but shortly before he was to graduate, in 1941, he was drafted into the army.

During his three years in the South Pacific, Shapiro wrote four books, "which must be some kind of record for a foot soldier," he notes in "American Poet?", adding: "I was the company clerk in the Medical Corps and something of an adept at goofing off to write poems. It had long since become expected of me in my outfit, and I do not recall ever having suffered any abuse because of my 'hobby,' as it was thought to be." Back in the States, his future wife, Evalyn, helped get his work published, and the poems in *Person, Place and Thing* (1942) were well received. Those in his next volume, *V-Letter and Other Poems* (1944), were even more impressive, and the book won the Pulitzer Prize.

Both collections are remarkable for their intellectual energy, hard and clear surfaces, brilliant use of concrete details (in this regard he followed Ezra Pound's advice and precise Imagistic techniques), and for their philosophical and social import. *Person, Place and Thing* contains some of Shapiro's strongest poetry, including the much-anthologized "The Dome on Sunday," "Washington Cathedral," "Auto Wreck," "Buick," and "The Fly." (On her program, Maxine Kumin remarks that this work, with its broad and unexpected range of subjects and use of modern language, had a powerful effect upon her own poetry and caused her to revise her ideas about the art.)

On "Poets in Person," Shapiro reads his war sonnet "Full Moon: New Guinea"; other poems from *V-Letter* are equally impressive: "The Gun," "Ballet Mécanique," "The Leg," "Elegy for a Dead Soldier." A recurring motif here is the dehumanization and brutality that have followed from man's technological triumphs. This theme is further developed in "The Progress of Faust" (also read by the author), which was published in Shapiro's 1947 book, *Trial of the Poet*. In the poem, Shapiro traces the story of Faust in legend and literature since the Renaissance, suggesting that inquisitive, rational Western man, like Faust, has made a disastrous pact with science which may lead to self-destruction. "The Progress of Faust" is notable for its skillful use of verse form, as well as for the fact that it was the first poem to be written about the atomic bomb.

While stationed in New Guinea, Shapiro also composed a

poem of over 2,000 lines called *Essay on Rime* (published in 1945), "a kind of 20th-century neoclassical treatise on the art of poetry" which initiated his protracted opposition to modern literary theory, particularly the New Criticism and its emphasis on rational analysis, and to Eliot's ideas about impersonality in literature. In its cantos, Shapiro also reassessed the problems facing the contemporary poet trying to write in the wake of the disintegration of the Great Tradition. The influential critic and Harvard professor F. O. Matthiessen praised the *Essay* as one of the most important books to come out of the war, but Shapiro notes that it "was widely resented by poets and critics alike". His preliminary arguments there would be pursued at length in the acerbic essays about the hyperintellectualizing of art and against Eliot, Pound, and the restrictiveness of academic dogma which he collected as *In Defense of Ignorance* (1960).

In this volume, Shapiro claims that for "saying what I thought and naming names [in the *Essay*] I was henceforth on the intellectual blacklist." Nonetheless, in 1947–48 he was appointed the Consultant in Poetry at the Library of Congress. His tenure began inauspiciously (Shapiro's curious first day is recounted in *Reports of My Death*, the second volume of his autobiography) and ended in controversy. While serving on the selection committee for the first Bollingen Prize (sponsored by the Library), Shapiro alone among the distinguished jurors voted against awarding the prestigious honor to Ezra Pound. Pound had been indicted for high treason because of broadcasts he made on Italian radio during the War, and Shapiro believed (and stated publicly) that Pound's actions, as well as his dubious political philosophy and disreputable attitudes, not least his anti-Semitism, made him unworthy of the Prize. Pound was eventually found mentally unfit to stand trial and was incarcerated in St. Elizabeths, a hospital for the criminally insane in Washington. In 1958, Eliot, Robert Frost, and Archibald MacLeish helped gain his release. Shapiro's positions on the poet and on the rightness of his Prize decision remain unchanged.

The Bollingen fiasco aside, Shapiro's longstanding quarrel with Eliot and Pound had more fundamental aesthetic or philosophical roots. As he mentions on his program, Shapiro felt the

Modernists had returned poetry "to the stacks" in their "museum-like poems" and had cut themselves off from life, certainly as actually lived in this country. In Eliot's later poetry in particular, the celebrated author and Anglican convert had become abstract and formal and, Shapiro believed, he had failed to deal with a central problem Eliot himself had identified: the dissociation of modern consciousness, the division between the rational and intuitive functions of the mind. Moreover, he notes in "T.S. Eliot: The Death of Literary Judgment" (in *The Poetry Wreck*): "The failure to achieve mystical consciousness (which indeed is one of the rarest achievements in mankind) drove Eliot back to metaphysics proper and to religion proper. . . . Eliot ends up as a poet of religion in the conventional sense of that term. And once having made the religious commitment he tried to visualize a religion-directed society; he thus becomes an official of the most conservative elements of society and a figurehead for all that is formalized and ritualized."

Elsewhere in *The Poetry Wreck*, Shapiro criticizes the Modernists for making "a cult of Intelligence." Further, "by plunging into the past and 'making it new'; by removing the arts from people and returning them to the classroom; by promulgating new theories of the Imagination, of the State, of the 'sensibilities' . . . this culture faction eradicated as best it could any influence by D. H. Lawrence, William Carlos Williams, Blake, Walt Whitman, and all other 'Romantics' and humanists."

As he notes on his program, Shapiro allied himself particularly with Whitman and Williams, who "really made a difference in the possibility of younger poets writing at ease in the American language." In his essay "William Carlos Williams: The True Contemporary," Shapiro writes of this indigenous American Modernist: "Poetry to him was a daily function of life, a means of seeing. In a sense, he is our first American poet since Whitman. . . . Williams accommodates himself to the brutal round of modern professional life." Williams made poetry natural, not literary, erasing the line between poetry and prose, life and art.

For the generation coming of age in the Thirties and Forties, the influence of Eliot's poetry, criticism, and theories was overwhelming. The expatriate literary elder statesman and Editor of the *Criterion*—the leading journal of the time—had become a repressive figure of Authority to younger native talents. Ironically, Shapiro was to find himself in a similar position of authority when, in 1950, he was asked to become the Editor of *Poetry*. Founded in 1912, *Poetry* first published many of the early Modernist masterpieces (Eliot's "Love Song of J. Alfred Prufrock," Pound's first *Cantos*, Wallace Stevens's "Sunday Morning") and had continued to print important works by major writers and to present emerging talents. Many influential critics also contributed essays and reviews to the magazine. During his tenure, Shapiro maintained and enhanced this tradition. With his high standards and broad taste, he chose a vigorous mix of pieces by established and promising writers, including Robinson Jeffers, Marianne Moore, James Merrill, Muriel Rukeyser, W. H. Auden, Louise Bogan, Richard Wilbur, W. S. Merwin, Frank O'Hara, Randall Jarrell, and Galway Kinnell.

Despite the high quality of its editorial content, the magazine continued to have financial difficulties, as it had done since its founding. Raising money was a constant burden, and following some disagreements with its board of trustees, Shapiro left *Poetry* in 1955. He then became the editor of another well-regarded literary journal, *Prairie Schooner*, published at the University of Nebraska, where Shapiro also became a professor in the English Department. But again controversy eventually arose; after a dispute with university administrators and editorial staff, who opposed his decision to publish a short story about a homosexual, Shapiro resigned both positions in 1966.

By then he had published several other books, including *In Defense of Ignorance* (1960). For their blunt and witty opinions of old masters and the contemporary literary scene, these essays still make lively reading; but, as Shapiro has noted, the volume alienated nearly everyone, including his friends. Shapiro had long considered the question of his Jewish identity and he collected several poems he had written on the subject in *Poems of a Jew* (1958), which also caused a stir. "The title aroused indignation from Jews and Gentiles alike," he notes in *The Poetry Wreck*, adding: "My chief reason for the book was to make people and myself say the word without any feedback. It would be a word like any other." The collection contains several memorable poems, including "The Jew at Christmas Eve," "The Crucifix in the Filing Cabinet," and "The Alphabet" (also read on the program).

*The Bourgeois Poet* appeared in 1964, and marked a major departure stylistically. The somewhat paradoxical title was suggested by a remark by Theodore Roethke, the influential poet and director of the writing program at the University of Washington. On "Poets in Person," Shapiro says, "I knew what he meant. I thought this was a very good definition of what I was trying to do . . . [it] defined, really, what I was up to. All, almost all of my poems are 'bourgeois' poems in the sense that the subject matter is American middle-class people and their values." In *The Bourgeois Poet*, he now adopted the prose poem format, which easily accommodated his free-ranging approach. "What I was searching for," he explains in "American Poet?",

> was a medium in which I could say anything I wanted—which for poets is something like finding the philosophers' stone or the elixir vitae. For one thing, I wanted to be able to use the ridiculous, for another the nonsensical, for another the 'obscene.' I wanted to be as personal as I liked, as autobiographical when I felt like it, editorializing or pompous, in short to be able to drop into any intensity of language I liked at any time.

In this large collection he considers many subjects, including his home in Nebraska and his own character and sensibility. In its openness of form and autobiographical content, the book indicates Shapiro's growing affinity now with the views and practice of the younger generation, including the "confessional" poets, as well as those who considered Whitman as the true originator of American poetry. Shapiro has always been too original himself to be anyone's follower, however. Throughout his career, he has demonstrated a profound knowledge of American and English literary traditions, while continuing to create his own unique forms. Perhaps one reason he tends to be neglected today is his unpredictability, the very diversity of his poetry over the years.

After leaving Nebraska, Shapiro taught at the University of California, Davis, until his retirement, in 1984. Despite his long career in the classroom (he also taught at Johns Hopkins, the University of Wisconsin, and Loyola, Chicago), Shapiro has said he did not feel at home there, and was not so much a professor as "sort of a mad guest." In any case, throughout the years he has remained active as a poet and critic. Among the most affecting of his later volumes are *White-Haired Lover* (1968), where he returned to writing in highly polished formal verse, and *Adult Bookstore* (1976). In addition to *The Poetry Wreck: Selected Essays 1950–1970* (1975) and his two-volume autobiography, other recent books are *Collected Poems 1940–1977* (1978), *Love and War, Art and God* (1984), and *New Selected Poems* (1987). Besides winning the Pulitzer, Shapiro has been recognized with a Guggenheim Fellowship, the Shelley Memorial Award, and membership in the American Academy of Arts and Sciences. And in 1969 the great dissenter, despite himself, also won the Bollingen Prize.

# MAXINE KUMIN

"Darlings, it's all a circle," reads a line in Maxine Kumin's poem "Family Reunion," and it is this sense of community which inspires all her work. For Kumin is a poet of attachments—to the family, to the natural world, to the details of everyday life, as well as to the techniques of her craft. During a publishing career spanning four decades, she had been an acute observer of the complex bonds between parents and children and a compassionate witness to the lives, and deaths, of animals. In her reflections upon the body, intimate relations, and women's place in the modern world, she recalls her close friend and literary confidante Anne Sexton, though Kumin's range is broader and her methods different. She has been compared to diverse other writers, as well: to Robert Frost, in her clear-eyed pictures of New England farm life and variations upon the tradition of the pastoral lyric; to Robert Lowell, in her sense of history, generational ties, and religious heritage; and to Elizabeth Bishop, in her precise observations, use of vivid particulars, and mastery of form. But whether on public or private matters, Kumin's writing shows a directness and degree of human warmth distinctly her own.

Maxine Kumin was born in Philadelphia in 1925. Asked about her beginnings as a writer on "Poets in Person," Kumin tells Alicia Ostriker, "I think I started out as one of those awful precocious kids who write little rhyming poems about the first robin and was hailed in the family—a not very literary-type family—as a budding writer." In high school, she notes, she found two mentors, her Latin teacher, who introduced her to the pleasures and discipline of literature, and her English instructor, "who opened me first to poetry." But entering Radcliffe College at age 17, she discovered "a whole new environment, where creative writing was frowned upon." She was further discouraged by a young English professor who told her she had no talent and "would be better advised to say it with flowers." So she did not write for almost a decade.

Kumin took her bachelor's degree in 1946 and her master's in 1948. In 1946 she also married Victor Kumin, and they soon had a son and two daughters. Kumin's experience was typical of that of many women during the years immediately following World War II. In a 1977 interview reprinted in her prose book *To Make A Prairie*, Kumin remarked:

> I was programmed into one kind of life, which was to say: get a college degree, get married, and have a family. It was just after the war, and this was what everyone was desperately doing; the tribe *was* seen as the saving centrality in a world that had gone totally awry. And I came to poetry as a way of saving myself because I was so wretchedly discontented. It just wasn't enough to be a housewife and a mother. It didn't gratify great chunks of me.

On her program, Kumin adds that she when began writing again, it was "in the closet" because "I didn't have anyone to show poems to." She then started sending out light verse to publishers during her third pregnancy. "I made a little pact with myself that I would either sell something before this baby was born or I would give it up entirely." Soon she developed "a cottage industry," with frequent appearances in *Good Housekeeping*, *The Saturday Evening Post*, and other popular magazines. It should be noted (although Kumin is too modest to mention it herself) that "light verse" does not mean "easy verse"; considerable technical skill and wit are required to make a generally short and humorous piece effective. Kumin's extensive practice with tight structures, strict metrics, and ingenious rhymes provided the foundation for the poetry to come.

Kumin traces her transformation from light versifier to serious poet to John Holmes's poetry workshops at the Boston Center for Adult Education, which she attended in the late Fifties. It was there that she met and began her long friendship with Anne Sexton. Kumin once called Holmes "my academic Daddy," but in Sexton she "had found a sister." During the next eighteen years, until Sexton's suicide in 1974, the two read and criticized each other's draft compositions regularly, sometimes daily, often over the telephone. As poets, the two women were and are very different; but in the 1977 interview Kumin recalled, "We didn't try ever to moderate or tamper with the other's voice. We were there as a sounding board to say: that's very strained, that image is wrenched, this is dreadful . . . . She was my closest contact." Kumin also credits her friend as a poet who was "in every way an innovator, both in terms of prosody and subject matter."

As Kumin has stated, Sexton was very daring in breaking taboos and writing about incest, menstruation, abortion, and other topics once considered improper for poetry. In the 1977 interview, Kumin continued, "She made it possible for women to write about the quality of womanhood in a way that just could not have been taken seriously twenty years ago." On the program, Kumin reads an elegy to her friend, "How It Is." She also acknowledges Sexton for encouraging her "to put aside academic concerns and be more open, to confront my own being, confront the world around me."

While this openness has grown over the years, Kumin has always been a very conscious artist and in control of her material (as Sexton often was not). Using all the technical skills at her command, she has been as concerned with form as with feeling. Like Marianne Moore, Kumin is a poet of reticence, and for that she has sometimes been accused of withholding or not being totally honest. But, again like Moore, Kumin prefers "poetic tact" or understatement to hyperbole. "Hyperbole has been so overused that it, like cliché, has lost its power to evoke feeling," she observes in *To Make a Prairie*. "If by understating, one is being not totally honest about the subject, then I guess I would have to say, yes, that I have not been totally honest in poems. But as far as telling the truth as I see it, I would have to say that I think I am always as honest as I can be." Asked directly if the *I* in a poem referred to a character or to the poet herself, Kumin told the interviewer in 1977: "It can be either and it can be a little of both, because the *I* is the persona that the poet is hiding behind. . . . Sometimes it can be very much a persona poem, and sometimes quite an autobiographical poem."

This division—or happy medium—is apparent in Kumin's first book, *Halfway*, published in 1961. In the collection, she treats several subjects that remain central throughout her career: family and cultural heritage, the relation of mankind to nature, and the tenuousness of life. Some of the pieces—the shaped poem "400-Meter Free Style," the sestina "High Dive: A Variant"—describe and employ metaphors from swimming, a recurring symbol in Kumin's work for the skill, practice, and daring required, as well as the risks and dangers faced, in life. Among the most touching poems in the volume are the elegiac "One Dead Friend," dedicated to K. C. Wang; "Poem for My Son," describing the boy at age six learning to swim; and "The Journey," written for her daughter Jane upon her leaving for school at age 13. "It is a dangerous time," "The Journey" concludes, "We exchange kisses; I call your name / and wave you off as the bridge goes under." Here, as in most of her personal poems, Kumin maintains a delicate balance between sentiment and restraint.

In *The Privilege* (1965), Kumin writes of her own parents and childhood, and recalls pivotal moments concerning her religious identity. When the poet was growing up, her family lived next door to a Catholic school and convent, a circumstance that produced internal conflicts for the sensitive child. "Sisyphus," for example, describes the young girl helping a legless man by pushing his cart up a hill: "Up past the sisters of Saint Joe / I pushed my stone so God would know." The man thanks her, calling her "a perfect Christian child." The poem ends: "One day I said I was a Jew. / I wished I had. I wanted to. / / The basket man is gone; the stone / I push uphill is all my own." In "Mother Rosarine," the poet remembers visiting the convent, where the Mother Superior "swung on the door to His Kingdom / through which I did not dare pass." (Kumin discusses her friendship with the nun and the genesis of the poem in *To Make a Prairie*.) Other poems are addressed to her family, as in "The Pawnbroker," a bittersweet elegy to the poet's father which turns lists of commonplace items into extraordinary expressions of love and loss. "It's a catalogue poem to a large extent," Kumin has commented. "It relies on a thickness of listing things to carry the notion. I wrote that elegy, 'Pawnbroker,' initially in syllabics as well as rhyme. That's how terrified I was of writing it." *The Privilege* also contains some of Kumin's strongest love lyrics and presents, under the title "Joppa Diary," a journal in verse describing with meticulous detail and ingenious metaphor the natural life surrounding her country home in New Hampshire.

Precise observations combined with surprising but strikingly appropriate analogies drawn from ordinary objects are hallmarks of Kumin's style, particularly in her writings about nature. Equally characteristic is her use of a variety of challenging poetic forms and conventions, especially in works which deal with the author's most intimate relationships and feelings. Contrary to the prevalent notion that formalism constricts free expression of ideas and emotions or is somehow incompatible with "authenticity," Kumin believes that rigorous form and technique can be liberating. On "Poets in Person," she attests to the value of traditional methods in her own practice:

> I have found over the years that the poems which have been emotionally painful, difficult, personal for me to write—those are the poems that I am most likely going to hammer into a really tight metrical pattern, because the form gives you permission to say the hard things. It's exactly like building a building . . . you excavate for the cellar, and then you put up these wooden forms, and then you pour the concrete, and then after it's hardened, you knock the

wooden forms away. And that's what the formal pattern does for the poem.

Elsewhere, she has said: "The tougher the form the easier it is for me to handle the poem, because the form gives permission to be very gut-honest about feelings. The curious thing for me is that rhyme makes me a better poet. . . . It raises my language to heights that I would not be up to on my own. When I'm writing free verse, I feel as though I am in Indiana, where it's absolutely flat and you can see the horizon 360 degrees around. . . . I lose, I have no sense of, the line."

In the Seventies, Kumin published four collections which further extended her range and established her among the leading writers on family, nature, and the environment. *The Nightmare Factory* (1970) concludes with a series of verses about sickness and death set in "The Old Bad Times," but is largely concerned with love, the natural world, and ties between the generations. The book opens with several "Pasture Poems" drawn from her experiences living on a farm and raising animals. Then follow several pieces set in Amsterdam, Boston, Washington, and other locales in "Going From Here to There." With the third section of "Tribal Poems," Kumin turns to a recurrent theme, the continuum of the family, notably in "The Fairest One of All" (again on her daughter Jane), "Father's Song," and "For My Great-Grandfather: A Message Long Overdue," which concludes: "Welcome, ancestor, Rosenberg the Tailor! / I choose to be a lifetime in your debt."

Kumin was awarded the Pulitzer Prize for her next collection, *Up Country*, published in 1972. Set in rural New England, these pastoral lyrics, like Robert Frost's, present clear-eyed views of the natural world and unsentimental accounts of mankind's relation to it. In a series of "Hermit Poems," Kumin's persona describes bird sounds, a dog's encounter with a skunk, berry picking, and other incidents of country life. Along with wit and humor, the volume is marked by somber reflections, as in "One Small Death in May" and "Woodchucks." One of Kumin's most famous poems, "Woodchucks" describes the angry gardener's warfare upon the destructive rodents; when cyanide fails, she resorts to a .22 shotgun—"I, a lapsed pacifist fallen from grace / puffed with Darwinian pieties for killing"— and manages to eliminate all but one old "wily fellow," and her sense of shame. As in "The Vealers" and "How It Goes On" (read by the author on the program), the poem is an eloquent statement about our domination and frequent mistreatment of animals. "Woodchucks" is also an good example of Kumin's unobtrusive use of meter and rhyme. On "Poets in Person," she remarks on the importance in poetry of maintaining "a conversational tone of voice, as if two intelligent friends were talking to each other." She also recalls with some amusement: "I had a high school student say to me once, after a reading, 'I love your woodchuck poem, and the nicest thing about it is that it doesn't rhyme!' "

*House, Bridge, Fountain, Gate*, published in 1975, takes its title from a phrase by Rainer Maria Rilke, who said that poets may exist "only to say house, bridge, fountain, gate"—that is, to name things. Kumin has stated, "Naming things is a way of owning them"; and referring to the title, she has reiterated that she believes strongly in "the particularizing of things. . . . I think that the one thing that's been consistently true about my poetry is this determination to give authenticity of detail." This credo is illustrated here in Kumin's meticulous attention to the facts of everyday life. The book also includes several poems about the poet's uncles, cousins, and other relatives. Of the autobiographical poems, "Life's Work" is perhaps the most poignant. In introducing her reading, Kumin terms it a "feminist poem" and notes her ambition in adolescence to become a professional swimmer, an aspiration which, like her mother's dream of being a concert pianist, was thwarted by male authority.

*The Retrieval System* appeared in 1978 and was followed by the new and selected poems in *Our Ground Time Here Will Be Brief* (1982). In several poems, Kumin writes of an old neighbor, Henry Manley, who is "sundowning," slowing down and forgetting words because of a stroke or the deterioration of old age. Losing the names of things is terrifying, a severing of contact with reality; so when after much effort Henry regains his memory of common objects like a cup or wristwatch, it is a kind of triumph in which the poet and the reader rejoice. Kumin's sympathy here may reflect her own growing consciousness of mortality in middle-age, and both of the volumes have a melancholy cast. Besides the elegy to Anne Sexton in "How It Is," *The Retrieval System* includes another poem to her friend in "Progress Report," as well as the somber visions of "How It Goes On" and "Changing the Children," with its theme of anger and disappointment with now-grown offspring. But the collection also presents a more positive view of the family continuum, as in "The Envelope," the final reading on the program. Likewise, *Our Ground Time Here Will Be Brief* speaks in "Regret" of "all those annulled connections / all those missed chances / and time running out"; but it also includes "Rejoicing with Henry," the shared joy with a disabled brother in "Out-of-Body Travel," and the celebration of "Family Reunion."

*The Long Approach* (1985) returns to favorite topics of family history and farm life. But the collection also addresses the present time and the larger world "Out There," particularly the specters of terrorism in the Middle East, famine in Africa, and nuclear holocaust. In *Nurture* (1989), Kumin again contemplates the themes of loss and the wonders of nature, but with a new sense of urgency. Speaking of her abiding interest in animals and of the poem "How It Goes On" in response to a 1977 questionnaire, Kumin wrote that for her "the animals in general and horses in particular represent a kind of lost innocence in our technological society and they often stand as a symbol for mute suffering." Now that the triumphs of technology seem to threaten existence itself, creating doubt whether it *will* go on, Kumin reaffirms her faith with "More Tribal Poems," and her hope in a section called "Catchment," in praise of imperilled animals. In *Looking for Luck* (1992), Kumin's urgent concern for animals continues. The collection is bracketed with a prologue and an epilogue that adapt Kiowa and Tlingit legends in which bears figure as symbols of magical power and regeneration. In "Looking for Luck in Bangkok," the poet follows local custom by walking under an elephant for luck, and reflects on the elephant's own misfortune as possible prey to ivory poachers. "Taking the Lambs to Market" reprises the themes of early poems such as "The Vealers" and "How It Goes On." Other poems in the collection return to family matters, as in "A Brief History of Passion," which counterpoints details of her parents' courtship and marriage with contemporaneous literary events. On "Poets in Person," asked whether she felt she was becoming a "political poet," Kumin tells Alicia Ostriker:

> For more years than I care to remember, I felt that poetry was too fragile a vessel to carry the weight of polemical conviction, and that it would sink if we stressed it in this way. And as the situation world-wide has deteriorated, a lot of my more recent poems have just occurred—they have been cries from the heart. A lot of the poems in *Nurture* which are about endangered species, for example, I didn't really set out to write them. They arrived, and they insisted that I deal with it.

In *Nurture* and *Looking for Luck*, as in her other books, when Kumin addresses issues of political and social import, she does so through the individual instance. Avoiding easy rhetoric, she persuades by illuminating the worth of what she cherishes with meticulous attention to detail and care for the language itself. "Well, words are the only 'holy' for me," she has said. Whether writing about public affairs or private affections, she continually surprises with metaphors and lucid perceptions which prove that, indeed, "it's all a circle."

Besides her several poetry collections, Kumin has published four novels, a collection of short stories, and over twenty children's books. Her prose has been collected as *To Make a Prairie: Essays on Poets, Poetry, and Country Living* (1980), as noted, and *In Deep: Country Essays* (1987). Kumin has taught at Tufts, Washington University, Brandeis, Columbia, Princeton, and MIT. In addition to the Pulitzer Prize, her awards include Fellowships from the Academy of American Poets, the National Council on the Arts, and the Bunting Institute. In 1983 she participated in the Arts America Tour, sponsored by the USIA, and in 1981–82 she served as the Consultant in Poetry at the Library of Congress.

# A. R.  A M M O N S

Lydia R. Johnson

"I process life by shaking, / I'm a sifter," A. R. Ammons writes in *The Snow Poems*. The statement, though modest and tinged with more than a hint of self-mockery, is an accurate, partial description of the author's procedures. One of the very few contemporary poets with a background in science, Ammons approaches the world with the eye of a naturalist, closely observing the myriad particulars of daily existence while calmly "sifting" the plethora of data to discern their relationships, and possibly an order within or beyond the infinite diversity of experience.

Archie Randolph Ammons was born in 1926 on his family's small farm near Whiteville, North Carolina. It was a subsistence farm, as he notes on "Poets in Person," and growing up in the country during the Great Depression gave him not only an intimate acquaintance with the works of nature but also a keen sense of the precarious nature of existence. Memories of rural poverty have prompted some of Ammons's most poignant poems, "Hardweed Path Going," "Silver," and "Nelly Myers." After high school, Ammons worked in a shipyard, then served on a destroyer escort in the South Pacific during World War II. It was there, after reading and imitating poems he found in an anthology, that he began writing poetry.

Though he recounts, with some humor, his schoolboy attempts at verse, he tells Alice Fulton in his interview that the reason he continues to write is that "I've been given to a certain more or less recurrent anxiety, and under the stress of that, I look for distraction." Walking, reading, playing music (Ammons is also a pianist), the poet sees "a configuration outside" which "seems to have in it the capacity of meeting the feeling that I have inside, so that this internal stress or tension seems to be released onto what one sees. . . . Writing poems is a marvelous distraction for some other anxiety which may be far worse."

After the war, Ammons attended Wake Forest College in North Carolina on the G.I. Bill and graduated with a B.S. degree in biology in 1949. He served as a grammar school principal in Cape Hatteras until 1951, when he joined his wife, Phyllis Plumbo, in graduate school at the University of California, Berkeley. On campus he met the highly regarded poet and teacher Josephine Miles; and though he did not take classes with her, she agreed to read his poems. She worked with Ammons informally and continued to encourage him when he returned to the East Coast, and suggested that he visit William Carlos Williams.

In 1952, Ammons became an executive with a manufacturer of biological glassware in Millville, New Jersey, a position he held for almost a decade. (On the program, he reads "Gravelly Run," which is set in a place the poet liked to stop on his business trips.) Eventually, Ammons contacted Dr. Williams, as Josephine Miles had suggested, and went to see him several times at his home in Rutherford. By the postwar period the aging Modernist had became a mentor and model for many poets of the younger generation, who were inspired particularly by Williams's emphasis upon spontaneity, open structures, the use of concrete details and colloquial language. As Ammons notes, "There are very few people, I think, not touched by that work." His own forms frequently draw upon Williams's example, as in "Corsons Inlet" and many of the short poems.

After Ezra Pound's command to "make it new," Williams's aesthetic motto, "no ideas but in things," has become the most famous dictum of contemporary poetry. But taken at face value, this insistence upon the specific, local, and immediate particu-

lars of material reality is too limited and constricting for a poet
of Ammons's complex vision and philosophical temperament.
After all, Williams's slogan is itself an idea; and with his characteristic serious humor, Ammons would enlarge the simple in-
junction by adding: "no things but in ideas," "no ideas but in
ideas," and "no things but in things." For Ammons, ideas and
things are inseparable, and never static; what interests him is
connection and motion, how mind and matter relate and inter-
act. As a student of the sciences, the poet understands that
everything in nature is interconnected while in flux; and in his
imaginative constructs, he prefers fluidity to dogma and set
forms.

In spirit Ammons shares much with his Romantic fore-
bears in the 19th Century, Walt Whitman and Ralph Waldo
Emerson. Like Whitman, he has a democratic sensibility that
seeks to embrace the universe and to celebrate its plenitude. He
says in "Still": "everything is / / magnificent with existence, is
in / surfeit of glory". With Emerson, he delights in the concrete
details, complexities, and contradictions of life, but at the same
time is drawn like that philosopher-poet by a desire to find
some transcendent truth which might connect the separate aspects or encompass the several processes that comprise earthly
reality.

Ammons is very much a product of this century, however,
and the revelations of science and his own skepticism prevent
him from making easy assumptions about transcendental Unity
and absolute Truth, despite their abiding allure. Like many other modern artists and thinkers, the poet focuses instead upon
the epistemological questions of how we know what we know
(if indeed we do know). Thus, the conflict between empirical
details and rational abstractions, between the universal (or
community) and the individual (autonomy)—"the one:many
problem," as he says in "Sphere"—and the complex relation
between matter and the mind perceiving it form both back-
grounds and major subjects in Ammons's poetry. The tensions
between these dichotomies also create the subtle motions and
quiet dramas in his work.

Leaving aside dry generalities, probably the best explanation (and demonstration) of Ammons's method appears in his most famous poem, "Corsons Inlet." The setting is a stretch of dunes along the New Jersey shoreline, and as the poet takes a leisurely ramble he makes minute observations of nature which lead to larger insights:

> the walk liberating, I was released from forms,
> from the perpendiculars,
> > straight lines, blocks, boxes, binds
> of thought
> into the hues, shadings, rises, flowing bends and blends
> > of sight:
>
> > > I allow myself eddies of meaning:
> yield to a direction of significance
> running
> like a stream through the geography of my work:
> > you can find
> in my sayings
> > > swerves of action
> > > like the inlet's cutting edge:
> > there are dunes of motion,
> organizations of grass, white sandy paths of remembrance
> in the overall wandering of mirroring mind:
>
> but Overall is beyond me: is the sum of these events
> I cannot draw, the ledger I cannot keep, the accounting
> beyond the account:

If the overall design of nature or meaning of existence is beyond the poet's (and our) comprehension, the process of observing and discovering the vital particulars, including the workings of the human "mirroring mind," seems reward enough in Ammons's poems.

By avoiding "boxes" or the habits of categorization—whether the heady abstractions of the philosopher or the reductive formulas of the scientist—the poet remains open to "the swerves of action" in which life expresses itself. The shape of the poem itself, as in "Corsons Inlet," reflects the meandering movements of nature and the human mind. In place of closed forms or poetic conventions, Ammons prefers to take his chances with openness and improvisation. One of our most prolific experimentalists, Ammons is comfortable with the provisional, willing to allow himself "eddies of meaning." As he says on "Poets in Person," "I write each poem as a kind of trial of a possibility." In Ammons's poems, "arguments" flow rather than follow "straight lines." The poet tends to circle his subjects, suggesting several points of view. Likewise, in place of "boxes," he offers (a favorite Ammons figure) the sphere. Like another literary ancestor, Emily Dickinson, Ammons is a poet of "Circumference" whose secular hymns celebrate both the central and peripheral aspects of existence in their search for wholeness.

Ammons's first volume was called *Ommateum*, and was dedicated to Josephine Miles. The title is particularly appropriate, as the term means "compound eye," as of an insect. (Borrowing from the scientific lexicon is another characteristic of the poet's style, which also mixes the language of the Bible, folk songs, and technology with the vernacular.) In his preface to the volume, the author explains the poems "suggest a many-sided view of reality; an adoption of tentative, provisional attitudes, replacing the partial, unified, prejudicial, and rigid . . . ." Almost forty years later, Ammons's poetic objectives have not changed. On "Poets in Person," he tells Alice Fulton that his work aims

> to dissolve positions that people take that seem rigid—political, philosophical, religious. Any kind of too-much-conviction that could lead to, for example, massacres or wars or things like that frightens me . . . what I like to do in my poems is to sort of lift those structures into some kind of examination, in which you show the many sides and a little uncertainty breaks out. I'm wary of people too certain of what they have to say.

*Ommateum* expresses the poet's urge toward transcendence, and the thirty lyrics in the collection might be considered "lenses" through which the poet examines, among other things, history, the earth, the nature of reality, and man's place in the universe. Although its opening poem, "So I said I am Ezra," is often anthologized today, the ambitious volume was virtually ignored when it first appeared, from a "vanity" press, in 1955.

Ammons waited almost a decade before publishing another book. In *Expressions of Sea Level* the poet focuses on themes which have become central to all his work: what mankind can and cannot know, and the conflict (and desire for unity) between flesh and spirit. In contrast to the forced and sometimes strident tone of his first book, Ammons's stance now is calm, often meditative, and even religious, as the poet comes to terms with human limitations. A number of the poems recall the Romantic attitudes of Emerson and Whitman in their quest for transcendence and unity. One may note, in particular, "Guide" and "Hymn," another poem read on the program. In "Guide," the irresolvable conflict between spirit and matter is accepted from the start: "You cannot come to unity and remain material: / in that perception is no perceiver." In "Hymn," the poet addresses a "you" (as he explains on the program, "whatever one conceives ultimate reality to be . . . that which is"), whom he seeks to find: "I know if I find you I will have to leave the earth / and go on out / over the sea marshes . . . ." But Ammons begins with the conditional "if": he cannot share Emerson's confidence in his quest. With his modern scientific perspective, he considers two directions. One leads outward (the macrocosm) and "farther than the loss of sight / into the unseasonal undifferentiated empty stark". The other route delves inward (the microcosm), "going right on down where the eye sees only traces". However, the "you" is "everywhere partial and entire . . . on the inside of everything and on the outside"—and the poet-seeker must remain on the earth of his origins: "if I find you I must stay here with the separate leaves." The poem's total lack of punctuation suggests the ongoing, unending nature of his quest.

Other poems in the volume employ what has become the hallmark of Ammons's style: the colon. On "Poets in Person," the poet wryly explains: "I never liked poems that had capital letters and periods . . . I don't know why that should be objectionable, but I thought, democratically, all the letters should be the same size. If you have a colon, you don't have a capital letter." Alice Fulton adds that the colon also indicates equivalence, as it equates both sides of the poet's phrases. While establishing this balance, the colon alerts readers and pushes them on to the next steps in the continuing process of the poem.

In 1965 Ammons published one of his most novel experiments, *Tape for the Turn of the Year*, a book-length meander consisting of necessarily short-line notations originally typed on a roll of adding-machine tape. Over a period of about a month (December 1963 to January 1964), the poet recorded a kind of journal combining commonplaces with astute observations. Of particular interest are his comments about his role as a writer, as in this key passage:

> *ecology* is my word: tag
> me with that: come
> in there:
>     you will find yourself
> in a firmless country:
>     centers & peripheries
>     in motion,
>     organic,
>         interrelations!

In *Corsons Inlet* (1965), Ammons continues to explore the one:many question, trying to find order by concentrating on the external realities and his own perceptions. As noted, the title poem presents a compact exposition of Ammons's poetics, as well as an admission of the limitations of his method. Still, the prospect of continuation offers hope of further discoveries: "tomorrow a new walk is a new walk." A rather darker image of the journey is conveyed in the final poem of the volume, "Gravelly Run." After looking and reflecting on the beautiful scene where "the air's glass / jail seals each thing in its entity," he concludes: "no use to make any philosophies here: / I see no / god in the holly . . . stranger, / hoist your burdens, get on down the road."

About this time, Ammons himself "got on down the road," by radically changing his career path. In 1964 he accepted a position as an English instructor at Cornell University, and within the short space of seven years he rose to the rank of full professor. This shift in direction resulted in an equally remarkable increase in his production as a poet. By the end of the decade, he published two other volumes, *Northfield Poems* and his first *Selected Poems*, which were followed by seven full-length collections in the Seventies; to date he has published over twenty volumes.

Throughout his career, Ammons has alternated in his writing between long or medium-length meditative poems and short (often very short) lyrics. In many of the longer compositions, the poet is apt to combine the perspective and vocabulary of the botanist, biologist or astronomer with the speculative stance of the philosopher. A singular example, and one of Ammons's most ambitious experiments, is *Sphere: The Form of a Motion* (1974), a book-length poem which draws upon his several resources to contemplate the flux and stable center of life—in one sentence 1,860 lines long. Although it employs regular, arbitrary patterns (155 stanzas of four tercets), its movement is flexible, working, like the mind, by association. And as it proceeds—with pointed comments, curious musings, conflicting ideas—the poem reflects the complex mental and emotional life of its creator.

Perhaps inevitably, given their scope, not all the longer poems are of equal quality, or at least not equally appealing to some critics. Ammons's eloquence can be interrupted by dull passages. The short poems, on the other hand, are among his most popular and memorable; which is to say, one wants to memorize them because of their witty wordplay, sly humor, pithy perceptions, and sometimes tart interpretations of the human condition. To take but two examples, here is "Weathering":

> A day without rain is like
> a day without sunshine

and "Success Story":

> I never got on good
> relations with the world
>
> first I had nothing
> the world wanted

> then the world had
> nothing I wanted

Since it's hard to resist—a third example, "Small Song"—

> The reeds give
> way to the
>
> wind and give
> the wind away

—in which sound and sense and form are cunningly fused. Many of Ammons's short poems remind one of William Carlos Williams's intricate, economical "little word machines" (as he called them) at their elegant best.

On "Poets in Person," Ammons has a good deal to say about his motives and methods in writing. He tells Alice Fulton, "I am not so much interested in the subject matter of a poem as in the dynamics . . . the way it moves. I like for the poem to imitate action." He illustrates by making an analogy between writing a poem and performing ordinary actions like dancing or playing football. "To me the same dynamics of action are involved in those as in poetry." Most telling are his remarks about the distinctions between scientific or descriptive discourse and poetic creation:

> I think one of the great potentialities of poetry is that, while it moves on the surface with image and color and motion and sense, it develops, not an exposition finally, but a disposition . . . what art does, and what explanation can't do, is that it stops. The poem ends. And at that point, it become a construct, a disposition rather than an exposition, and it is silent at that point and indefinable. And this cures us of the fragmentation that words imposed on us from the beginning. You see, by the use of words and sentences and sense, we're able to break down a silent world into certain clear things to say about it. But then we need to be rescued from the fragmentation we've made of the world. And we do that by art,

by putting these motions back together and actually reaching the indefinable again. . . . it's not a piece of knowledge that you put in books, but something you encounter, something you live with as if it were another person, as you come back again and again to a piece of sculpture and just stand and be with it. When we get to that point in a poem, where we be with it rather than ask what it means or explain how it got there, then we are back with the indefinable, we are restored to ourselves and feeling can move through us again.

In 1972, Ammons published his *Collected Poems 1951–1971*, which won the National Book Award, one of several honors which now include the Bollingen Prize (1975), a MacArthur Fellowship (1981), the National Book Critics Circle Award (1982), and membership in the American Academy and Institute of Arts and Sciences (1982). In the Eighties, he supplemented *The Selected Poems 1951–1977* with the *Selected Longer Poems* of 1980 (which includes the important "Essay on Poetics" and "Hibernaculum"), and published five other collections, as well: *A Coast of Trees* (1981), *Worldly Hopes* (1982), *Lake Effect Country* (1983), *The Selected Poems: Expanded Edition* (1986), and *Sumerian Vistas* (1987). Ammons first collected his short pieces in *Briefings: Poems Small and Easy* (1971), to which may now be added *The Really Short Poems* (1990), some 160 of them representing his entire career.

In all this impressive outpouring, "sifting" or "shaking," Ammons has shaped a body of work that confirms the understanding he expressed in "Corsons Inlet":

> I will try
> to fasten into order enlarging grasps of disorder,
>     widening
> scope, but enjoying the freedom that
> Scope eludes my grasp, that there is no finality of vision,
> that I have perceived nothing completely,
>     that tomorrow a new walk is a new walk.

# W. S. MERWIN

"I suppose I prayed to be obsessed with writing, I very much did," W. S. Merwin tells James Richardson on "Poets in Person," recalling his college days. In a career now spanning five decades, that obsession has resulted in a voluminous body of work, including fifteen books of poetry and nineteen of translations from many languages, which have made him one of the most prominent of the postwar poets. All of Merwin's ten full-length original collections remain in print: an unusual achievement for any contemporary poet, and all the more remarkable given the complex, inward character of much of this work.

In many ways, Merwin's is a very private poetry. Over the years, it has become the record of a spiritual journey spoken in voices which have evolved as the author has pursued an elusive quest for the authentic, in the self and in art. But these several voices—haunting, mysterious, compelling—have obviously spoken to, and for, a great number of others. For in their changing tones, Merwin's poems have continued to address fundamental issues.

Merwin is primarily a philosophical poet whose lyrics and narratives ponder the dilemma of contemporary men and women facing and trying to find their place in a universe now devoid of discernible meaning. His themes center on the questions of human identity, isolation, and estrangement from the rest of creation; how, in its confu-

sion, fear, and self-deception, mankind considers itself superior
to nature, and becomes destructive in its attempts at domination. So baldly summarized, this rich and protean body of work
may sound forbidding. But it has in fact proved bracing, often
exhilarating, not least because Merwin's engrossing voice and
his extraordinary vision repeatedly evoke a sense of wonder at a
universe which lies just beyond the grasp of words.

William Stanley Merwin was born in New York City in
1927, and grew up in Union City, New Jersey, and Scranton,
Pennsylvania. As the poet recounts on his program, his first
attempts at writing were hymns for his father, a Presbyterian
minister: "I thought the least he could do was to include them
in the Sunday services. He didn't do that." A number of poems
in Merwin's 1960 book *The Drunk in the Furnace* depict several
relatives who are, with the exception of his grandmother, un-
pleasantly conventional and narrowmindedly religious. And in
his prose collection, *Unframed Originals: Recollections* (1982), as
well as its poetic companion, *Opening the Hand* (1983), the author paints a delicately devastating picture of a family that was
emotionally cool and spiritually impoverished, particularly his
miserly father.

Merwin attended Princeton and graduated in 1947, then
spent another year there studying foreign languages. His teachers
included the noted critic R. P. Blackmur and the brilliant young
John Berryman, the subject of a fascinating autobiographical
poem read by the author on the program. From 1949 to 1951,
Merwin lived in France and Portugal, where he worked as a
private teacher and translator. He also travelled to Majorca to
meet Robert Graves. Arriving unannounced, he was greeted at
the door by the poet himself, who invited him in to tea; after
talking into the evening, Graves asked Merwin to be his son's
tutor.

Graves was that rarity, a poet who supported himself (and
several dependents) entirely by his writing, with translations
and extremely popular novels like *I, Claudius* sustaining what
he considered his primary vocation, poetry. Like the master,
Merwin too has been able to live by his pen, rather than a
professorship. His many translations—from both classical and

modern Western and Oriental literature, including Euripides, Persius, Neruda, and Mandelstam; *The Poem of the Cid* and *The Song of Roland*; and other Spanish, French, Chinese, Japanese, and even Sanskrit poetry—are as renowned as his original work. On "Poets in Person," Merwin recalls his early years working as a translator: "It seemed to be a way of practicing writing, or learning literally how to write, how to deal with the language itself. . . . I didn't have a very high standard of living, but I could live that way and remain independent."

Merwin has never held an academic position, nor has he been a member of a literary school or movement, though critics have associated him with certain contemporaries and styles of poetry. Merwin's extensive interest in world literatures has given him a deep knowledge of the Great Tradition, and this has been an abiding influence on his own poetry, as is evident in his use of myths, legends, and folktales in his longer narrative poems. Particularly in his early books, Merwin uses the wisdom contained in this ancient heritage to re-examine modern-day realities.

*A Mask for Janus*, Merwin's first book, was selected by W. H. Auden for the Yale Younger Poets Series and published in 1952. As the title implies, the collection looks in two directions: to the past through, for example, the archetypal themes of voyage-and-discovery and the birth-death-rebirth cycle, and to the present time of disillusionment and fragmentation. Here the poet conveys his vision through traditional verse forms (odes, ballads, sestinas) and deliberately archaic diction. In his *Selected Poems* (1988), Merwin chose to represent the volume with only three poems, including "The Ballad of John Cable and Three Gentlemen," which recasts the story of *Everyman* but without the morality play's hopeful conclusion promising redemption.

In *The Dancing Bears* (1954), Merwin returns to old myths to construe new meanings. The most famous poem in the collection is "East of the Sun and West of the Moon," a retelling of the story of Cupid and Psyche (also translated from Apuleius by Graves). In Merwin's version, the tale becomes a vehicle conveying the poet's several ideas about the nature of reality and love, and the power of belief and art. Central to the fable—and to Merwin's artistic philosophy—is the idea that "All magic is metaphor": language, man-made signs give order and meaning to life.

*Green with Beasts* (1956) signals a shift in the poet's subject matter and style. From classical myths elaborately, and sometimes too self-consciously, rendered, Merwin turns to Biblical stories, fables, and fictions of his own making to express the mystery of the world, and speaks with a simpler voice. Of the several admirable poems in the collection, "Leviathan," "The Prodigal Son," and "The Annunciation" deserve special notice. In "The Annunciation," the speaker tries, with difficulty, to tell the reader of her remarkable experience; but despite specific details and repetitions, ordinary language is incapable of communicating the extraordinary, indeed ineffable experience she has undergone. The reader sympathizes and shares her wonderment, a sense of the otherworldly manifesting itself amid ordinary "reality."

In "Learning a Dead Language," Merwin reflects more directly on the mysteries of his métiers as translator and poet: "There is nothing for you to say. You must / Learn first to listen." Learning, remembering, the poet may discover the origins of poetry in what precedes the words: "You may find at last the passion that composed it . . . what passion may be heard / When there is nothing for you to say." A leitmotif through Merwin's work is the idea that poetry somehow exists even before it is expressed in words (perhaps like the Word's existence before the Creation).

*The Drunk in the Furnace* (1960) contains a number of poems about Merwin's family, as noted, and presents some of the poet's darkest visions of American community and the human condition generally. Several other pieces—notably, "Odysseus," "The Ice-Berg," "Bell Buoy," "The *Portland* Going Out"— center on the sea and voyages, ancient symbols of menace, delusion, and danger, where the drama of man, with his spirit of hope and adventure, is played out against the strength of pitiless nature. Appearing last in the collection, the title poem does, however, suggest some hope. The drunk (a figure for the

poet) is an outcast living in an abandoned furnace, to the irrita-
tion of the villagers "in their tar-paper church." They shun him
(with "Their Reverend," they "nod and hate trespassers"); but
when he bangs on the sides of his shelter, their children are
drawn "to its siren / Crescendo, and agape on the crumbling
ridge / Stand in a row and learn."

Beautifully crafted, bold in its reimaginings of ancient
myth and lore, and beguiling with its original ideas, Merwin's
work in these first books established him as one of the important poets of his generation. But the writer himself was not
satisfied. "I just felt that I'd come to the end of something, that
this was a way of writing I couldn't continue," he says on "Poets
in Person." There followed two years of silence, "and all of a
sudden the day came when I simply sat down and the first
poem of *The Moving Target* was there."

Published in 1963, the collection marks a major turning
point, when Merwin re-emerged drastically self-transformed.
In the words of James Richardson: "Suddenly—or so it seemed
to readers, though it was no doubt slow and agonizing for Merwin himself, and though in hindsight the change seems logical
—we had a new poet. The grandiloquent traditionalist was suddenly turning out elliptical, unpunctuated free verse that leapt
vertiginously from image to image and seemed governed by a
secret logic."

In his "Inscription for a Burned Bridge," Merwin indicates
he has left the old ways behind. Abandoning tradition and received forms—and along with these conventions, even punctuation and the rules of syntax—he begins a harrowing journey
into the interior. Thus he cautions: "I have gone in with the
river. / I will serve you no longer but you may follow me." For
the poet, it is necessary to strip away the artifices that order (and
conceal) the fluid complexities of consciousness in order to confront the alienation of the self. For the reader, this new style
may be confusing, but it commands attention.

In *The Moving Target* and the works following, Merwin lays
bare his struggle to deal with the existential dilemma of discovering purpose and a way of acting authentically in a world that

no longer has objective meaning. Merwin considers the present age in its disillusionment in his poem "The Gods" (printed in his next book, *The Lice*), which accepts the stark new reality that

> The gods are what has failed to become of us
> Now it is over we do not speak
> Now the moment has gone it is dark . . . .

In an age of unbelief following the "death of God," history and social structures cannot show the way, and indeed they further alienate human beings from themselves by forcing them to assume false or preconditioned identities.

In "Acclimatization," for example, the poet expresses the predicament we all share living in a society where wholeness, true selfhood, is exchanged for the illusory rewards offered by the dehumanized powers that be ("them," "the empire"). Repeatedly Merwin depicts aspects of this divided self, with its dissociation of feelings from perception, using his new idiosyncratic, disjunctive style and several personal symbols (since authenticity demands each person find his own answers, his own way). Favorite images—stone, hand, glove, mirror, window, door, lock and key—are situated in dreamlike, haunted landscapes reflective of the poet's psychic condition. Because of such figuration, Merwin is sometimes termed a "deep image" poet and associated with contemporaries like Robert Bly, Galway Kinnell, and others who try to evoke the subconscious through such concrete yet multivalent symbolism. And because of his use of ellipsis, seemingly arbitrary combinations of objects, and imaginary landscapes, he is often called as a surrealist. But such classifications are inadequate, and misleading; Merwin's work is not so easily categorized.

On "Poets in Person," Merwin himself rejects such labelling. In his discussion of surrealism and "deep image" poetry with James Richardson, he notes: "It's very easy to sort of use the word 'surrealist' as a way of saying, 'Well, I don't have to say anything more about *that*.'" Likewise, he points out that the use of dreams or dream imagery is far from new to poetry: "You could go through *The Divine Comedy*—that wonderfully rational, apparently rational poem—and keep mining out those images of the deep, deep unconscious that Dante's using." Merwin also calls into question the notion that images and metaphors are solely the product of the poet's fantasy or that so-called surrealist effects are constructed from figments of his imagination. On the program, he offers as a striking illustration an actual incident with Robert Bly in which Merwin showed how a supposedly surrealistic image in fact arose from a commonplace natural occurrence—flies circling a shaft of sunlight in a barn. Equally telling is the poet's description of the origin and setting of "The Shirts," which he also reads on his program.

"The Shirts" and "Bread" (as well as other poems presented on the program) are not without their challenges; their images and structures are perhaps more evocative than obvious in their meaning. But even on first encounter they do communicate. This is certainly true when the poems are *heard*, particularly in the author's own superb oral interpretations. In this connection, it should be noted that the speaker in many of Merwin's poems adopts an oracular tone, the poems become a kind of incantation, which suggests that the words presented are not so much scripts to be analyzed as utterances to be experienced.

Merwin's work has been the subject of much literary criticism; indeed, his ambiguities and opacities seem to invite scholarly speculation. And poems that resist interpretation, even by learned critics, are often considered "difficult." On the program Professor Richardson asks the poet if he thinks the term applies to himself. While he admits the "ellipses and leaps in the poems in *The Moving Target* and *The Lice* and *The Carrier of Ladders* have always seemed difficult to some people," he denies that he has been "willfully obscure," pointing out "the fact that children have always responded to those poems. . . . And you know, children don't stop to wonder about whether they understand a poem or not. They either respond to it or they don't."

Still, it must be admitted, many of Merwin's poems remain obscure, especially those toward the end of *The Moving Target* and elsewhere in later books, including *Writings to an Unfinished Accompaniment* (1973). But in most instances, elegant clarity or logical continuity would be inappropriate and incapable of expressing the sense of the poet's angst or spiritual struggle. In *The Lice* (1967), various aspects of this turmoil are revealed, as the poet explores man's alienation from the rest of creation. As noted, "The Gods" suggests a world from which the deity and traditional belief have fled, leaving man to himself. Thinking himself superior, man now turns to (and on) the world, and abuses his power. But, the poet asks at the conclusion of the poem,

> What is man that he should be infinite
> The music of a deaf planet
> The one note
> Continues clearly this is
>
> The other world
> These strewn rocks belong to the wind
> If it could use them

Several other poems in the collection—notably, "Fly," "The Finding of Reasons," "December Night," and "Watchers"—consider man's irresponsible behavior in assaulting the rest of creation.

"For a Coming Extinction" considers our self-importance as we exterminate other species, while "The Last One" provides an acerbic parable on mankind's greed: "Everywhere was theirs because they thought so." But after the thoughtless destruction ("Well they cut everything because why not."), "the shadow" of nature has its revenge, as man himself faces extinction: "The ones that were left went away to live if it [the shadow] would let them." Other poems in the volume, like "For the Anniversary of My Death" (also read by the author), speak in a more direct and personal manner of the poet's own relation to the world.

In 1970 Merwin published *The Carrier of Ladders*, which was awarded the Pulitzer Prize. These poems, written when the poet was in his late forties, are more subdued in tone and indicate a greater acceptance of his fate and share in the human condition, its paradoxes, and often intractable problems. But the poet's sympathy with his fellows is perhaps even greater now. One of the many memorable works from the volume is

"The Removal." As noted on the program, the sequence was written during the Vietnam war and depicts the plight of Native Americans who were dispossessed and driven from their land in the 19th Century. Merwin presents these events in the third person, but also from the victims' point of view in the opening and closing sections of the poem. The two perspectives, together with the poet's masterful use of simple but striking images, recreates the historical scene with a palpable immediacy. Dedicated *"to the endless tribe,"* the poem also offers poignant testimony to a shameful episode whose effects continue to this day.

In *Writings to an Unfinished Accompaniment* (1973), Merwin's approach is again through the private symbols and ambiguous imagery of earlier volumes, which seem calculated to keep the reader disoriented or on guard. Particularly haunting is the poem read by the author, "Bread," which portrays the estrangement of modern man—"wandering on / searching"—and the poet asks:

> have they forgotten the pale caves
> they dreamed of hiding in
> their own caves
> full of the waiting of their footprints
> hung with the hollow marks of their groping
> full of their sleep and their hiding . . . .

In "Habits," the poet presents an unnerving picture of himself being destroyed by these unconscious kinds of behavior: "they go on handing me around . . . then they hang onto my memory / thinking it's theirs . . . they borrow / most of my tongues to tell me / that they're me . . . ."

*The Compass Flower* (1977) gives other examples of man's sense of loss, but the collection is more hopeful and contains a number of tender poems. Particularly engaging is "Kore," a twenty-four-part sequence celebrating beauty and the power of love to renew life. From this collection, the poet reads sections of "St Vincent's," which describes and meditates on the hospital building as seen from the poet's Greenwich Village apartment.

*Opening the Hand* appeared in 1983 and contains a number of family portraits, as noted, as well as other autobiographical pieces which carry an elegiac note. And more recently, in *The Rain in the Trees* (1988), Merwin again returns to the past in touching poems about childhood ("Being Early," "Memory," "Pastures"). Several others address the present and our continuing decimation of other species and poisoning of the biosphere. But in the midst of mourning, the poet, now in his sixties, also finds new love, and with it rebirth ("Late Spring," "Anniversary on the Island," "Travelling Together"). Ironically, Merwin rediscovers love in his sometime home, New York City, whose towers oversee much of the ecological degradation his poems decry.

Besides New York and the other countries noted, Merwin has also lived in Mexico and in England, where he wrote radio scripts for the BBC. About a decade ago the wandering poet settled on the island of Maui. It may be noted that the photograph on the jacket of *The Rain in the Trees* gives a glimpse of ohia forest in Hawaii National Park, and that for several decades Merwin has not only written poems in defense of the natural world but has been active in the environmental movement, working especially to save the rain forests. In addition to the many books of poetry and translations, Merwin has published three volumes of prose: *The Miner's Pale Children* (1970), *Houses and Travellers* (1977), and, as mentioned, *Unframed Originals* (1982). Other previously uncollected prose pieces—memoirs, essays, statements, stories, and interviews—were printed under the title *Regions of Memory* in 1987; eight of his plays have also been produced here and abroad. The fledgling author's prayer to be obsessed with writing was indeed answered, and in his inspired poetry Merwin has repeatedly fulfilled his aim: "to give utterance to the unutterable experience of being alive."

# GWENDOLYN BROOKS

If a true measure of an author's fame is how many have committed that writer's work to memory, Gwendolyn Brooks has achieved a status attained by few other American poets since World War II. In a time when, with the exception of song lyrics, poems are seldom learned "by heart," countless people can recite Brooks's "We Real Cool"—not only because it has become a staple of classroom anthologies, but because repeating the poem is enjoyable. Today Brooks remains the best known and best loved of the black poets; but she also holds interest on several levels besides the popularity of one poem. Brooks began her publishing career during World War II, and the changes in her verse style and attitude toward writing parallel some of the major transformations in American poetry, and society generally, in the following decades.

Gwendolyn Brooks was born in 1917 in Topeka, Kansas, but since early childhood has lived in Chicago, on the city's South Side, the setting for many of her poems. In her autobiographical *Report from Part One* (1972), Brooks recalls she was a shy and sensitive child who stayed close to home and spent her time reading. Her parents encouraged the precocious youngster when she began writing in grade school. In her "Poets in Person" interview with Alice Fulton, Brooks explains: "My mother told me that when I was seven years old, I brought her a page of rhymes, and she said, 'You are going to be the lady Paul

Laurence Dunbar.' That was high praise because Paul Laurence Dunbar was a very famous black poet, and we had all of his works in the house, and my father used to recite his poems to my brother and myself." Brooks also remembers that when a teacher did not believe the student had written her verses by herself, her mother would go to school and set the teacher straight.

When she was fifteen, Brooks also tells Alice Fulton, she discovered the work of several black poets, including Sterling Brown, Countee Cullen, Claude McKay, and Langston Hughes. "So it was a delight to me to find that it was not only Paul Laurence Dunbar who was writing poetry and being published but all these others. So I thought there was some hope for myself, because by that time I knew what I wanted to do was to write poetry." When she was 16, Brooks met Langston Hughes at a reading he gave in her family's church. Her mother insisted she show the famous poet and journalist a sample of her work, and after reading it Hughes predicted someday she would publish a book.

Brooks attended several high schools and Wright Junior College in Chicago. On the eve of World War II, she married Henry Blakely and they soon had a son and a daughter. Brooks's first poetry collection, *A Street in Bronzeville*, was published in 1945, just as the war was coming to a close. The name in the title was coined by a reporter at the *Chicago Defender* to describe a large section of the South Side, and the book presents several vignettes of ordinary people who live there amid poverty, frustration, violence, and loneliness. Brooks's street scenes are taken from daily inner-city life and from her own experience, as in "kitchenette building," as she notes before reading the poem. Brooks's other portraits—of an old married couple, a preacher, a woman haunted by her abortions, a handicapped girl—are also deftly drawn. The poet's tone is generally sympathetic, but can be witty and satiric too, as in the sketch of a glamour-seeker "at the hairdresser's" and in the detailed examination of "The Sundays of Satin-Legs Smith."

In *A Street in Bronzeville* Brooks pointedly treats subjects that are central to all of her work: the debilitating effects of poverty and prejudice, the resourcefulness as well as shortcomings of human character, and the resiliency of individual will in the search for happiness. The book also demonstrates the poet's skill and versatility in using or adapting a number of traditional forms, particularly the sonnet. Brooks's interest in the form began early. "Of course, I read Shakespeare's sonnets in school," she notes on the program, "and I liked them enough to read them at home." As late as 1969 she told an interviewer she thought "there are things colloquial and contemporary that can be done with the sonnet form." Ballads, blank verse, and quatrains are also favorite forms in the early work, where the influence of Frost, Dickinson, and Eliot is most apparent. In attitude she resembles Whitman, as well, particularly in her empathy for many different kinds of people and in her ability to represent diverse ways of life. But in spirit and style—particularly in the musical mix of colloquial speech with strong rhythmic patterns —Brooks's deepest affinities lie with the original black poetic tradition, particularly the blues, and with the practice of Langston Hughes. (See, for example, her incisive portrait of Mame in "Queen of the Blues" and her critique of hierarchies in the black community in "The Ballad of Pearl May Lee.")

In 1946 Brooks received a Guggenheim Fellowship and an award from the National Institute of Arts and Letters, which supported her work on her next collection. *Annie Allen* was published in 1949 and received wide recognition, including the Pulitzer Prize for Poetry. The book is divided in several sections, portraying Annie Allen through different poetic approaches. The first part traces her early family life in eleven brief scenes and is followed by "The Anniad," an elaborate mock-heroic narrative of Annie's later life told in rhymed, seven-line stanzas. The final and strongest section, "The Womanhood," describes the realities of day-to-day life in verses similar to *Bronzeville*'s urban ballads and sonnets. The opening sequence considers "the children of the poor," with Annie Allen asking in the second poem, "What shall I give my children? who are poor, / Who are adjudged the leastwise of the land". In prefacing her reading of the fourth poem, a Petrarchan sonnet, Brooks notes that Annie "has been thinking about whether or not she should expose her children to 'culture' . . . and she has become very desperate and says that first line in a fit of semi-hysterical anger: 'First fight. Then fiddle.' " The poet points out that her protagonist is very much like her own mother, "who of course had her moments of sadness and discouragement, but took her children to the Art Institute and to the Field Museum, the Museum of Science and Industry, and got them books at Christmastime. So it is far from being advice to the young to get out their guns." The sestet concludes:

> Win war. Rise bloody, maybe not too late
> For having first to civilize a space
> Wherein to play your violin with grace.

"There's a little hint there, of course," Brooks dryly observes, "that it's rather hard to concentrate on the delicacies and sweetnesses of art if you're hungry and you're not in a place that is civilized so that you can attend to those wonders."

Brooks continues her social commentary in other poems in the section. In part VII, "I love those little booths at Benvenuti's" portrays the attitudes of whites of the period out on a "slumming" tour. They go to a Bronzeville restaurant (in New York, it would be a Harlem nightclub) and expect to be entertained by an exotic show of "dusky folk, so clamorous!" But they are disappointed when "Nobody here will take the part of jester. . . . The colored people will not 'clown.' " The following poem depicts "Beverly Hills, Chicago," an affluent suburb, as viewed by a black couple as they drive by. They admire the lifestyle of the rich, with their "golden gardens": "Even the leaves fall down in lovelier patterns here." The speaker realizes, however, that these people may also have troubles, and even sympathizes: "Nobody is saying that these people do not ultimately cease to be." But the disparity between rich and poor prompts the observation: "It is just that so often they live till their hair is white." As the couple move on, they note: "Nobody hates these people. / At least, nobody driving by in this car. . . . But it is only natural that we should think we have not enough."

Those who truly do not have enough are the subjects of Brooks's next poetry book for adults, *The Bean Eaters* (1960). (In

1956, she published a collection for children, *Bronzeville Boys and Girls*, following her 1953 novel, *Maud Martha*.) The title is taken from Van Gogh's painting "The Potato Eaters," and the poet recalls, "I said to myself, 'The Bean Eaters' is probably more appropriate for this collection of blacks who are not very rich . . . because a pound of beans in such a family will go farther than a pound of potatoes: you just add more water." After Brooks's reading of the title poem, Alice Fulton notes the final line suggests the dispossessed who live on the fringes of society, not only the old couple in the poem but the rest of the ghetto dwellers in the book, including the teenagers in the volume's most famous poem. In introducing her reading of "We Real Cool," Brooks says she was inspired when she passed a pool hall in her neighborhood.

> And I said to myself, Why aren't they in school? . . .
> And I wondered, however, how they felt about them-
> selves, and I decided that they felt that they were not
> cherished by the society. Therefore, they were out
> thumbing their noses at said society. Though secretly
> it pleased me to think they would have enjoyed being
> respected, given some little attention by the society.
> So that's why I put 'we' at the end of each line until
> you get to the bottom, so that the reader could give
> them that little split-second's attention.

Throughout the collection, Brooks's tone is one of compassion mixed with irony. Many of the poems center on the lives and struggles of black women, North and South. But while most of the characters in the book are deprived, it is not only material goods they lack; driven by insecurity, they wander in search of spiritual fulfillment, as well. The desire for escape to a better life is depicted in "The Ballad of Rudolph Reed," the story of a black man who moves his family to a white suburb. The "oaken" man hopes the new house will be a haven from ghetto misery, but when a rock flies through a window and strikes his daughter, he rushes out with a gun and a knife, wounds four men, and is killed. Brooks's tale is baldly melodramatic, but her message about racism and her growing concern are clear indeed.

Reactions to the book were mixed. In an interview with George Stavros in 1969, Brooks recalled: "Many people hated *The Bean Eaters*; such as would accuse me of forsaking lyricism for polemics, despised *The Bean Eaters* because they said it was 'getting too social. Watch it, Miss Brooks!'" But younger black writers felt that the poet had still not gone far enough. In his preface to *Report from Part One*, Don L. Lee looked back on Brooks's career: "Her work in the late Fifties and early Sixties like that of James Baldwin and Ralph Ellison appealed to a wide cross-section. The mood of the land was integration. . . . The Sixties for Gwendolyn Brooks was to be an entrance into a new life; however it didn't start with *The Bean Eaters*."

By the early Sixties, Lee (Haki R. Madhubuti), LeRoi Jones (Amiri Baraka), Nikki Giovanni, and others in the new generation of black writers began to demand a distinct African-American literary identity that emphasized the black oral tradition, used the urban black dialect, and was committed to raising black consciousness. Brooks's work to this point, while socially committed, had concentrated on individual personalities and internal psychological struggles, while melding received poetic forms with black patterns of expression in a style that was both intimate and ironic. In new work included with her *Selected Poems* (1963), Brooks still saw the possibility of racial harmony and cooperation. Nor was she alone, of course, during this era of freedom marches and coalitions for racial equality. But as the decade progressed, a more militant mood arose. The cries of "Black is Beautiful" were joined by "Black Power," and calls for separatism. In the Black Arts movement, this came to mean a rejection of white literary and cultural standards. Unlike the writers of the Harlem Renaissance forty years earlier, the authors of the new movement had little faith in the conscience of white America. Etheridge Knight spoke for many when he wrote: "To accept the white aesthetic is to accept and validate a society that will not allow [blacks] to live. The black artist must create new forms and new values . . . create a new history, new symbols, myths and legends . . . ."

Brooks became associated with the movement, and in 1967 she attended the second Black Writers' Conference at Fisk

University, where she met several of the younger and more militant poets. On "Poets in Person," she recalls:

> These people knew a lot about what was happening in the society. I was an optimist, and I still am by way of being an optimist, but I was a complete optimist then. . . . Well, these young people that I met in those times, '67–'68, would have none of that kind of attitude. They felt that their address should be to themselves. They felt that blacks had so much to say to each other. And that's what they were about the business of doing.

In the late Sixties, as political and social changes rapidly swept the black community and the country, a major shift in emphasis and style occurred in Brooks's work, as well. In 1968, she published *In the Mecca*, returning to the scene of the *Bronzeville* poems with a heightened sense of realism but a considerably diminished sense of optimism. While she did not completely abandon her old forms and techniques, Brooks now experimented with free verse and looser structures, particularly in the title poem. Set in a South Side landmark, the once-luxurious Mecca apartment block, the 26-page narrative depicts a large cast of characters who share the building but little else besides self-interest. The plot centers on Mrs. Sallie Smith, the mother of nine children, and her attempts to locate her daughter Pepita, who is missing. In her frantic search, she encounters neighbors absorbed in their own lives and indifferent to the child's plight, such as the fraudulent "Prophet" Williams, the gun-collecting revolutionary "Way-out Morgan," Great-great Gram who was born in slavery and lives in the past, and Edie Barrow who "fell in love with a Gentile boy" and was jilted. Sallie Smith finally discovers Pepita, after she has been raped and murdered by another resident of The Mecca.

In keeping with the seriousness of the story and its social critique, "In the Mecca" displays a new severity, and little of the subtle satire, humor, and ironic tone of Brook's earlier work. In his preface to *Report from Part One*, Don L. Lee observes: "This was to be her epic of black humanity. She wanted to exhibit all its murders, loves, loneliness, hates, jealousies." As counter-balance to these unflattering portraits, the second part of the volume presents elegies to Medgar Evers and Malcolm X and a number of laudatory occasional pieces. As if to underscore Brooks's new direction and attitude, an epigraph (from Ron Karenga) is attached to one of the last poems in the book: "The fact that we are black is our ultimate reality."

About this time, Brooks ended her relationship with Harper & Row, her longtime publishers. In switching to the black-owned Broadside Press in Detroit, she explained: "my first duty is to the estimable, developing black publishing companies." (*Blacks*, which reprints her books from *A Street in Bronzeville* through *In the Mecca* with selections from subsequent works, is available from Third World Press in Chicago.) In 1969 Broadside issued Brooks's chapbook *Riot*, which presents a sympathetic picture of the rioters and looters; and in 1970 the press published *Family Pictures*. On the program, Brooks reads from the first poem in the latter collection, "The Life of Lincoln West," a free-verse ballad which depicts how "the ugliest little boy / that everyone ever saw" ironically turns a racial slur and prejudice about his appearance into a source of pride.

In the early Seventies, Brooks travelled to East Africa, which deepened her interest in the black heritage and the Third World, as well as her appreciation of the contrasts between African-American and native African cultures. (Brooks's experiences and impressions are recorded in "African Fragment" in her autobiography.) In 1975 she wrote an essay with Dudley Randall called *A Capsule Course in Black Poetry Writing*, with this message to aspiring black writers: "ESSENTIAL black literature is the distillation of black life. Black life is different from white life. Different in nuance, different in 'nitty-gritty.' Different *from* birth. Different *at* death." In many ways, Brooks's own writing since has been an illustration of that belief. In the Eighties the poet published a number of thin volumes, including *To Disembark* (1982), *The Near-Johannesburg Boy* (1986), and *Gottschalk and the Grande Tarantelle* (1988). On "Poets in Person," the author reads a section from *Winnie*, her most recent book, as well as an affecting poem of consolation and encouragement, "To the Young Who Want to Die," from *The Near-Johannesburg Boy*. Throughout her career, Brooks has devoted time and energy to young people. As early as the Thirties, she worked for the NAACP Youth Council in Chicago, and in the Sixties she taught poetry writing to members of the Blackstone Rangers street gang. For several years she has sponsored poetry contests and awarded cash prizes to students in Chicago area elementary and high school systems. Besides the Pulitzer, Brooks's many awards include honorary doctorates from Columbia College, Brown University, Lake Forest College, and Northwestern University. In 1976 she received the Shelley Memorial Award and, in 1989, a Lifetime Achievement Award from the National Endowment for the Arts. Since 1969 Brooks has been the Poet Laureate of Illinois, and she was appointed the 1985–86 Consultant in Poetry at the Library of Congress, where she organized poetry programs which were among the most popular in the history of the capital. Now in her seventies, Brooks still maintains a very active schedule of readings and other appearances throughout the country.

# JAMES MERRILL

"We want to find a way of presenting our lives to ourselves, as well as to other people . . . that retains some kind of coherence and plausibility and perhaps has more of a happy ending to a given episode than it might have, if we were not concerned to make a shapeliness out of it," says James Merrill on "Poets in Person," commenting on the need to find meaning and resolve the difficulties in our lives.

Making a "shapeliness" of the episodes, accidents, and paradoxes of his own life through his art, Merrill has also illustrated the truth of his aphorism, "Life is fiction in disguise." In over a dozen volumes—which he once called his "chronicles of love and loss"—the poet has continually transformed the several aspects of his domestic and romantic autobiography into the elegant patterns of his verse, creating a single, multifaceted artifact. Long acknowledged a great stylist, Merrill has written in nearly all the major poetic forms, renewing the traditions of the personal lyric and the epic, the latter in his massive trilogy, *The Changing Light at Sandover.*

Merrill has said that music was his first love, and an acute sense of sound, rhythm, and phrasing governs the elegant modulations of his lines. Composing with a Mozartian sensibility, the poet exquisitely counterpoises sharp intelligence and poignant emotion. A melancholy strain lies just beneath his shimmering surfaces, though pathos is contained in (or held in check by) graceful forms and transposed by wordplay. On the program, when J. D. McClatchy remarks on the poet's linguistic "sleights of hand," and the surprising ways he makes words convey more than their usual meanings, Merrill observes:

> Language subverts itself. Language, words run away with you. And I've always liked the feeling that language runs away with me. I've always trusted where the words go . . . rather than tried to rein them in, through having something I want too much to say. I want to say what can be said. And that leads you into jokes. It leads you into ambiguities. But, you know, I think you have a more pleasant ride than you would if you stuck to the macadam.

James Ingram Merrill was born in New York City in 1926, the son of Charles E. Merrill, a co-founder of the brokerage firm now known as Merrill Lynch, Pierce, Fenner & Smith. He attended a number of private schools and graduated from Lawrenceville, in New Jersey. Even as a boy he wrote verse, producing a poem a day, especially sonnets; he has said his models were both French and English and that as a teenager he admired Elinor Wylie and Rainer Maria Rilke. Merrill's parents divorced when he was 12. It was a "spectacular divorce," as J. D. McClatchy notes, and made the front page of the *New York Times*. It was also a traumatic episode which left lasting marks on the author's character and work. The boy's experience is recorded in one of Merrill's most famous poems, the sonnet sequence "The Broken Home," sections of which he reads on the program. Responding to McClatchy's observation that the subject "goes right to the heart of a great deal of your poetry," Merrill agrees that

> almost any set of opposites, any set of dualities, that I encountered intellectually after those years were tinged with the estrangement of my father and my mother. When I say in "The Broken Home," "Father Time and Mother Earth, a marriage on the rocks," it

seemed to me that the geography and history in our own epoch have begun to pull apart as if they were, had originally been, a happily married couple. This is absolutely part of my seeing and probably a part of my sense of saying in language, as well, that there are two sides to every question, and that the issues fray and diverge.

Merrill has returned to the pivotal event of his parents' divorce repeatedly over the years, in "Scenes of Childhood," "The World and the Child," "Days of 1935," "Lost in Translation," and "The Ballroom at Sandover," the concluding section of the trilogy (also read on the program). Later poems revisit earlier ones, and each poem gives different insights and nuances. This kind of incremental, self-referential layering is a major characteristic of all Merrill's work, giving the poetry its complex resonance.

Merrill attended Amherst College, where he began to study modern literature and was strongly attracted to the work of Wallace Stevens, whose musical phrasing, wit, and lush visual sense are emulated in Merrill's own richly textured poems. He wrote his senior thesis on another literary forbear, the novelist Marcel Proust, whose account of the recovery of lost time and lost love has become a leitmotif throughout the poet's own work. Always precocious, Merrill started publishing as an undergraduate. Asked whether his privileged background may in fact have been a disadvantage to him as a writer, he tells McClatchy:

> I thought it was a terrible handicap until I was perhaps 30 years old. Until, that is, I had begun to establish myself as a writer. Because until then, I wouldn't have had any real sense that I was justified in leading a literary life, even though I began to publish quite early—even in the pages of *Poetry* Magazine when I was still under 20. It took two or three books to convince me, and perhaps to convince my family, that this was not just affectation.

Merrill's college career was interrupted by World War II—it was in the army that he began reading Proust ("basic training," he says in "Days of 1941 and '44")—but following the service, he returned to Amherst and took his degree in 1947. He had already produced two volumes: the privately printed *Jim's Book: A Collection of Poems and Short Stories* (1942) and *The Black Swan and Other Poems*, published in Greece in 1946.

Merrill made his professional debut with *First Poems* in 1951. The collection was praised for its formal elegance and persuaded the critics, and probably his family, that the young poet was a serious artist. In "The Black Swan," "The Broken Bowl," "Willow," and indeed all the pieces in the volume, Merrill proves himself a skilled craftsman. Two poems in particular sound themes replayed often with variations in later work. In "The House," which ends the book, the speaker reflects on the swiftness of time's passing and the tenuousness of the human condition; and "Hourglass" concludes: "Love only is replenishment of halves."

While reviewers admired the technical mastery and high finish of the early work, some critics thought the poems overly reticent, perhaps too cool in their perfection. Beautifully shaped, the lyrics do tend to be too self-consciously artful, as well as static. Merrill himself soon realized something was missing, after giving his first public reading at the 92nd Street YMHA in New York City. "I'd never read my poems aloud before," he recalls, "and I didn't read them to myself to hear how they sounded. They were always visual artifacts. But I realized as I was reading them that there was nothing of a living voice in them. They were musical in a way but not in any sense declamatory." So he tried to make a change, using the techniques of prose dialogue and adapting the methods of the dramatist and the novelist. (Indeed, his next poetry collection was entitled *Short Stories* [1954]; he has also published two novels, *The Seraglio* [1957] and *The (Diblos) Notebook* [1965]). Still, in his poetry, Merrill has continued to avoid straight narration, preferring to work more subtly by implication and indirection; he notes: "I like the idea of hinting at a story, at a narrative."

*The Country of a Thousand Years of Peace* appeared in 1959. As the title and other poems indicate—"Amsterdam," "Hôtel de l'Universe et Portugal," "In the Hall of Mirrors"—Merrill's many travels now provide occasions for his work. An elegiac tone pervades the collection, notably in "A Dedication," commemorating the death of the poet's friend Hans Lodeizen in Switzerland (the country of the title). In "The Octopus," "Mirror," "Stones," and the other poems, Merrill's gifts for imagery and euphony are again abundantly evident. But while he now adds more dialogue (or internal monologue) and narrative elements, he leaves out so much "plot" information (as in "A Narrow Escape") that the reader feels like an eavesdropper on a clever private conversation, an outsider overhearing an inside joke. And although Merrill's convoluted syntax cannot muffle his music, his voice is oddly detached and the poems often remain murky. The poet himself seems aware of these weaknesses. "But in the end one tires of the high-flown," begins another poem, "About the Phoenix"; and one may readily agree: "despite / Its pyrotechnic curiosity, the process / Palls." In "The Doodler," he professes, too modestly: "Indeed, nothing I do is at all fine / Save certain abstract forms. These come unbidden."

In 1962, Merrill published *Water Street*. Titled after the location of his home in Stonington, Connecticut, the collection shows a new openness, as the poet contemplates his past and his present situation, literally and emotionally, as he nears middle age. In "An Urban Convalescence," viewing the razing of a building near his apartment in New York City, he reflects, "Well, that is what life does," and feels "the dull need to make some kind of house / Out of the life lived, out of the love spent." He returns to his youth, in "A Vision of the Garden" and "Scenes of Childhood," and to the inevitable waning of Eros in a long relationship, in "Poem of Summer's End." Sharing perhaps his sense that "time is running out," he pays tribute to his literary mentor in "For Proust," and affirms that master's maxim: "the loved one always leaves." For all their nostalgia, Merrill's journeys into the past do not stray into sentimentality. And, less inclined now to dazzle, the poet speaks more directly from the heart and to the reader. In "A Tenancy," the host stands on the doorstep of the house on Water Street to greet his guests:

> And then, not asking why they come,
> Invite the visitors to sit.
> If I am host at last
> It is of little more than my own past.
> May others be at home in it.

In *Nights and Days*, published in 1966, the poet's fortieth year, Merrill treats his dual themes of Love and Time, as well as home and displacement, with both warmth and the ironic humor maturity brings. The book was widely praised and won the National Book Award. Besides "The Broken Home," the collection includes a number of poems which enlarge upon his central subjects and introduce characters who will figure in later work. Most important among them is "Days of 1964," whose title and deft manner pay graceful tribute to another favorite author, Constantin Cavafy (1863–1933); like the Alexandrian Greek poet, Merrill paints incisive portraits of friendship and erotic attachment, combining witty detail and rueful insight.

In 1959, Merrill and his friend David Jackson bought a house in Athens and for the next twenty years were to divide their time between Greece and Connecticut. In "Days of 1964," Merrill depicts "Kyria Kleo who cleaned for us" and who lives with her mother and "wastrel son. She called me her real son. // I paid her generously, I dare say. / Love makes one generous." The cause of this benevolence is the poet's unexpected happiness with his new (and as yet unnamed) lover: "I had gone so long without loving, / I hardly knew what I was thinking." In comic-serious contrast, he presents an incident involving the maid. Though fifty-something, Kleo (for the poet, a figure for Eros) still pursues her ancient profession, and when he accidentally sees her one afternoon, heavily made-up ("Her face was painted / Clown-white"), he thinks of "the erotic mask / Worn the world over by illusion / To weddings of itself and simple need." Though the brief episode is amusing, Merrill's narrative imbues the story with deep psychological meaning, prompting a central Cavafyan question: "was love illusion?" The answer, of course, is yes, as the poet realizes even in the midst of passion. But as with other emotionally charged subjects, Merrill returns to this question repeatedly, and to his changing feelings about his love affair, which are recorded in "To My Greek," "Flying from Byzantium," "Another August," "After the Fire," "Strato in Plaster," and "Days of 1971," included in his next two volumes.

On the program, J. D. McClatchy talks with the poet about his life abroad and many travels and asks, "What is it that a new place gives you for a poem?" Merrill responds,

> I've recurrently throughout my life been somewhat in flight from what I already know, and maybe I have even a kind of reluctance or distaste for getting to know anything too well. I believe in rapid impressions. . . . At times, it seems to me that the visible world is really there to teach us about ourselves, so that any new configuration of it, responding to the exhilaration that we feel when we go to a new place, shows us to ourselves in a new way. I don't believe very much in the direct expression of feeling. But I think that the *oblique* feeling that comes back to us when we verbalize in front of new scenes and unfamiliar places is a great instrument of self-knowledge.

Merrill's preference for the oblique and his growing self-knowledge are expressed in his next volume, *The Fire Screen* (1966). The title suggests a certain shielding from intense experience, a holding back that is the product of aging and mid-life ennui but also, in part, the result of his fluctuating emotions and disappointments in love, especially as recalled in "Flying from Byzantium." In "Matinees," the poet remembers the thrill of first hearing, as a boy, the great singers and the romantic flights of Wagner and Richard Strauss. But now he wishes to withdraw from the high drama of Grand Opera—and its more mundane domestic counterpart—and is content simply to play the piano: "Enough to know the score / / From records or transcription /

For our four hands." In the course of the finely rendered (and very touching) sonnet sequence, he reflects on the relation, for him, between reality and art:

> What havoc certain Saturday afternoons
> Wrought upon a bright young person's morals
> I now leave to the public to condemn.
>
> The point thereafter was to arrange for one's
> Own chills and fever, passions and betrayals,
> Chiefly in order to make song of them.

*Braving the Elements* (1972) contains some of Merrill's best-known poems, including "Willowware Cup," "The Victor Dog," and "Syrinx." Stylistically, the poet works more gracefully than ever within his chosen forms (both received and refashioned) with an artistry that conceals his art, just as he moves effortlessly between levels of language, from the arcane and sophisticated to the casual and slangy. On "Poets in Person," J. D. McClatchy notes that Merrill started and has continued to write as a formalist, "employing meter and rhyme and all the other traditional tools of the poet's craft, even after they fell out of favor." Merrill explains: "I always loved the idea of received space. It's never occurred to me to build my own house. But I love to fit myself into existing rooms. And the same way with forms. . . . The idea, it seems to me, is to use the elements of the form that are still viable nowadays." In her review of *Braving the Elements* (reprinted in *Part of Nature, Part of Us*), Helen Vendler finds:

> These poems are gripping because they are quiet and
> conversational: it is as though a curtain has been
> drawn aside, and we were permitted a glimpse of the
> life inside the house, a life that goes on unconscious
> of us, with the narrator so perfectly an actor in his
> own drama that his presence as narrator is rendered
> transparent, invisible.

Besides looking back to "Days of 1935," Merrill continues his story from "Days of 1964" to "Days of 1971," a sonnet sequence tracing the disintegration of the poet's love affair during the course of an automobile trip from France to Greece. Analyzing his disillusionment in retrospect, he summarizes the wisdom he has gained as a twofold "Proust's Law":

(a) What least thing our self-love longs for most
Others instinctively withhold;

(b) Only when time has slain desire
Is his wish granted to a smiling ghost
Neither harmed nor warmed, now, by the fire.

In "After the Fire," returning to inspect the damage and repairs to his place in Athens, he realizes: "Everything changes; nothing does." Likewise, in "Strato in Plaster," he finds that time has not been kind to his once-handsome Greek lover ("The god in him is a remembered one") and fears that "the fracture's too complex, / Too long unmended, for us to be friends." Yet, their bond of affection remains; like the broken arm in the cast, friendship endures, despite its fragility. These poems attest that life is unpredictable and alters all, but also that love is never wholly lost, only "translated," transformed—the major theme of the lines which will soon develop into Merrill's masterwork, *The Changing Light at Sandover*.

As unusual in origin and it is unique in organization, the trilogy was first published separately in three volumes, "The Book of Ephraim" in *Divine Comedies* (1976), *Mirabell: Books of Number* (1978), and *Scripts for the Pageant* (1980). But the inspiration for the poem extends back much further, to the mid-Fifties, when the author and his friend David Jackson moved to Stonington. At first, Merrill explains on "Poets in Person," they had few friends in the small town, and entertained themselves by experimenting with a Ouija board. "We found that it worked like a charm, and we could get the most thrilling conversation from using the Ouija board." What started as a diversion became a major endeavor, as Merrill transcribed the messages from the board over the next twenty years, and transformed them into an epic of some 17,000 lines. "It never occurred to me at the time that I could use these transcripts for a piece of writing. I was so convinced in a way, in those early years, that it came from some realm outside myself that it would have been like a kind of plagiarism to incorporate them into the work." The board became his medium for contact with "Voices From the Other World" (as first revealed in 1959 in the poem of that title, referring to the unorthodox "muses" speaking through the board); but it was the poet's imagination and skill, honed over thirty years of practicing his craft, which made the transcriptions, whatever their origin, into an artistic tour de force.

"The Book of Ephraim" is preceded in *Divine Comedies* by several poems which look back to the past while foreshadowing themes in the epic. The poet's father is elegized and refigured as Ali Pasha in "Yannína," for example, while an old friend from Athens is recalled in "Manos Karastefanís" (another poem read on the program). "Lost in Translation" returns to the subject of "the broken home" and acts as a kind of preface, succinctly stating many of Merrill's perennial themes, chief among them:

> But nothing's lost. Or else: all is translation
> And every bit of us is lost in it
> (Or found . . . .

"The Book of Ephraim" is itself an extended prologue to the books to follow, though the author was not at first wholly aware of that when it was being written. The passive voice is intentional here, for the poet presents himself in the poem as a scribe taking dictation; he has also confirmed the fact in interviews about its composition. The problem of the poem's credibility (and the poet's credulity) is itself a major topic in "Ephraim." On the program, Merrill admits:

> I was embarrassed to think that I would have to
> somehow produce a poem that, even in somebody
> else's voice, contained so much pop ideology and
> mythology, flying saucers—I mean, the kind of de-
> tail was out of a comic book. All those things had to
> be somehow rationalized or at least had to be sur-
> rounded by a kind of ambiguous tone, a tone of faint
> disbelief. Much as we became moved and thrilled by

the increasing seriousness and beauty of the messages, our own temperaments infused into those
messages a kind of humor, a kind of playfulness.

As a character expressing skepticism, Merrill (JM in the poem's
shorthand) acts as a surrogate for the reader, of course. At one
point (section I) JM consults his ex-psychiatrist, who suggests
he and DJ (David Jackson) are engaged in a *folie à deux* or that
the voices of the Ouija board come from the unconscious, the
revelations projections "Of what already burned, at some obscure / Level or another, in our skulls." Or, since (according to
Jung) God and the unconscious are one: "*He* was the revelation / (Or if we have created him, then we were)."

In any case, despite initial doubts, as the poem progresses
JM and DJ (and, it is hoped, the reader) forget to question their
sources and simply enjoy the messages. A great part of the
pleasure, and persuasive power, of the poem arises from its
playfulness. Humor and a self-critical stance are hallmarks of
Merrill's previous work, but here the wit brings qualities un-
precedented in the epic. In contrast to the bellicose tradition of
the genre which depicts jealousy, rage, revenge, cruelty, siege,
and destruction, Merrill recasts the conventions, portraying oc-
cult knowledge gained through laughter, gentleness, courtesy,
and good will. War cries are exchanged for polite conversations;
and in place of the old epic "machinery," the poet presents an
original mythology combining science, particularly biology,
with personal history and the memory of departed family and
friends.

"Compared with 'The Book of Ephraim,' other long
poems of our time are structurally primitive," David Perkins
observes in *A History of Modern Poetry*. Within the intricate overall framework of all three books, Merrill interweaves several
poetic forms (sonnet, sestina, ode, terza rima, canzone), metri-
cal patterns (syllabics, blank and free verse), complex intercon-
necting themes and patterns of imagery, about which only the
briefest notes are possible here. (On the program, the poet discussions some of these aspects.) The structures of the individual
books are derived from the print on the Ouija board: "Ephraim"

consists of twenty-six sections, named for each letter of the alphabet. (Throughout the texts, the otherworldly voices are presented all in capitals.) *Mirabell*, a "Book of Science," is divided into ten sections (0–9), each subdivided into ten parts (6.0, 6.1, . . . ). *Scripts* has three major divisions, "Yes," "No," and "&"; "Yes" and "No" are further divided into eighteen parts, the central "&" section into fourteen. The trilogy, printed as *The Changing Light at Sandover* in 1982, has an extensive coda, "The Higher Keys," in which the poet prepares to read the entire trilogy, from the beginning, to his friends and influential forbears, arranged alphabetically and diplomatically from Jane Austen; the long guest list includes Dante, T. S. Eliot, Pope, Proust, Gertrude Stein (and Alice B. Toklas), Stevens, Wagner, and Yeats.

Like Dante, but far more cheerfully, JM and DJ encounter those in the afterlife through intermediaries. Instead of a grim Virgil, their first guide is a chatty, even campy, character identified as a Greek Jew who died in 36 A.D. As the Willowware cup races across the Ouija board, Ephraim communicates with them, as do eventually several of the departed, notably Merrill's great friend and mentor, the poet W. H. Auden, and Maria Mitsotáki, a recently dead friend from Athens. As their instructor, Ephraim finds that JM and DJ are quick studies, and exclaims: "I FEEL WE HAVE / SKIPPING THE DULL CLASSROOM DONE IT ALL / AT THE SALON LEVEL." He reveals that mortal beings are incarnated spirits or patrons and that after the deaths of their hosts these spirits pass into other bodies. The recently deceased Charles Merrill (CEM), for example, was between lives, but Ephraim tells JM that his father "WAS BORN YESTERDAY / To a greengrocer . . . in Kew"; Mozart, another of the "untamed dead," is at present "A BLACK ROCK STAR / WHATEVER THAT IS." As they undergo repeated reincarnations, the spirits "rise in station" through nine stages, each providing "a degree of PEACE FROM REPRESENTATION."

As the book progresses from A to Z, many other real and fictional people appear, including Robert Morse, a Stonington neighbor, and DJ's aged parents (who die in the course of the epic) and characters from an abandoned novel by JM. In this way, Merrill merges memory and imagination, present and past—friends, loved ones, places visited, personal and cultural history. Ephraim provides "huge tracts of information," much of which JM paraphrases or versifies (in lower-case), but his messages are often incomplete, and some are later shown to be inaccurate. For all their serious philosophical and theological content, the conversations are lively, and sometimes Ephraim seems frivolous; JM and DJ protest at one point, "Must *everything* be witty?" But after all, these are *Divine Comedies* in several senses, and Merrill balances the poem's potentially solemn elements with the saving graces of humor and irrepressible wordplay. Toward the end of the poem, however, a different and sterner voice is heard. It is the unidentified Mirabell, who cuts in to announce: "MYND YOUR WEORK      SIX MOONES REMAIN." JM must complete this book soon, for "Ephraim" has been in fact only a preparation for a larger task ahead, the composition of "POEMS OF SCIENCE."

While "The Book of Ephraim" was some twenty years in the making, the much longer *Mirabell: Books of Number* was transcribed and written in the summer and fall of 1976. (It won the National Book Award in 1979; *Divine Comedies* received the Pulitzer Prize in 1977.) First known only as 741, the new guide is finally named Mirabell, and he provides a much more complete vision of the universe. As it unfolds, this novel cosmology grows ever more detailed and intricate, and JM's charge becomes more serious: to help "WARN MAN AGAINST THE CHAOS." Mirabell and his cohorts are described variously as pure reason, negative energy, bats or gargoyles. They once dared to tamper with the universe and black holes resulted, but now they serve God B (Biology). Since man first achieved sustained atomic fission, they have tried to preserve the now threatened greenhouse of Nature and to prevent chaos and nuclear annihilation. (In this account, radiation can not only kill the body but destroy the soul.)

God B is described as a good, if remote, force that selects a few souls who are recloned in his Research Lab and serve to improve the human race. This they do by performing "v WORK" (for the French "vie," life, and the five chief protagonists), creating art, music, poetry, developing cultures, thus returning earthly life to an Edenic state. In opposition to God B there is a vague negative force, at times referred to as "CHAOS," "THE OTHER," "THE UNDOER," or "THE VOID." (Merrill suggests a Manichean dialectic in the universe, but leaves the philosophical problem of evil rather undefined; for him, the greatest evil is death.) When WHA asks why he, JM, DJ, and MM are among the few chosen to do V work, Mirabell explains that they are childless, like him, and "THIS TURNS US / OUTWARD TO THE LESSONS / & THE MYSTERIES." JM remains skeptical and asks him to "admit that certain very great / Poets and musicians have been straight"; but the assertion has been made. In any case, the spirits need creative mortals for their expression—Mirabell, especially, since he is not only a "bad angel" but a boorish one. Through communication with JM and DJ, he learns the value of courtesy and affection. Moreover, at first a mere number, he becomes humanized, capable of language and feeling (not just formulas): "B4 OUR MEETINGS I WAS NOTHING . . . YR TOUCH LIKE A LAMP HAS SHOWN ME TO MYSELF . . . I HAVE ENTERED A GREAT WORLD    I AM FILLD / WITH    IS IT MANNERS?"

This humanizing drama is one of the most attractive aspects of the epic. At the same time, Merrill (or his muses) spin out an extremely elaborate narrative of creation filled with curious lore, not all of it compelling. The baroque profusion of "plot" strands and their complications are fascinating but at times tedious (machinery indeed), though the poet alternates typically luminous lyrical passages with the duller narrative—much like operatic arias inserted between prosaic stretches of recitative. At one point, JM himself seems weary, complaining to WHA that after "Ephraim" he wanted to return to "private life, to my own words. Instead, / Here I go again, a vehicle / In this cosmic carpool." Defending epic convention, Auden chides him: "WHAT A MINOR / PART THE SELF PLAYS IN A WORK OF ART / COMPARED TO THOSE GREAT GIVENS."

Like JM, Merrill played the part given to him and started work on *Scripts for the Pageant* immediately, in 1977. In the final and longest installment of the epic, JM and DJ have yet another guide, the archangel Michael. (Ephraim, we learn at the end of the trilogy, is a manifestation of Michael. As Merrill explains on the program, he also hearkens back to Michael, his Irish setter in "The Broken Home"; "setter" also refers to the sun, the archangel's symbol, and Apollo's.) In tone, Michael's voice resembles that of the poet, urbane, witty, ever courteous, as he provides even more revelations about the order of the universe and about other, lost worlds. In *Scripts*, the cast of Speakers (listed at the start) is large, as Mirabell, WHA, MM, and the old crowd are joined by the important character of Gabriel (Michael's opposite, identified as "an *Angel of Fire and Death*"), The Nine Muses, Jesus, Mohammed, and several friends and immortal guest artists (Maria Callas, Kirsten Flagstad, Stevens, Richard Strauss, W. B. Yeats). God B is paired with Nature, "*His twin. Known also as* Psyche *and* Chaos," indicating their complementary duality. In the divine scheme of things, mankind is bound to Nature, but bound for destruction for disobeying God B and misusing its new knowledge of science. Thus the traditional story of the Fall is revised in the epic's psychodrama of "Yes & No."

If God and the unconscious are one, the duality of the deities constitutes human "nature" or character, as well. Mankind's opposing creative and destructive tendencies are likewise represented by Michael and Gabriel and treated symbolically through the trilogy. On its higher levels of abstraction, the allegory of *Sandover* urges a message or "moral" of salvation—of mankind and of the earth in the face nuclear holocaust. But on the profoundly personal level, the poem is the grand summation of Merrill's lifelong endeavor to stay the forces of Time and Loss through his art. Summoning all his resources, he has reinvented an ancient form to find another means to retrieve the past, to recover and immortalize the growing number of his beloved dead—"The Dead" who, the first book informs us, "are the surround of the living"—prolonging their existence even into the afterlife through this epic communion. In *Mirabell*, his guiding spirit promises JM that after the cycle is finished, "U WILL BE RETURND TO YR CHRONICLES OF LOVE & LOSS." But the trilogy itself is Merrill's most imposing record of those abiding emotions.

Following its publication in one volume as *The Changing Light at Sandover* in 1982, Merrill presented his selection *From the First Nine: Poems 1946–1976* (1983). In *Late Settings* (1985), Merrill returns to his earlier interests and lyrical mode, although the collection retrieves some of the epic's discarded passages, "From the Cutting-Room Floor." Following the extended conversations with the dead in *Sandover*, a somber note is sounded throughout the book, as the poet addresses his own mortality more directly and marks several significant changes in his life. In "Santorini: Stopping the Leak," he bids farewell to Greece, where "Things just aren't what they were—no more am I," and confronts the specter of cancer. (He undergoes radiation therapy for a plantar wart and envisions his existences draining out through the "leak" in his foot.) In "Clearing the Title," he details the acquisition of a new winter home in Key West (sometime residence also of Wallace Stevens and of Merrill's great friend Elizabeth Bishop). Other Florida poems include "The Pier: Under Pisces" and "Palm Beach with Portuguese Man-of-War," an almost surreal vision and a curious elegy to the poet's tycoon father, who (a note informs us) is buried in West Palm Beach, "off the Interstate."

Merrill's dreadful sense of his own declining health spills over into his treatments of dangerous recent history, where an uncharacteristic bitterness enters. Under "Topics," for example, he considers terrorism, nuclear combat between the super powers, and, once again, the destruction of a world that began as a "glow of cells in the warm Sea". "Page from the Koran" castigates the religious warfare in Beirut, where "God's very word, then, stung the heart / To greed and rancor." In "Channel 13" (also read on the program) and "Developers at Crystal River," the poet muses ruefully on the fate of endangered species. Though each of the book's highly varied pieces is impressive, the autobiographical poems are the most affecting. Besides "Santorini," one may note especially "The School Play" and "Days of 1941 and '44," recollections of adolescence, the latter poem an acute recreation of a painful episode and its poignant aftermath; and "Bronze," the longest poem and set at the center of the collection, another extraordinary example of Merrill's ability to merge past and present, art and life.

In 1986, Merrill's essays and interviews were collected in *Recitative: Prose by James Merrill*, enlightening pieces filled with casual aperçus and learning worn lightly. In 1988 *The Inner Room* appeared, a diverse volume including not only four long poems among the shorter lyrics, but also a play and an extended prose piece. "The Image Maker," a one-act play for two actors and three puppets, stars Manuel the santéro, who carves the figures; the plot involves romantic bewilderment and warring dark and bright spirits. "Prose of Departure" juxtaposes brief but vivid travel notes from Japan interspersed with rhymed haiku. Here and in many of the other poems in the book, death hovers over the living. The late poet Howard Moss is remembered with "Morning Glory," and two moving elegies are dedicated to the critic David Kalstone, "Investiture at Cecconi's" and "Farewell Performance," an unforgettable performance itself. Most of the lyrics revolve about love and memories of it. "A Room at the Heart of Things" is the most complex, a series of sonnets which intertwines strands of narrative about and meditations upon a youthful romance, written in an oblique manner reminiscent of Merrill's earlier work. In all, the book shows the poet's continuing versatility and unpredictability.

At the end of the program, Merrill talks with J. D. McClatchy about the use of autobiography in his work and the relation between life and language. Looking over his career, he reflects: "I've tried to portray myself as happy. I've tried to bring humor and understanding as much as I can. I've tried to keep things from sounding too serious and too gloomy." He adds:

> It seems to me that I'm at home with the idea of telling myself the story of my own life. It seems to me that a lot of people get through the day that way, just making sense. A kind of not-even-articulated inner monologue of saying to yourself: "This is what I'm doing." And I mean, the words are there, ready to support you, if for a moment you hesitate or black out.

# A D R I E N N E   R I C H

"In many ways, I think of being in relationship to a poem as being in a relationship with a person . . . you draw on your fullest integrity, you try to speak the truth, and you want to be heard, you want to be understood, but you don't sacrifice any complexity for that," Adrienne Rich explains on "Poets in Person."

For over forty years, Rich's on-going conversation has been as intellectually stimulating as it has been emotionally intense. In over a dozen books, she has been engaged in a vigorous dialogue, both with the world and within herself. The internal dialectic has been a bold inquiry into the conflicts she has experienced as a woman—daughter, wife, mother, lover—and an artist in America. Searching for the sources of her psychic distress, she has confronted her own life, history, and the deep-seated prejudices, pressures to conform, and other spirit-deadening powers in modern civilization.

Gradually finding and coming to terms with her own identity, Rich has extended this process of discovery into a wider social analysis and philosophical debate, and then into political action. During the Sixties and Seventies, as she struggled for self-determination, her compassion for other women, and indeed all the oppressed, compelled her participation in the several liberation movements of the period. These activities made her redefine her role as a writer and enlarge her vision as a woman poet. Her early style, formal and contained by convention, was in turn transformed into a distinctive voice capable of addressing both her personal concerns and public issues directly. As it has it evolved, Rich's work has reflected the major changes in American life and poetry since the Fifties. It has also been an unfolding spiritual autobiography, a story of mind and heart which speaks to, and for, an ever larger audience.

Adrienne Rich was born in Baltimore in 1929. Her father was a physician and her mother a musician; both parents set strong examples with their wide interests in and disciplined approaches to the arts. On "Poets in Person," Rich recalls that her mother "practiced the piano several hours a day, every day, for much of the time I was growing up. There were chamber music groups that met in our house. My parents knew artists." As a child Rich did not know any poets, but her father encouraged her to write. "He was an amateur poet, an amateur musician, an amateur everything except scientist," she notes, and as a doctor, he was "a very, very serious professional." He emphasized the importance of technical training, and very early "gave me a book of poetic forms with many examples and told me to write villanelles and triolettes and quatrains." Reflecting on the cultural milieu of her childhood, Rich says: "I was a very lucky and privileged child who was growing up in a house where people read poetry aloud to me, where there was a lot of music played, where very early I was impressed with the power of the written word. And so when I began to do what all children do, which is imitate what they see around them, I was given a great deal of encouragement." That support included the printing of her poems and plays when she ten and twelve.

On the program, Rich recalls she began writing verse about the age of four, but did not identify herself as a poet until much later. She tells Diane Wood Middlebrook: "That vocation seemed something very far off and distant, and something that you would apprentice yourself for." In high school, she realized that poetry was "perhaps the most important activity that I knew, for me." But such was her seriousness about her vocation that

for a long time into my adult life, although I was

publishing poems and acknowledged as a poet, I still found it very hard to say I was a poet, for very complex reasons. I think it had to do with, first of all, the problem of defining oneself as an artist or a poet in America. But I think it also had to do with being female and the problem, particularly, for a young woman coming to maturity and starting out as a poet in the Fifties, of defining herself by a vocation at all.

Rich attended Radcliffe College and graduated with honors in 1951, the year her first collection of poetry was published. *A Change of World* was selected by W. H. Auden for the Yale Younger Poets Award, and in introducing the book, Auden praised the 21-year-old author for her technical mastery and "capacity for detachment from the self and its emotions". Auden's influence, as well as that of older masters, can be seen in these early poems, which demonstrate the principal characteristics of postwar "academic" poetry: clarity of intellect, a formal style, a focus upon the Tradition, and use of personas—the legacy of T. S. Eliot's theories about impersonality and the New Criticism which had dominated the teaching and writing of poetry since the Thirties. Looking back on her early work twenty years later in the essay "When We Dead Awaken: Writing as Re-Vision," Rich acknowledges, "I know that my style was formed first by male poets," and cites Robert Frost, Dylan Thomas, John Donne, Auden, Louis MacNeice, Wallace Stevens, and William Butler Yeats. "What I learned chiefly from them was craft."

Written during the late Forties, the poems in the first book convey in part the atmosphere after World War II. On the program, Rich reads from "Storm Warnings," one of the poems in the volume, and notes the historical background: the explosion of the atom bomb at Hiroshima and Nagasaki and the revelation of the Nazi death camps only a few years earlier, as well as the "tremendous anxiety in this country about the Cold War . . . when World War III was actually talked about." The sense of "powerlessnesss in the face of immense disaster," especially among the younger generation, and the poet's own turning inward and withdrawal from a world seemingly out of control, is vividly conveyed in the concluding stanza of "Storm Warnings":

I draw the curtains as the sky goes black
And set a match to candles sheathed in glass
Against the keyhole draught, the insistent whine
Of weather through the unsealed aperture.
This is our sole defense against the season;
These are the things that we have learned to do
Who live in troubled regions.

As a first book, *A Change of World* was more than promising—the poet was already very proficient—and its title now seems prophetic; for Rich's subsequent work would mirror the radical changes about to occur in American society, her own life, and poetry in the coming decades.

After graduation, Rich travelled for a year in Europe and England on a Guggenheim fellowship, then settled in the Boston area. Several of the poems in her second book, *The Diamond Cutters and Other Poems* (1955), were occasioned by places she visited abroad; others show the influence of various literary forbears. While the book demonstrates Rich's characteristic intelligence, grace, and skill, it does not mark a development of her talent; the poet herself has said she was already dissatisfied with the volume by the time it was published. She did not produce another collection for eight years, and for the reasons many another woman has seen her professional career interrupted, if not ended.

In 1953 Rich married Alfred Conrad, an economist at Harvard, and in quick succession had three sons, the last born in 1959. At this time, Boston was home to Robert Lowell, Sylvia Plath, Ted Hughes, Anne Sexton, and other younger poets just coming to prominence. Although she met and knew most of them, Rich was not able to participate in the lively Boston literary scene. "I was over there in Cambridge," she recalled in her interview for the program, "trying to keep up with three children and domesticity and hiring a baby sitter so I could go up to the third floor of the house and write. Or quite often, not write—just sit." On "Poets in Person," she reveals deeper reasons for her dissatisfaction:

> It was difficult to be writing poetry. Nothing had prepared me for what motherhood was going to be like. As I think of it now, it was not simply a question of time and energy, although it was that too, but it was the question, which was ever under the surface for me, of what did it mean to be a poet at all, and particularly to sort of go for broke as a poet and to be a woman who was a wife and mother? And what themes were permissible, were recognized, were validated at that time? To have written about my life in that domestic sphere, with all its passions, tensions, contradictions, would not have been validated, I felt. So it was a large part of my experience that I was only able to write out of obliquely or not at all.

Rich's frustration, mingled with guilt and long-held anger, finally surfaced in *Snapshots of a Daughter-in-Law* (1963), an important collection which marks a major shift in the poet's attitude and style. Here Rich begins to examine in detail the question of female identity, the position of women in society, and the relationship of women to one another. The ten-part title poem addresses several aspects of these issues through contrasting "snapshots." The poem opens with a vignette of the mother-in-law, a woman whose self-image has been formed by society. The young daughter-in-law recognizes, however, that her own identity is compromised; immersed in domestic routines, she denies the inner voice telling her: "*Save yourself; others you cannot save.*" She then realizes how women replicate a sad history of opposing each other ("The argument *ad feminam*, all the old knives / that have rusted in my back, I drive in yours") and of adapting themselves to patriarchal models, particularly the stereotypes of woman as sex object (thus "she shaves her legs") and intellectual mediocrity (her "slattern thought styled intuition"). But the poem also recalls Emily Dickinson and Mary

Wollstonecraft, authentic individuals who broke the old patterns and prefigured modern, independent women. In "The Roofwalker," Rich writes:

> A life I didn't choose
> chose me: even
> my tools are the wrong ones
> for what I have to do.

Though "exposed, larger than life, / and due to break my neck," the roofwalker also suggests a new freedom awaits those who are willing to risk the dangers acquiring independence may entail.

Stylistically, *Snapshots of a Daughter-in-Law* also marks a transition. Moving from her earlier tightly controlled, rhymed and stanzaic forms, the poet now begins to experiment with more open structures and more rhythmically flexible lines. This looser approach was encouraged by Denise Levertov, "whose friendship was tremendously important to me, because she was the first woman poet I knew, and she also had a child," Rich remarks on the program. Levertov offered alternatives to the academic standard authors that Rich emulated, bringing "into my range of consciousness poets like William Carlos Williams, Robert Creeley, Robert Duncan, the Black Mountain Poets, Charles Olson, and, to a certain extent, the Beat poets." Rich adds that Levertov

> was very strongly of the persuasion that you could no longer write good poetry in iambic pentameter. . . . it was exactly when I felt that my own experience, the terms of my own existence, were exploding the forms I had been using and the traditions I had been using. It was tremendously important, I want to say, too, that this was coming through a woman, and this was very pre-feminist, I have to tell you.

Although at this stage Rich was not prepared to write the kinds of extremely self-revealing pieces that Sexton, Plath, Lowell, and other "confessional" poets produced, she began to draw more extensively upon her own experiences as an American woman, wife, and mother. The conventional poetic persona of the "objective," gender-neutral "he" was gradually replaced by "she" and then by "I," as Rich moved closer to speaking in a truly personal voice.

These shifts in perspective and style were not appreciated by the critics. *Snapshots* "was ignored, was written off as being too bitter and personal. Yet I *knew* I had gone beyond in that book. I was very conscious of male critics, then, and it was like flunking a course," the poet observed in a 1975 interview. Undeterred, in 1966 Rich published *Necessities of Life: Poems, 1962– 1965*, whose title poem announces: "Piece by piece I seem / to re-enter the world." The collection demonstrates the author's confidence in her new course, as she probes more deeply into the complex relations between parent and child, and husband and wife, as well as the nature of her own psyche. Rich is at her most incisive in "Like This Together," "In the Woods," "Night-Pieces: For a Child," and other emotionally complex poems centered directly on her experiences of marriage and motherhood.

Rich moved to New York in 1966, when her husband accepted a professorship at City College. The next years were a tumultuous period for the country, and pivotal for the poet's developing consciousness of herself as a woman and as a writer. As U. S. involvement in Vietnam escalated, Rich and her husband became active in the anti-war protests. In her interview with Diane Middlebrook, Rich remarked she viewed her participation as "not only a challenge to me as artist, but also as an education. . . . I was learning a great deal about my country and the world in which we were situated, and my location within all that, that I hadn't had to think about before." The poet also began teaching and was "very active on the Columbia faculty in the 1968 strike at the School of the Arts, and then in support of the Black and Puerto Rican Students Coalition at City College."

After the assassination of Martin Luther King, Rich had applied for a position in City College's SEEK program, which was "designed to bring young, largely black and Puerto Rican high school students into the college mainstream—students who had been previously discarded by the colleges as not being capable of absorbing higher education, but who had been profoundly betrayed by the public school system in the city." The experience proved an "education in democracy": "It had a tremendous impact on *me*, and therefore on my poetry. In many ways, it was the beginning of my political education."

Her consciousness was furthered raised by the writings of black authors such as the novelist James Baldwin and the Algerian political philosopher Frantz Fanon, whose analyses of power and oppression began "to coalesce for me with works that I had been reading about women." Feminism for Rich had been taking shape very gradually, "in a very isolated . . . way almost without a language." In the early Sixties, she had read Simone de Beauvoir's classic *The Second Sex*, "which opened my mind very wide, except that there seemed to be no one with whom I could talk about it." By 1967, however, following the "second wave" of the women's liberation movement, "there was an explosion of women talking to each other . . . of pamphlets, of leaflets, of mimeographed position papers," she recalls. "There was a tremendous sense of passionate opening and anger, validated anger, anger that was no longer suppressed or whispered, and creativity."

Rich's own creativity and, even more, her anger are expressed in her next collection, *Leaflets: Poems, 1965–68* (1969), a record of her responses to the war, the college campus rebellions, Black Power, and other social and political upheavals during the period. The poet's feelings toward these events are intense. In the title poem she insists, "I want this to reach you," but her manner of expressing her urgent concern was not always viewed sympathetically by the critics. The collection enlarges her formal repertoire, however, with a section of *ghazals*, composed after the manner of the Persian poet Mirza Ghalib (1797–1869), another poet "writing in an age of political and cultural break-up," Rich's note explains. Employing a minimum of five autonomous couplets, the *ghazal* allows the poet to experiment, juxtaposing ideas within a flexible form.

In 1971 Rich published *The Will to Change*. The collection includes a section of "Blue Ghazals," and two of the poet's most famous works. On the program, she reads "Planetarium," a tribute to Caroline Herschel (1750–1848), an astronomer who discovered eight comets but whose accomplishments were eclipsed by the fame of her brother William. In the closing lines of the poem, Rich speaks in the voice of Caroline Herschel:

> . . . I am an instrument in the shape
> of a woman trying to translate pulsations
> into images      for the relief of the body
> and the reconstruction of the mind.

Just as she melds the poet and the persona, Rich now attempts to join the private and public worlds in her work, making the words speak to large issues of political change and social justice. In "The Burning of Paper Instead of Children," she combines poetry with prose passages to address the problems of violence and poverty. In *Leaflets*, she had emphasized the importance of language, while recognizing its inadequacy; and in "Burning" she states: "there are books that describe all this / and they are useless". Language has been abused to support power: "knowledge of the oppressor," she realizes, "this is the oppressor's language / / yet I need it to talk to you." In "Images for Godard" and the 12-part "Shooting Script," Rich adapts the "jump cuts" and other cinematic techniques of French New Wave directors, to convey her meaning or message through quick bursts of images rather than argument or narration: "the poet is at the movies / / dreaming the film-maker's dream but differently . . . the mind of the poet is changing / / the moment of change is the only poem".

How radically Rich's mind and poetry were now changing can be gauged in *Diving Into the Wreck: Poems, 1971–1972* (1973), a collection which garnered accolades and generated much controversy. With Audre Lord and Alice Walker, Rich received the 1974 National Book Award for Poetry, which she refused as an individual but accepted on behalf of all women. And justly so, for the book not only voices her own indignation and frustration but speaks to the condition of women generally, "the matrix of need and anger" they endure amid destructive forces in a male-dominated society. Rich's sense of outrage in such poems

as "The Phenomenology of Anger" and "Rape," especially, provoked great hostility, in turn, from many critics. In her bitterness, Rich sometimes lapses into stereotypes, unfairly branding
all men as adulterers, rapists, and murderers, and the poet's
polemical pitch overwhelms her more usual aesthetic poise. In a
lengthy, balanced review, Helen Vendler observes: "The truth of
feeling ('I felt this way, I wrote it down') has never been coter-
minous with the truth of art. And since the truth of art has
always been Rich's securest claim on our attention, even in her
tidiest poems, it gives a reader a wrench of pain to see her play
false to her own standard." But in the 1973 essay (reprinted in
*Part of Nature, Part of Us*), Vendler hastens to add: "Unwelcome
though some of Rich's sentiments may be to those who do not
share her recent activist feminism and other political activities, it
would be unfair to let ideological difference obscure the presence, felt and conveyed in these poems, of finely discriminated
emotions—of the numbed, the stricken, the defrauded, the mis-
erable."

*Diving Into the Wreck* presents a penetrating examination
of Rich's developing consciousness, while continuing her analysis of the controlling force of language. In "Trying to Talk with
a Man," the woman says: "we talk of people caring for each
other . . . but you look at me like an emergency"; and in
"When We Dead Awaken," she finds: "the words / get thick
with unmeaning— / yet never have we been closer to the
truth / of the lies we were living . . . ." Those lies, the "dazed"
and "lost" speaker in "Waking in the Dark" declares, are "The
tragedy of sex" and "A man's world. But finished. / They themselves have sold it to the machines." To find the truth, the meta-
phorical diver in the title poem must delve into "the deep element," the unconscious:

> I came to explore the wreck.
> The words are purposes.
> The words are maps.
> I came to see the damage that was done
> and the treasures that prevail.

In her explorations, the "mermaid" discovers she is also a

"merman"—"I am she: I am he . . . we are the half-destroyed instruments / that once held to a course". The androgynous figure suggests the possibility of wholeness or the reintegration of the divided self, for "We are, I am, you are / by cowardice or courage / the one who find our way . . . ." In commenting on the book's concluding "Meditations for a Savage Child," Helen Vendler also notes: "Rich forsakes distinctions between men and women . . . and sees us all as crippled creatures, scarred by that process of socialization and nurture . . . the whole edifice of civilization, of which she now sees the dark side—war, exploitation, and deadening of instinct."

Following her *Poems: Selected and New, 1950–1974,* Rich published a lengthy prose study which examines the topic of nurture and socialization at its most fundamental, *Of Woman Born: Motherhood as Experience and Institution* (1976). Combining autobiography with extensive research, Rich attempts to provide a historical context for the significant distinction indicated in her title, by showing how the concept of motherhood has been (mis)shaped in a society dominated by "the power of the fathers." Men's subordination of women and their nurturing qualities—particularly as exemplified in the differences between delivery by midwife at home and by (male) obstetrician in hospital ("Hands of Flesh, Hands of Iron," "Alienated Labor")—is seen as part of a larger pattern: a patriarchal system with its "warrior mentality" and "death-culture of quantification, abstraction, and will-to-power." Rich notes she wanted to write on the subject "because it was a crucial, still relatively unexplored, area for feminist theory"; and the book has been criticized for exhibiting a radical-feminist bias and an intemperate style. But the validity of many of Rich's observations cannot be denied, among them: that birth "is neither a disease nor a surgical operation," that women should be allowed to choose how they will give birth, that men "need a kind of compensatory education in the things about which their education as males has left them illiterate."

As the Seventies progressed, Rich continued her work as an activist, becoming a very popular speaker at the forefront of the feminist movement, while remaining highly productive as a writer. Confronting the complex questions of race, class, and gender, she also came to terms with her own sexuality. In 1976 Rich published *Twenty-One Love Poems*, tender celebrations of her lesbian relationship. On "Poets in Person," she tells Diane Middlebrook, "It was enormously important to me that lesbian poets . . . were clearly writing and visibly writing as lesbians; and so I feel as though I was very much empowered to go on and write out of those parts of myself by the fact that other women were already doing that." (It may be noted that, speaking of "sensual relationships, pacifism, sex" in the essay "When We Dead Awaken," Rich stresses, "I mean sex in its broadest significance, not merely sexual desire".)

These love lyrics are included in *The Dream of a Common Language* (1978), and as its title suggests, the collection presents a more hopeful vision of community, especially among women. Rich offers as examples the friendship of the painter Paula Modersohn Becker and the sculptor Clara Westhoff Rilke, a team of Russian mountain climbers ("Phantasia for Elvira Shatayev"), and her own sister ("Sibling Mysteries"). Still the poet is concerned with the problem of communication—"It is an old theme even for me: / Language cannot do everything—" she says in "Cartographies of Silence." Rich prefaces her reading by indicating the poem is "political," since it "concerns the breaking through of silences that smother identity, that smother who we are." Responding to Diane Middlebrook's observation that "many people consider politics to be deadly to poetry," Rich points out: "That's an attitude that I think is prevalent in the United States, but in very few other cultures."

> It's certainly not prevalent in Latin America, for example, it's certainly not prevalent in Europe . . . the notion that politics—defined as the struggle to grasp who we are in the world and what our place is in the world and how we've been empowered or disempowered and how we can transform the disempowerment—why should poetry, why should any art be asked to stand outside that great human enterprise?"

In 1979 Rich published *On Lies, Secrets, and Silence: Selected Prose, 1966–1978*, which provides a detailed commentary on her evolving aesthetics, personal life, and political engagement during this crucial period. In her introduction, Rich states her purpose is "to define a female consciousness which is political, aesthetic, and erotic, and which refuses to be included or contained in the culture of passivity." Besides offering a valuable companion to her own poetry, the collection presents feminist critiques of Emily Dickinson, Anne Bradstreet, Charlotte Brontë, and other women writers and a provocative essay on education, "Toward a Woman Centered University." In "Women and Honor: Some Notes on Lying" (1975), she writes: "There is no 'the truth,' 'a truth'—truth is not one thing, or even a system. It is an increasing complexity." Though she does not always avoid the simpler, reductive "truths" of ideology, in the poetry that follows Rich tries to trace that complexity.

Always prolific, she produced four poetry collections and another substantial prose volume (*Blood, Bread, and Poetry*) during the Eighties. In these books from middle age, the author reprises many of the autobiographical subjects and social themes treated in earlier work. But now the mood is rather darker, as she views a world still little changed and seeks to revise her own poetic means or frames of reference. In *A Wild Patience Has Taken Me This Far: Poems, 1978–1981* (1982), she returns to her mother-in-law and asks, "before we part / shall we try again?" But twenty years later, the chances for mutual understanding seem no better than before. Again, revisiting the streets of Boston in 1979, she encounters police brutality and the same male victimization of women she formerly decried. While the author's sincerity is beyond question in these and similar poems, one wishes that the stereotyping were less pronounced and that equal sympathy would be extended occasionally to the male half of the race; also that some distancing irony or even humor might leaven the unrelieved solemnity. In "The Images," Rich asks, rhetorically, "when did we ever choose / to see our bodies strung / in bondage and crucifixion . . . to be lynched on the queasy electric signs / of midtown . . . to become the masturbator's fix," and the rhetoric seems overwrought. Later she says, "I can never romanticize language again / never deny its power for disguise for mystification"; and she questions the value of art, because its beauty "translat[es] / violence into patterns so powerful and pure / we continually fail to ask are they true for us." Yet, for all her disappointment with the imperfect world, she realizes a separate existence is not possible. In "The Spirit of the Place," she affirms

> The world as it is:     not as her users boast
> damaged beyond reclamation by their using
> Ourselves as we are     in these painful motions
>
> of staying cognizant:     some part of us always
> out beyond ourselves
> knowing     knowing     knowing

In *The Fact of a Doorframe*, Rich offers an updated Selected Poems covering the years 1950 to 1984. Among the six new poems in the collection, "In the Wake of Home" is also retrospective, with the poet reaching back to the site of her early rage, her tense relation with her demanding father, "my Jewish father writing me / letters of seventeen pages / finely inscribed harangues / questions of loyalty and punishment . . . a bad daughter . . . ." The poet tries to conjure a more perfect family life in an imagined past world—"a little kingdom . . . a village of shelters"—but again finds her place in the troubled present. Translating her personal unhappiness and psychological distress into sympathy for others who are oppressed, she asks: "What if I told you your home / is this planet of warworn children / women and children standing in line or milling / endlessly calling each others' names"—but the monologue abruptly stops. Again, the message of solidarity, mere language, is not enough: "—will any of this comfort you," she asks, "and how should this comfort you?"

In the books that have followed—*Your Native Land, Your Life* (1986), *Time's Power: Poems, 1985–1988* (1989), and *An Atlas of the Difficult World: Poems, 1988–1991* (1991)—Rich has continued to alternate her sights between her personal life and the larger social causes she has long espoused, a bifocal vision identifying a deep and integral sensibility. Many of the more recent poems retrace the past, including Rich's Jewish heritage, her husband's suicide in 1970, the lot of women in history. (On the program, Rich reads "Baltimore: a fragment from the Thirties," from *Your Native Land, Your Life*.) Others pieces arise from current events, topical poems that reiterate themes made familiar over Rich's long career as artist-witness to the violence, exploitation, and injustice of our difficult times.

While she has not lost her sense of outrage, warmth often supplants the angry tone of previous work, just as the impersonal pronouns of earlier poems are now replaced by "you" and "I" and "we." This usage is not simply rhetorical. Because of her own intellectual and spiritual struggles for authenticity—the painful process of discovery recorded in her work—Rich has (despite her doubts) the moral authority, achieved only by personal effort, to speak for others, and to us, as individuals. In her 1975 essay on Emily Dickinson, she writes of the poet's vocation and the ancient idea

> that she is endowed to speak for those who do not have the gift of language, or to see for those who— for whatever reasons—are less conscious of what they are living through. It is as though the risks of the poet's existence can be put to some use beyond her survival.

The paragraph, of course, applies as well to Adrienne Rich and her life's work.

# JOHN ASHBERY

© Anna Tomczak

"I'm trying to accurately portray states of mind, ones of my own that I think might have a general application, and the movements of the mind and the way we think and forget and discover and forget some more," says John Ashbery on "Poets in Person," offering the shortest and in some ways clearest statement we have about his work.

Over the last three decades, Ashbery has become one our most prolific authors, and one of the most often imitated. No poet of his generation has elicited more critical commentary. Yet for all the ink expended, neither his interpreters nor his imitators seem quite able to capture the qualities which make his work so uniquely affecting. Like reality and consciousness themselves, Ashbery's meditations on the relation between the two remain elusive, while his influence upon American poetry continues to be inescapable.

Ashbery's poems are "about" time, love, loneliness, art, death, the traditional subjects of poetry. Their purview seems to take in the whole world, from the most artistic and intellectual artifacts to the very ordinary, even banal, aspects of American life and popular culture. His diverse range of interests is registered in an equally capacious vocabulary that accommodates the lexicons of technology, philosophy, music, art, and high culture as easily as the overworked jargon of newspapers, textbooks, office memos, advertising copy, and casual conversation. Like experience itself, the protean structure of Ashbery's work is unpredictable. In his flexible lines the reader confronts suddenly changing perspectives, paradoxes, non-sequiturs, and baffled expectations.

Ashbery's tone is extremely variable: by turns witty, wistful, intimate, matter-of-fact, nostalgic, arch, ironic, self-critical, amused, ambivalent. In the fluid movements of his poems, meanings shift as readers are made aware of the myriad ambiguities of their own consciousness, and their participation in the poetry: a process of constant readjustment. Life is an untidy affair, and Ashbery's work refuses to neaten things up with the usual narrative structures, arguments, or convenient closures that art contrives. As he announces in the first lines of his *Selected Poems*: "We see us as we truly behave: / From every corner comes a distinctive offering."

Abandoning most poetic conventions, Ashbery has evolved his own poetics. Continually reformulated, Ashbery's inventions make curiously diverting if ultimately inconclusive inquiries into the complexities of contemporary life and consciousness. While critics attempt to explain his fascinating and frustrating methods, non-specialist readers seem undeterred by the difficulties the scholars find. Despite their challenges, his poems speak to an ever-growing audience less interested perhaps in pondering aesthetic puzzles than in enjoying the thoughtful pleasures they provide.

John Ashbery was born in Rochester, New York, in 1927, and grew up on a farm in western New York State. His childhood was relatively isolated, though the loneliness and boredom were alleviated by visits to the home of his grandfather, a physics professor at the University of Rochester. As a teenager, he was a radio "Whiz Kid" and attended Deerfield Academy, in Massachusetts. He was attracted not only to literature but to painting and music. Music—from the Baroque period to the Second Viennese School and from the obscurer reaches of the operatic repertoire to John Cage—remains a strong interest; his verse has been set to music by Cage, Elliott Carter, Ned Rorem, and others.

"I began by wanting to be a painter," Ashbery relates on the program. "I took art classes at the local art museum for about five or six years, when I was a kid, weekly classes. At that time, I was very excited by the Surrealists, who had been the subject of an essay in *Life* magazine . . . I was about ten years old at that time. So I think I decided at that age that I was probably a surrealist. I don't think so still, by the way." He notes that William Carlos Williams also painted but said that he gave it up because "he found it easier to carry around a manuscript than a wet canvas. And this may have been a little the case with me, too."

As a child Ashbery wrote poetry. In high school he won as a prize Louis Untermeyer's *Anthology of Modern British and American Poetry*, "most of which was unfamiliar to me. And reading those, I began writing poems in the style of some of the more accessible ones, such as Edna St. Vincent Millay and Elinor Wylie."

> The modernist poets still kind of eluded me, and I think it was Auden, whose work completely baffled me when I first read it—although now it doesn't seem to present much difficulty for anybody. But I was confused by his use of colloquial speech, which I didn't think you were supposed to do in poetry. I then wrote a lot poems almost embarrassingly in the style of Auden. As so often, one is blind to one's imitating of one's favorite models, and to me at the time they seemed completely original, and very good.

Ashbery studied English and wrote an honors thesis on W. H. Auden at Harvard, where he met fellow student Frank O'Hara. He graduated in 1949, then took an M. A. in literature from Columbia in 1951. In New York City he became a member of the lively art crowd which included the experimental poets Kenneth Koch, James Schuyler, and his friend O'Hara, as well as the avant-garde painters Willem de Kooning, Franz Kline, and Jackson Pollock, soon to be famous as "action painters" and

Abstract Expressionists. O'Hara eventually became a curator at the Museum of Modern Art and was more deeply involved with the visual arts than Ashbery.

On the program, Ashbery says that O'Hara "prodded" him to look at the work of the Abstract Expressionists, but he acknowledges: "I do think, though, that their conception of what a picture is undoubtedly influenced my method of writing, by just plunging in . . . [their idea that] the work of art is somehow a history of its own making is in there, too." In conversation with the poet, David Bromwich quotes Jackson Pollock's remark: "When I'm in the painting, I don't understand what I'm doing. It's only after a sort of get-acquainted period that I see what I've been about." Ashbery agrees that he shares that feeling, and recalling the novelist Heinrich Böll's quip, "Inspiration begins on page 60," he adds:

> I, like Pollock, can be writing for quite a long time
> without having any idea what I'm writing about. I
> begin writing with no clear idea of what I'm going to
> say. I'm not sure that I have ever had anything to say,
> in the sense of a message that one can extract from
> the poem and carry home with one, as it were. In
> that sense, writing a poem is a sort of embarking on
> a voyage toward some unknown point—and per-
> haps not ever arriving there, either.

Often, but inaccurately, Ashbery is classed with O'Hara, Koch, and Schuyler as a member of the "New York School of poets." It is true that all of them were living in Manhattan in the Fifties, and their poems share an "urban" aesthetic which reflects the multiplicity and energy of city life. (O'Hara light-heartedly includes bits of telephone calls, movies, lists of his diverse activities, names of people and places—as if to cram in as much of his experience of the metropolis as possible while capturing the zest and spontaneity of the moment.) But the term "New York School" is a misnomer and, as Ashbery explains, merely a convenient label first affixed to the then unknown authors in an anthology compiled by the art dealer and critic John Bernard Myers, who "thought that the prestige of the New York School of painting might rub off on the poets whom he published." He adds, "I feel that each of us is quite distinct from the others. One thing I think linking us together is a kind of experimental attitude towards poetry, but . . . this produces different results in each case."

That experimental attitude is evident from Ashbery's earliest work. In 1956, Ashbery published *Some Trees*, which was selected by W. H. Auden for the Yale Younger Poets series. The collection includes a number of formal verses (sonnets, sestinas, a canzone, an eclogue), which show his technical mastery, and the artificiality of the conventions. Other poems are more inventive and display what became Ashbery's characteristic diffident tone and quizzical style. "He," for example, begins each line with that pronoun and contains these statements: " 'He is his own consolation prize.' " "He walks in his sleep into your life." "He is invisible to the eyes of beauty and culture." In "Illustration," people try to dissuade a suicidal woman from jumping off a building; she responds: " 'I want to move / / Figuratively, as waves caress / The thoughtless shore. You people I know / / Will offer me every good thing / I do not want. But please remember / / I died accepting them.' " The daydreamer writing "The Instruction Manual" imagines a vivid scene in Mexico and concludes: "How limited, but how complete withal, has been our experience of Guadalajara! . . . What more is there to do, except stay? And that we cannot do." "*Le livre est sur la table*" offers the odd aperçu: "All beauty, resonance, integrity, / Exist by deprivation or logic / Of strange position." Throughout the book, as in the work that follows, Ashbery's supple lines are touching, while they tease us into a variety of interpretations.

Ashbery was awarded a Fulbright Fellowship for 1955–57 and went to France. He ended up staying for ten years in Paris, where he wrote art criticism for the European edition of the *New York Herald Tribune* and *Art International* (Lugano) and was a correspondent for *Art News* (New York). Later, on his return to

New York following the death of his father in 1965, he became executive editor of *Art News*, a post he held until 1972; from 1976 to 1980, he was the art critic for *New York* Magazine, and then for *Newsweek*, from 1980 to 1985. His reviews and essays are collected in *Reported Sightings: Art Chronicles 1957–1987*.

On "Poets in Person," Ashbery tells David Bromwich, "Although I was an art critic for many years, this was kind of an accident. I mostly did it very reluctantly." Still, as he notes, the methods of the avant-garde painters did influence his work during this period, particularly the poems in his next collection, *The Tennis Court Oath* (1962). On the program, Ashbery gives the context for the composition of this controversial volume:

> I had finished a first book of poems at the time when I arrived in a new country where I didn't speak the language, and it was perhaps this that caused the more experimental poems in *The Tennis Court Oath* . . . much of the poetry of that period was made up of almost automatic writing and lots of use of collage. I read a lot of American magazines and newspapers at that time, just somehow to keep in touch with the kind of American conversational voice, and sometimes cut those things up and pasted them into my poetry. And I wasn't very satisfied with [those] . . . works.

Some critics have not been very satisfied with the poems, either, especially the very lengthy, much remarked upon "Europe." The shorter poems in the volume are not so dissimilar stylistically from those in the previous book; most are quite evocative, for example, "An Additional Poem," which concludes: "we / Rise with the night let out of the box of wind." But the cut-and-paste of "Europe" results, over the long haul, in a dispiriting collage. The approach is not, of course, original with Ashbery; Pound's *Cantos*, Williams's *Paterson*, and Eliot's *The Waste Land*, and other long Modernist works use disjunctive techniques to convey the sense of fragmentation in contemporary life. But Ashbery's pastiche, composed as it is of newspaper clippings and other dull, ephemeral scraps, compresses their banalities into an opaque mass.

Ashbery's procedures in "Europe" have doubtless contributed to the notion that he is a surrealist writer, which the poet denies, and with reason. Elsewhere he does employ odd juxtapositions, elliptical constructions, and discontinuities, and his phrases can seem interchangeable. But he does not, by and large, arrange his materials randomly; far from automatic writing, most of his work is quite consciously, usually cunningly, devised. While he has rejected and parodied the old verse conventions, as well as the New Critical principles of the well-made poem—and the ideas or systems of order they presume—he has devised what have become his own conventions for expressing the flux of thought, emotion, and indeed the world.

"The Skaters," the long and poignant poem which concludes his next collection, *Rivers and Mountains* (1966), offers a good illustration of some of Ashbery's methods. In an 1974 interview, the poet describes it as "a meditation on my childhood which was rather solitary. . . . I think the boredom of my childhood was what I was remembering when I wrote that poem—the stamp albums, going outside to try and be amused in the snow . . . Also an imaginary voyage prompted by the sight of a label or a postage stamp was again a memory of childhood." These details evoke other memories and occasion the imaginary trips (flights indeed) Ashbery notes. The four parts of the poem proceed by means of associations, with transitions smooth and abrupt: "True, melodious tolling does go on in that awful pandemonium, / Certain resonances are not utterly displeasing to the terrified eardrum," he says in a passage about musical instruments which suggests the aleatory or chance compositional techniques of John Cage. (Elsewhere echoes of poetic forbears, Eliot and Stevens particularly, can also be heard.)

"I simply wanted to see how many opinions I had about everything," Ashbery told the critic David Shapiro in discussing "The Skaters." But one must be wary of "opinions" in any of Ashbery's works, since they usually cancel each other out. "Who, actually, is going to be fooled one instant by these phony

explanations, think them important?" he says toward the end of
the first section of the poem.

> So back we go to the old,
>     imprecise feelings, the
> Common knowledge, the importance of duly suffering
>     and
>         the occasional glimpses
> Of some balmy felicity. The world of Schubert's lieder.
>     I am fascinated
> Though by the urge to get out of it all, by going
> Further in and correcting the whole mismanaged mess.
>     But am afraid I'll
> Be of no help to you. Good-bye.

But "explanations" about the vast confluences of experience are
not what the poet is after; rather than trying to rationalize the
"mess," he is more interested in tracing its movements. Thus,
skaters and skating make apt metaphors: "skaters elaborate
their distances, / Taking a separate line to its end. Returning to
the mass, they join each other / Blotted in an incredible mess of
dark colors, and again reappearing to take the theme / Some
little distance . . . different parabolas, / Taking the exquisite
theme far, into farness, to Land's End, to the ends of the earth!"

"Life for Ashbery . . . is motion," Helen Vendler notes in
*The Music of What Happens.*

> We are on boats, on rivers, on trains. Each instant is
> seen "for the first and last time"; each moment
> is precious and vanishing, and consequently each
> poem is unique, recording a unique interval of con-
> sciousness. This is a consoling aesthetic, since by its
> standards every utterance is privileged as a nonce
> affair; it is also mournful, since it considers art as
> fleeting as life.

A little later in the passage cited earlier, Ashbery says, "the
carnivorous / Way of these lines is to devour their own nature,
leaving / Nothing but a bitter impression of absence, which as
we know involves presence, but still." From a more positive

perspective, however, the poet views the movement of the skater (and the figuration of the creative artist) in an image of infinity: "The figure 8 is a perfect symbol / Of the freedom to be gained in this kind of activity." Such "freedom" is (as we know) severely limited: the movements form an unending loop. As so often, Ashbery asserts and denies at the same time.

In the late Sixties, Ashbery published his first *Selected Poems*, three small-press books, and a novel, *A Nest of Ninnies*, co-authored with James Schuyler. In 1970 he published *The Double Dream of Spring*, a highly self-referential volume in which the author repeatedly questions the ability of poetry (his own especially) to order, or "author," his experience. The poems cite many truisms while treating conventional wisdom ironically; or perhaps not, since the poet's tone encourages us to sympathize with his (and our) predicament. "Definition of Blue," for example, states: "In our own time, mass practices have sought to submerge the personality"; and "Soonest Mended" observes: "Barely tolerated, living on the margin / In our technological society, we were always having to be rescued. . . .

> To step free at last, minuscule on the gigantic plateau—
> This was our ambition: to be small and clear and free.
> Alas, the summer's energy wanes quickly,
> A moment and it is gone. And no longer
> May we make the necessary arrangements, simple as they
>      are.
>            . . . . . . . .
>                . . . We are all talkers
> It is true, but underneath the talk lies
> The moving and not wanting to be moved, the loose
> Meaning, untidy and simple like a threshing floor.

All of us talkers, poet and non-poet alike, remain ambivalent, although (the poem concludes) "our conforming to the rules and living / Around the home have made—well, in a sense, 'good citizens' of us . . . For this is action, this not being sure, this careless / Preparing, sowing the seeds crooked in the furrow, / Making ready to forget, and always coming back / To the mooring of starting out, that day so long ago." In "For John

Clare," he rephrases the thought: "the whole history of proba-
bilities is coming to life, starting in the upper left-hand corner,
like a sail."

In 1972 Ashbery took a new tack with *Three Poems*, in
which he experiments further with the prose poem, breaking
away even from the artifice of lineation. "It's sort of an uncomfortable term, 'prose poem.' Lots of people would deny that
there is such a thing," Ashbery tells David Bromwich on the
program.

> But I began writing them, I think, as a kind of reac-
> tion . . . the poet tends to suddenly become an ora-
> tor, and there's a built-in rhetoric to prose poetry,
> which I wanted to get away from. And also, since
> I like common, if even demotic forms of prose, I
> wanted to examine these and see if there was any
> possibility that there might be poetry in this kind of
> speech or prose. Therefore, I used a lot of different
> tones in those poems in a kind of democratic jum-
> bling of different voices and different styles.

Certainly the book displays Ashbery's ease in mixing a variety
of dictions—slang, proverbs, philosophical phrases, clichés—
replicating or further complicating, as he says in "The System,"
"the already complicated texture . . . through which we have to
stray". But the poet finds that each part of the jumble is important: "not one of these tendrils of the tree of humanity could be
bruised without endangering the whole vast waving mass . . .
that gorgeous, motley organism would tumble or die out unless
each particle of its well-being were conserved as preciously as
the idea of the whole." Thus, even clichés are accorded unusual
respect in Ashbery's work. On "Poets in Person," he explains:

> Everybody laughs at clichés, and they're not sup-
> posed to be part of "literature" . . . to me there's
> something almost slightly sacred about clichés, just
> because so many people have used them to express
> their strong emotions. And it's, I suppose, part of
> what Mallarmé calls "the language of the tribe,"
> which, unlike him, I'm not interested in purifying
> but perhaps just preserving.

In 1975 Ashbery published *Self-Portrait in a Convex Mirror*, which won the Pulitzer Prize, National Book Award, and National Book Critics Circle Award for poetry. In the brilliant title poem, Ashbery examines the famous painting of that name by the 16th-century Mannerist artist Parmigianino. His detailed observations lead to a stream of reflections on the nature of time, the self, the creative process, and particularly the mysterious and often distorting relation between the work of art and the world it represents. Like the painting, the ideas it occasions for the poet are complex and paradoxical. At one point, he is struck by the feeling

> that the soul is not a soul,
> Has no secret, is small, and it fits
> Its hollow perfectly: its room, our moment of attention.
> That is the tune but there are no words.
> The words are only speculation
> (From the Latin *speculum*, mirror):
> They seek and cannot find the meaning of the music.
> We see only postures in a dream . . . .

Unlike the precisely controlled realm of the artwork, the world of "the turning seasons and the thoughts / That peel off and fly away" cannot be contained, nor its chaos organized. Comparing the present time with the Renaissance (and the orderly universe it posited), he addresses the artist: "Long ago / The strewn evidence meant something . . . Impossible now / to restore those properties in the silver blur that is / The record of what you accomplished . . . ." In place of the abandoned myths, theological systems, the other narrative frames that once supported society and the arts, we are left with the present moment. But

> Today has no margins, the event arrives
> Flush with its edges, is of the same substance,
> Indistinguishable. "Play" is something else;
> It exists, in a society specifically
> Organized as a demonstration of itself.

No more than any other Ashbery poem can "Self-Portrait" be summarized. But it may be noted that his idea of art as "play" or performance, prized in itself apart from former justifying value systems, is a principal motive and leitmotif in all his work. Ashbery does not lament the loss of the old systems; there is more than enough matter and motion to engage his attention in the present. "You and I and the dog / Are here, this is what matters for now," he says in "Hop o' My Thumb." In the past, it was "civilization that count[ed] . . . we are as much of it as anybody else / Only we think less about it, even not at all . . . ." In its meditation on time, "Grand Galop" asserts:

> Nothing is partially complete, but the wait
> Invests everything like a climate.
> What time of day is it?
> Does anything matter?
> Yes, for you must wait to see what it is really like,
> This event rounding the corner
> which will be unlike anything else and really
> Cause no surprise: it's too ample.

In the books which follow *Self-Portrait*, while he continues his explorations of time, consciousness, the self, and other favorite topics, Ashbery shows if anything an even greater openness to the flux of daily experience. Despite a mid-life preoccupation with death, his mood seems lighter, his humor—and Ashbery is one of our wittiest poets—more direct and less turned to irony. *Houseboat Days* (1977) is in some ways his most accessible volume. Or perhaps it merely seems so; after twenty years, familiarity with his idiosyncratic style (the mannerisms of which have been so often imitated) seems to have lowered the rhetorical barriers he is often accused of erecting. In the title poem, he writes

> The mind
> is so hospitable, taking in everything
> Like boarders, and you don't see until
> It's all over how little there was to learn
> Once the stench of knowledge has dissipated . . .
>            . . . . . . . .
> But I don't set much stock in things
> Beyond the weather and the certainties of living
>      and dying:

The rest is optional. To praise this, blame that,
Leads one subtly away from the beginning,
   where
We must stay, in motion. . . .

In "Pyrography," he says, "To be able to write the history of our time, starting with today, / It would be necessary to model all these unimportant details," such as colored wallpaper and painted furniture; but "No sighs like Russian music, only a vast unravelling / Out toward the junctions and to the darkness beyond."

*Houseboat Days* is expansive and includes many slices of popular culture: "Street Musicians" (with its "forgotten show-tunes" and picnics in pine forests), "The Other Tradition" ("endless games of Scrabble," "The celebrated omelette au Cantal"), as well as "Unctuous Platitudes," "Business Personals," and "Daffy Duck in Hollywood." The last poem indicates the poet's appreciation for the movie industry's ability to assimilate everything, from grand opera to "acajou harpoons," high culture and pop culture (a distinction that doesn't trouble him overly), into a "finished product."

Ashbery's *ars poetica*, the subject of so much earnest self-examination in earlier poems, receives a curiously blithe (though no less complex) treatment in "And *Ut Pictura Poesis* Is Her Name." Taking off on Horace's saying that poetry is like a picture, Ashbery retorts: "You can't say it that way any more. / Bothered about beauty you have to / Come out into the open, into a clearing, / And rest." Poetry need not portray things outside itself or justify itself with meanings in the usual sense. After pausing abruptly after nine lines (" . . . So much for self-analysis."), the poet continues with a mock-serious list of "What to put in your poem-painting," and concludes: "Something / Ought to be written about how this affects / You when you write poetry:"

The extreme austerity of an almost empty mind
Colliding with the lush, Rousseau-like foliage of its desire to
   communicate
Something between breaths, if only for the sake

Of others and their desire to understand you and desert you
For other centers of communication, so that understanding
May begin, and in doing so be undone.

*As We Know* was published in 1979 and stirred considerable controversy with its almost 70-page opening poem,
"Litany," whose two columns, Ashbery notes, "are meant to
be read as simultaneous but independent monologues." Even
the imperturbable Helen Vendler was somewhat taken aback
by the format, which she found "a somewhat trying imitation of
the bicameral mind." (The intrepid Harold Bloom considered it
two poems, reflecting two sides of one psyche, and preferred the
right-hand column.) Although one can read across the page,
the two columns (roman and italic) go their separate ways for
the most part (there are some parallel and contrasting passages),
and it wise to take Ashbery at his word, that these are independent texts. Obviously, this "antiphonal" poem does not permit
short summary, except to say its (or their) many topics revolve
about Ashbery's perennial interests, particularly art and criticism. As in his other long poems, here subjects are only loosely
related and one topic is soon replaced by another.

In contrast, the second part of the collection contains
mostly short lyrics, forty-seven of them, whose subjects include
autobiography, death, "My Erotic Double," "Homesickness."
There are a few one-liners: following the title "The Cathedral
Is," "Slated for demolition."; and after "I Thought Things
Were Going Along Well," "But I was mistaken." Of the group,
"Haunted Landscape" and "Landscapeople" make particularly
affecting inquiries into the nature of identity. In part II of *As We
Know*, as in his other books, it may be noted that Ashbery often
gives titles seemingly unrelated to the texts which follow them.
On the program, David Bromwich asks the poet if he makes up
the titles separately, since they seem distinct "poetic acts almost
in themselves." Ashbery replies: "For me, it's a way of kind of
expanding the meaning of the poem. If a poem has a title that
seems not to have anything to do with it, you are forced to try to
relate it to that title nevertheless, and to make sort of jumps that

you wouldn't if the title was a perfectly straightforward announcement of the poem that was to follow."

In *Shadow Train* (1981), Ashbery changed course yet again, using the same four-quatrain form in all fifty poems in the collection. "Since I'm known for writing very long ones, I thought I'd see what it's like if I don't," Ashbery has said. "It's as simple as that." The book was originally called "Paradoxes and Oxymorons," and as the poem of that title indicates, it deals with "language on a very plain level" and at the same time a "deeper outside thing." The apparent contradiction here is consistent with Ashbery's career-long linguistic practice and his penchant for probing into the equivocations and inconsistencies within systems and the speech from which they are constructed. The title poem begins,

> Violence, how smoothly it came
> And smoothly took you with it
> To wanting what you nonetheless did not want.
> It's all over if you don't see the truth inside that meaning.
>
> To want it is to be better than before. To desire what is
> Forbidden is permitted. . . .

The poem, "on a very plain level," adopts the tone and syntax of aphorism, seemingly in order to mock platitudes. At the same time, however, trying to "see the truth in that meaning" ("wanting what you nonetheless did not want"), one might interpret the poem as a warning against the seductive charms of advertising. The idea seems supported later, as "The great plumes / Of the dynastic fly-whisk lurch daily" while "You are half-asleep at your instrument table." But then again, perhaps not: a question is inserted, "Who can say / What it means, or whether it protects?" The sequence of statement, query and possible retraction, inconclusive conclusion is the characteristic Ashbery procedure which teases, amuses, frustrates here as throughout his other work. He says (warns) in "Paradoxes and Oxymorons": "Look at it talking to you. . . . You have it but you don't have it. . . . The poem is sad because it wants to be yours, and cannot." Is it play?

"Well, actually, yes, but I consider play to be / / a deeper outside thing, a dreamed role-pattern . . . Open-ended." And now, in this poem, "It has been played once more." And turning on the reader, the poet concludes:

> I think you exist only
> To tease me into doing it, on your level, and then you aren't
>     there
> Or have adopted a different attitude. And the poem
> Has set me softly down beside you. The poem is you.

"I'm always trying not to repeat myself," Ashbery has said, and shown by his continuing experimentation. Helen Vendler has remarked on "the element of playfulness (of not being, God forbid, boring or, worse, bored)" in his work, and noted how "very transparent Ashbery's poems can become over time". All of these aspects are demonstrated in Ashbery's most recent volumes. *A Wave* (1984) presents a variety of forms, including rhymed quatrains ("The Songs We Know Best"), "37 Haiku" (written as single lines), six "Haibun," prose poems (including "The Lonedale Operator," read by the poet on the program), and the long title poem, which concludes the volume. The author's abiding interest in the quotidian, however banal, is expressed in "Description of a Masque," a prose poem which gives equal notice to "Scenes from movies, plays, operas, television; decisive or little-known episodes from history; prenatal and other early memories from our own solitary, separate pasts; events yet to come from life or art; calamities or moments of relaxation; universal or personal tragedies; or little vignettes from daily life that you just had to stop and laugh at, they were so funny . . . ." The items "go on evolving eternally . . . all of the same series, which [is] creation itself."

In its twenty-two pages, "A Wave" forms a sustained meditation on mortality, brooding yet oddly beguiling, as the poet questions his purpose: "To be always articulating these preludes, there seems to be no / Sense in it . . . ." Yet, "certain that day will end soon and that night will then fall," he is calm, "not unhappy": "I mean I don't mind staying here / A little longer";

and in the end, it seems the writing will have been worth it. For,
because of the poems,

When they finally come
With much laborious jangling of keys to unlock your cell
You can tell them yourself what it is,
Who you are, and how you happened to turn out this way,
And how they made you, for better or for worse, what you
     are now,
And how you seem to be, neither humble nor proud, *frei aber
einsam* [free but alone].

In *April Galleons* (1987) and *Flow Chart* (1991), Ashbery's
thoughts turn increasingly toward last things, and a nostalgic,
Proustian tone dominates. Speaking of *Remembrance of Things
Past* on the program, Ashbery recalls, "I read it when I was still, I
think it was, 20. . . . And I think it was perhaps something that
one should read later on. In a way, it kind of illuminated and yet
saddened life for me. . . . It's very, very powerful, almost like
another substance or element, but the message, of course, is . . .
times, they are a-changing." The poems in *April Galleons* record
the changes with backward glances to childhood and meditations on maturity, decline, and death. These subjects also domi-
nate *Flow Chart*, Ashbery's second book-length poem, and at over
200 pages his longest. It is written in long lines and very long
sentences, as well, with a conversational tone that mixes several
levels of diction and evocative imagery. As in other Ashbery
works, the six parts of the poem move in a free-associational
manner, though the texture is varied by free-verse paragraphs,
stanzas, and occasional isolated lines. Though it is impossible to
abstract all its themes—the book is in a way a grand summation
of the ideas, as well as the techniques, of all that has preceded it—
one section may suggest its flavor:

Two nights ago when I was complaining about all the
     weather we've been having lately,
and about how no one can do anything about it—much as
     I'd like to—

I was still happy, but today it turns out the drought has been
    secretly installed for weeks:
we're only beginning to feel the brunt of it. Of course,
    measures will be taken


but that's scarcely the point. It won't like you any better for
    it.
And what about mud? If we lose it, we lose everything.
Distinctions would no longer get muddied. There'd be
    nothing in life to wriggle out of,
no ooze to drop back into. We need water, heaven knows,
    but mud—it's so all over the place,
like air, that the thought of its not being there is even scarier.
Like a home that must be abandoned quickly, whose carpets
    and wallpaper get that faintly
distressed look, earth would go on without us, leave us
    waiting in space
for a connection that never comes. Somehow we'd survive—
    we always do—but at what cost
of mud and cosmetics. Different forms of address
would have to be adopted. Manners would become pallid,
    and the plot of one's life
like a thin membrane in which one can still recognize the
    shapes
that brought us here, and lure us on, but stronger too, to
    survive business,
and that would wreck our average partygoing.
I live at the bottom of the sea now.
But I can still sense a stranger
even when far off
and count the threads of partings still to be formalized.

At the end of "Poets in Person," David Bromwich notes
that general readers seem to have "pretty good feelings" about
Ashbery's work, and the poet agrees that even people "who
have never read any poetry" have asked to see his poetry and
"didn't seem to have the problems with it that people who are

of a more literary bent often complain about." Asked who he thinks his readers are, he responds:

> Well, I don't know who they are, of course. Therefore, it's very difficult to communicate with them directly. Or course, every writer has the same problem. Well, I guess for that reason . . . I write, as Gertrude Stein said, "for myself and strangers."

# SHARON OLDS

"One of the major sources for poetry for me was silence, all that's not spoken about," Sharon Olds explains on "Poets in Person." She notes that "people have not thought that it was proper to speak about certain things in public or in art" and that "those who could speak of something from the inside didn't happen to be the speakers that we mostly had in poetry" when she was coming of age. But like nature, art abhors a vacuum, she suggests: "So the silences in our culture—I think, in a way, poems are sucked out of us by the magnetic attraction of that silence."

Breaking the silences—particularly those concerning the body and the taboos surrounding our most intimate relations—has been a major thrust in Olds's work. With unusual frankness and striking imagery, she focuses on the complex bonds between women and men and the loving but often troubled attachments between parents and children in poems that are both clear-eyed and disquieting. Her frequent journeys into the interior can become harrowing explorations of the human psyche. But only by confronting what is concealed, especially the traumatic episodes of her (and our) personal history, Olds insists, can safety or sanity or wholeness be found. Citing the Gnostic Gospel of Thomas, she states, "If you do not bring forth that which is within you, that which is within you will destroy you."

Sharon Olds was born in San Francisco in 1942. In her "Poets in Person" interview, she tells Alicia Ostriker that even as a small child she felt a desire "to create something." Constructing dollhouse scenes, "trying to create a replica of some kind," was a source of pleasure, as was having "the chance to take one's own turn to speak, to say what one thought oneself about something. . . . I wrote as a little kid." She credits as her earliest literary influence the Bible, particularly the Psalms her mother read to her: "Those were the poems that I heard from birth." She notes that as a teenager she wrote "in as narrow forms as I could find," and read Shakespeare, Dylan Thomas, Edna St. Vincent Millay, Emily Dickinson, e. e. cummings, W. H. Auden, and Walt Whitman. Then, in her 20s, she discovered more open forms and more contemporary authors: "Muriel Rukeyer and Galway Kinnell and Ruth Stone and Philip Levine have been the most important writers for me."

Olds attended Stanford University and graduated with a B.A. in 1964, then took her Ph.D. from Columbia in 1972. Her first book, *Satan Says*, appeared in 1980 and received the inaugural San Francisco Poetry Center Award. The book attracted wide attention particularly for its directness in treating such themes as birth and motherhood and the tensions between the generations. In a *Poetry* review, Lisel Mueller found the collection "uncompromisingly autobiographical"; and certainly many readers of this and Olds's subsequent books have shared the critic's feeling that Sharon Olds the author and the "I" of her poems are one. This impression is encouraged by the work itself, especially a poem like "I Go Back to May 1937," from Olds's third book, *The Gold Cell*. Here the speaker pictures her future parents just before their college graduation. They are about to be married, and knowing the pain to come ("you are going to do bad things to children"), she says, "I want to go up to them and say Stop"—but she doesn't, because "I want to live." Instead, "I say / Do what you are going to do, and I will tell about it."

Olds herself tells very little about her early years or any other aspects of her personal life. Indeed, beyond the most basic facts of her education, her literary affinities, and details of her professional career, the poet reveals virtually nothing, and demands that critics not inquire. (Of course, such silence may only prompt certain inquiring minds to further speculation.) With Sylvia Plath, Anne Sexton, Allen Ginsberg, and other "confessional" poets, it is tempting to equate the personas in their poems with the real-life authors. This is particularly true when correspondences are readily made between details in the poems and self-revealed facts about the lives. Ginsberg, Robert Lowell, Adrienne Rich, and other contemporary writers have been highly public figures, as well; and in assuming public roles, these authors have addressed large issues of the day and espoused political and social causes, further complicating response to their work. While Olds generally speaks "from the inside" and is not overtly "political," reactions to her writing have been no less complicated.

Because her subjects strike very close to home, literally, and her language and images are so vivid—not to say provocative—her poems are highly charged and tend to stir strong emotions. Readers' responses may be extremely personal, like or dislike of the poems and their author very subjective indeed. Perhaps by closing off discussion of her biography, Olds wishes to maintain distance, and avert confusion, between her private realm and the created world in her work. In any case, the truth of poetry (as with any fiction) usually lies beyond mere recitation of "facts": artists and their imaginative productions deserve to be judged by aesthetic criteria—the measures of their success as *makers*—while the authenticity of the work of art may be confirmed or denied by the individual reader's or observer's own experience. To Olds's admirers, the incidents and emotions portrayed in her poems ring all too true.

"The world of your poetry is so intensely physical, is so embodied always, so close to the flesh," Alicia Ostriker tells Olds on the program. "You write about childbirth, you write about sex, you write about death, you write about your own body and the bodies of those you love, with reverence and intimacy." Ostriker speaks for the many who have identified with the poet's depictions of the multiple roles of daughter, woman, and mother, titles which also form the section headings in *Satan Says*. The "Daughter" poems are especially passionate, and frequently bristle with hurt and anger. In the title poem, the speaker is located "in a little cedar box" and taunted by Satan to denounce her parents. She follows his commands and finds some relief, yet conflict remains: "I love them but / I'm trying to say what happened to us / in the lost past." This tension underlies and engenders the psychodramas in the poems to follow. Torn between filial love and the desire "to say what happened," the voice of the divided self in "Satan Says" suggests the collection is an attempt to exorcise the demons of the past.

Some of the "Daughter" poems depict scenes of an unhappy childhood marked by physical mistreatment and (in some ways worse) emotional abuse from a rejecting father. Here the images are arresting, the diction blunt, but occasionally overwrought, as well. In her review, Lisel Mueller observes that Olds "sometimes allows her rage to go out of control, using a voice so vehement, a language so hyperbolic, as to incur disbelief, at least in this reader." Olds's scenes can be unsettling, and, as Mueller notes, her metaphors at times (in "Love Fossil" and "Monarchs," for example) are "uneasy." On the other hand, when she distances herself and approaches the subject of violent anger through a historical event, Olds is more controlled and convincing. Returning to the scene of the crime in "Photographs Courtesy of the Fall River Historical Society," the poet coolly considers the savage murders of Lizzie Borden's parents and concludes: "Only a daughter could have done that."

On the program, Olds reads a number of poems from the third section of *Satan Says*, "Mother," which includes some of her most affecting work. In the first of five "Young Mothers" poems, she describes the cautious fears and hypersensitivity of the protective parent:

> Now she is alert for violation,
> hearing acute as a deer's, her pupils
> quick, her body bent in a curve,
> wet rope which has dried and tightened,
> a torture in some cultures.
> She dreams of death by fire, death

by falling, death by disembowelling,
death by drowning, death by removal
of the head. Someone starts to scream
and it wakes her up, the hungry baby
wakes and saves her.

Several other poems in the section are addressed to a daughter, revealing a range of complex emotions, not least the anxieties which are rooted in the mother's own history. Brief and incisive, "The Unjustly Punished Child" is likewise a telling profile, in this case of a young boy and his psychological transformation; following his rage, "He is stronger. The long impurification / has begun this morning."

"The Language of the Brag" is probably the best-known piece in the collection, an unabashed paean to "this exceptional / act with the exceptional body, / this giving birth"—and a poem which is itself extraordinary, both for its graphic descriptions and its bold, indeed epic, stance. Alicia Ostriker considers it "a revolutionary poem" because it declares that "childbirth is heroic" and "a perfectly acceptable and wonderful subject for literature." In saying "I have done what you wanted to do, Walt Whitman, / Allen Ginsberg, I have done this thing, / I and the other women," Olds not only celebrates the "exceptional act" but insists that it is in fact an "American achievement" equal to any masculine feat of strength and courage. In that sense, "The Language of the Brag" can be considered a "political poem."

"I think that every poem is political, both by what we include and what we leave out," Olds remarks on "Poets in Person." "I do tend to seem to get interested in writing about relationships of power between people, unequal power, between governments and citizens or parents and children or men and women." In an interview by mail conducted by the Poetry Society of America in 1989, Sharon Olds, Carolyn Forché, and Alicia Ostriker were asked: How important is it that your poetry make some sort of political statement? Do you use your poetry as a vehicle for your political views? Olds responded that "for a long time, the only things I felt intensely enough about to write a poem I'd end up liking were things very close to me." She

noted that she would hear "the work of those *out in the world*—
Muriel Rukeyser, Adrienne Rich, June Jordan, Carolyn Forché
—and 'know' I could never do that, and 'know' that private was
lesser than public. And it didn't cross my mind that family
poetry—involving power and size and the imprinting of the
soul—might be seen as political." She added, "I think I had
started out with a small heart, or a heart filled up with its close
concerns. Then gradually it grew." The degree of that growth
can be gauged in Olds's second book.

   *The Dead and the Living* was published in 1984 and won
the Lamont Poetry Prize and the National Book Critics Circle
Award. In this large collection, Olds continues the narration of
her family romance begun in *Satan Says*, examining both the
past and the present. But the first part of the book, "Poems for
the Dead," begins with a section titled "Public," poems situated
"out in the world" and implying larger moral or political imper-
atives. Here she catalogues 20th-century oppression and ele-
gizes the victims of famine and massacre in Russia and Armenia
("Photograph of a Girl," "Nevsky Prospekt," "Portrait of a
Child"), of racial hatred in Rhodesia and Oklahoma ("The
Issues," "Race Riot, Tulsa, 1921"), of political executions in Iran
("The Aesthetics of the Shah"), and torture in Chile ("Things
That Are Worse Than Death"). The poet's sympathy and sense
of outrage are apparent throughout these lines. Yet for all the
horrific detail, there is also a curious reserve in the pieces, perhaps because most of them are drawn from photographs. The
scenes she depicts are emotionally loaded, and given our residual feelings, the writer must exercise rhetorical control to
prevent sensationalism and sentimentality in considering them.
Despite her craftsmanship, this group is perhaps more effective
as protest than persuasive as poetry. But, then, Olds does not
need to persuade: we already agree with her condemnation of
mass starvation and genocide and share her revulsion against
the individual torments she describes.

   In the following "Private" section, Olds returns to her
"close concerns" in several elegies, to old friends, her grandmother, a child lost through miscarriage. Though most of these
"Poems for the Dead" are poignant expressions of love and loss,

Olds still harbors acerbic feelings toward a grandfather who "taught my father / how to do what he did to me"; and in "The Guild" (also read on the program), the poet recalls both men with the kind of ambivalent but mostly somber emotion that runs through her earlier accounts of her homelife. Alicia Ostriker observes that "The Guild" demonstrates Olds's ability to express opposite ideas simultaneously: "There is fear, there is anger, there is also profound love in a poem like that."

"Part Two: Poems for the Living" is divided into three sections. "The Family" returns to the past and includes several more poems addressed to the father, who is now considered with a new degree of compassion, although the title of "The Victims" indicates that the entire household has suffered by his faults. Here, however, and in "The Departure" Olds's comparison of the father to historical fallen figures (Nixon and the Shah of Iran) seem overdrawn, as does the analogy to Hitler entering Paris in a bitter poem about a bullying sister. Poems addressed to her mother show deeper understanding, but lingering resentment, as well.

Turning to the other men in her life in second section, Olds offers touching portraits of early sexual experiences, a husband's tenderness, and the affections and fears of devoted partners in marriage. This group carries an erotic charge and shows Olds's considerable skills with sensuous imagery and limpid lines to best advantage. These qualities are also evident in the several poems to "The Children" which conclude the book. In their mixture of tenderness and frank descriptions of the son's and the daughter's sexuality, these poems are quite unlike any other lyrics of parental love. The candor of "Exclusive," "Six-Year-Old Boy," "Son," "35/10" and others in the group allows a rare presentation of the erotic ties that bind. At the same time, Linda Gregerson has noted, the poet, "perhaps inadvertently, records the radical invasiveness of erotic proprietorship: Olds takes in these poems an owner's liberties" with the children's bodies.

Reviewing the book in *The Iowa Review*, Carolyn Wright found, "What makes these poems gripping is not only their humanity, the recognizable and plausibly complex rendering

of character and representative episode, but their language—
direct, down to earth, immersed in the essential implements
and processes of daily living." Olds's gifts for candor, precise
observation, and exceptional metaphor are also evident in her
next collection, *The Gold Cell* (1987). With more loosely structured lines, she continues her explorations in somewhat longer
poems about married love, reconciliation with aging parents,
the strains of adolescence, and the joys of children growing to
adulthood. As the title indicates, each subject carries ambiguities; the figure suggests both treasure and entrapment, that the
facts of family history, physicality, and emotional attachment
cannot be escaped. In "Why My Mother Made Me," for example, the poet muses: "Maybe I am the way I am / because she
wanted exactly that, / wanted there to be a woman / a lot like
her, but who would not hold back . . . I lie here now as I once
lay / in the crook of her arm, her creature". Many of the poems
in the book's last three sections retrace the themes concerning
mother and father, son and daughter, and sexuality of the first
two collections.

But Olds also expands her range in the first section of *The
Gold Cell* with narratives drawn from life in New York City, her
home of many years. "On the Subway" presents a white woman facing a black youth at the opposite side of the car. She is
wearing a fur coat, he has sneakers and "the casual cold look
of a mugger"; contemplating the differences in their lives, the
woman realizes they are each in the other's power. Another
poem considers "The Abandoned Newborn" who was found in
a shopping bag, rushed to the emergency room, and through
modern medicine brought back to life. But what kind of life?
On the program, Olds reads "Summer Solstice, New York City,"
in which the police try to coax a suicidal man from a rooftop.
The drama concludes:

> . . . they closed on him, I thought they were going to
> beat him up, as a mother whose child has been
> lost will scream at the child when it's found, they
> took him by the arms and held him up and
> leaned him against the wall of the chimney and the

tall cop lit a cigarette
in his own mouth, and gave it to him, and
then they all lit cigarettes, and the
red, glowing ends burned like the
tiny campfires we lit at night
back at the beginning of the world.

Commenting on the relation between the poet and the
community in her interview, Olds notes: "Someone who is born
with a certain gift for language, a passion for language, might
end up speaking for more than just herself or himself. Let's hope
so. To me that word 'I' in a poem is a worthless thing if it doesn't
really mean anybody at all." In daring to break the silences and
in attempting to tell of things "not spoken about," the poet has
given voice to some of the central human experiences. With
shocks of recognition, many readers have found in Olds's "I"—
autobiographical or otherwise—aspects of their own identity, as
her impassioned words have resonated with their most deeply
held feelings.

Sharon Olds has taught at Brandeis and Columbia, and
now directs the Creative Writing Program at New York University. She is very popular reader of her own work and is a frequent guest lecturer in workshops around the country, besides
conducting her regular writing classes at Goldwater Hospital on
Roosevelt Island in New York. Her other awards include a grant
from the National Endowment for the Arts and a Guggenheim
Fellowship.

# CHARLES WRIGHT

"I think of the self that I write about as being made out of words. He's been reconstructed constantly, over and over again, out of words. I think I am a product of language much more than other people I know," Charles Wright remarks on "Poets in Poet."

During the gradual evolution of his work, Wright has assimilated many of the major technical and philosophical elements of Modernist poetry and translated them into a voice, an aesthetic self, uniquely his own. The influence of Ezra Pound is most evident in Wright's striking use of imagery; like the old Modernist, Wright has discovered in the image "that instant when an outward and objective thing is transformed to a thing inward and subjective." In his metaphysical speculations, painterly methods, and musical phrasing, which subtly combines sound and sense, he is reminiscent of Wallace Stevens. Emily Dickinson, Gerard Manley Hopkins, Dante, Li Po, and many other forbears have also helped inform his highly individual sensibility and style.

Wright's recurrent themes are the pervasiveness of the past and the persistence of memory, the relation between the secular and the sublime, and his own life and personal quest for salvation. But while he uses religious terms and has never lost a longing for transcendence, his conviction remains that "salvation doesn't exist except through the natural world." In the poem "Reunion," he presents part of his artistic aspiration: "I write poems to untie myself, to do penance and disappear / Through the upper right-hand corner of things, to say grace." For Wright, language itself is a "sacred place," and in his own words he locates and often elicits mysterious dimensions within mundane reality.

Charles Wright was born in Pickwick Dam, Tennessee, in 1935 and grew up in eastern Tennessee and North Carolina, "a very rural, deprived, poor, dirt-poor area of the country," he notes on the program. His father was a civil engineer who supervised the construction of dams for the Tennessee Valley Authority. As a young woman, the poet's mother may have had literary aspirations herself and later harbored similar hopes for him. He says that she "always felt being a writer would be a wonderful thing—how many mothers think that it would be a wonderful thing for their sons to be writers!" Although he was a relatively "late bloomer," the seed of his vocation was planted as early as the fifth grade. "That was it for me," he tells J. D. McClatchy, for "the fifth grade is where I got interested in words and language."

On "Poets in Person," Wright reads a section from a sequence called "Tattoos" which describes the moment when, practicing the "Oval oval oval oval push pull push pull" of the Palmer method of handwriting, he discovered that words were charmed objects and things in themselves:

> The words, like bees in a sweet ink, cluster and drone,
> Indifferent, indelible,
> A hum and a hum:
> Back stairways to God, ropes to the glass eye:
> Vineyard, informer, the chair, the throne.
>
> Mojo and numberless, breaths
> From the wet mountains and green mouths; rustlings,
> Sure sleights of hand,
> The news that arrives from nowhere:
> Angel, omega, silence, silence . . . .

Equally indelible were his boyhood impressions of the South— its topography, its flora, its very atmosphere—which would provide the central images and become the most potent "material" for his work. "All of my South is locked into . . . 1940 to 1955, from the age of five to fifteen," he explains; the experiences of these earliest years were "an engendering force for my life."

Wright attended local public schools, except for his last two years of high school as a boarder at Christ School, an Episcopal academy near Asheville, North Carolina. On "Poets in Person," he recalls working on construction jobs as a teenager and meeting people who were more like "characters" from Southern novels than he considered himself to be. "But all of that informed me, in the same way that religion informs my work. It was always just there . . . religion just suffused the whole air and mentality of the South during the time I was growing up." Even as a young student, however, Wright became skeptical of traditional religion. "I was struck with the kind of spiritual awareness that I think I still have, but I was already beginning to be uncomfortable with the organization in which I had first discovered this spiritual awareness." Elsewhere he has spoken of the "sparring match I had for about ten years with the Episcopal Church, in which I was raised . . . and out of which I remain. But it had a huge effect on me . . . it has given me a sense of spirituality that I prize."

Wright attended Davidson College, in North Carolina, graduating with a B.A. in 1957 (after what he has described as "four years of amnesia, as much my fault as theirs"), and then signed up for four years in the army. He spent three of them in Italy as a second lieutenant in the Counter-Intelligence Corps (1958–61). It was there that he encountered the European poetic tradition and the work of Ezra Pound. While Wright was stationed in Verona, a friend learned he planned to visit nearby Lake Garda and gave him Pound's *Selected Poems*, telling him to read one of them, called "Blandula, Tenulla, Vagula": "It's about the place where you're going to go." On the program he recalls:

> And so I went and sat under an olive tree in the
> March sunshine and read this poem, and as Emily

Dickinson said, the hairs on the back of my neck stood up. Now, I don't know what it was about the poem that I particularly liked. I suspect nowadays it was the iambic pentameter, the blank verse that it was written in, but I didn't know what blank verse was or iambic pentameter was at the time—it just sounded good to me. . . . And I thought this was fabulous.

He read the rest of the poems and then the Italian edition of Pound's *Pisan Cantos*, "and I got very interested in poems at that particular moment." And so, at the age of 23, Wright began writing poems. Pound's example, particularly his imagistic and disjunctive techniques, were and have remained strong inspirations. Wright has said that he first used the *Pisan Cantos* as a travel guide book "to out-of-the-way places, then as a reference work and finally as a 'copy' book." He was also attracted to the Italian poets, from Dante to the present, and eventually translated Montale and Dino Campana.

After his tour of duty, Wright returned to the States and enrolled at the University of Iowa. Although he was in the graduate school, he discovered that he had not been formally admitted to the Writers' Workshop. At the time, the Iowa writing program was small, with only a few dozen students. "I just showed up and went to the first class," Wright recalled in his interview for the program. "It wasn't until April of the following year that I finally asked somebody, 'How did I ever get in here?' I knew nothing when I came." When discussion in the very first class turned to iambic pentameter, he found, "I didn't know what they were talking about. I thought, 'I'm in the wrong place.' But I kept my mouth shut for two years and picked up a few things. . . . All anyone thought about was writing poems, and that's all I was interested in doing. And basically that's all I've been doing ever since 1961. All my jobs have been adjuncts to that."

After receiving his M.F.A. in 1963, Wright was awarded a two-year Fulbright Fellowship and returned to Italy, where he translated modern Italian poetry and lectured at the University of Rome. In 1966 he joined the English department at the University of California, Irvine. He remained on the Irvine faculty for seventeen years, while also holding periodic visiting professorships at Iowa, Princeton, and Columbia. In 1968–69 he again went to Italy, as a Fulbright Lecturer at the University of Padua. In 1983, he returned to the South, to take his current position as Professor of English at the University of Virginia. The critic George F. Butterick has remarked that Wright's academic career "contains no surprises. All torment or danger or vagary has gone into the language and is to be found on the page, to our great benefit."

Finding such a language, and a voice distinctly his own, did not come quickly or easily for the poet. "I'd always wanted to write, as they say, but I thought to write meant to write stories and fiction, and I couldn't write stories," Wright tells J. D. McClatchy. But his reading of Pound proved a revelation:

> now I found something that I thought I could do, which is the lyric poem. I didn't know it was called "the lyric poem" at the time, but it was an associational kind of progression and not a straight Frostian, Dickensian narrative, and I thought, well, I could do that because that's the way my mind seems to work, in fits and starts—it jumps from one thing to another. And if you can jump from the right thing to the next right thing, then you can have . . . an associational organization to a poem. And I liked the sound, and all of my, I suppose, repressed musical ambitions were able to finally find a way of coming out.

In the work of Emily Dickinson he also found a kindred spirit, both for her questioning mind and for the musical measures in her secular hymns. Wright has referred to his own poems as hymns, as he explains on the program: "I wanted them to be musical . . . all my poems are poems of praise." He adds:

> I've always thought that the true purpose of poetry, at least in my case, was a contemplation of the

divine, however or wherever one finds that. And
everyone finds it differently for himself. Emily Dickinson affected me at my heart's core—and does—
because what she writes about is what concerns me:
the inability to get to heaven.

In his interview for the program, Wright elaborated: "I don't
think she ever believed truly in the accepted religious dogma or
attitudes of her day, although she was a religious person. I feel
the same things affect me. Whitman's 'Song of Myself' is a
religious poem, obviously, but it's of a different kind. Emily
Dickinson's poems are much more concentrated, condensed,
non-stories, as it were, exclamations of desire. I like to listen to
Walt talk, but she speaks to me."

Eugenio Montale also spoke to him, and for similar reasons. During his first Fulbright years, Wright translated *La Buf-
era e altro* (published as *The Storm and Other Things* in 1978) and
found in Montale's elliptical lyrics a sensibility that was con-
genial with his own temperament. As in Pound's work, he admired the Italian master's precise, hard-edged but elusive imagery, and even more the ways in which Montale deployed it. In a
1976 interview at Oberlin College (published in *Field* and reprinted in his prose collection, *Halflife*), Wright acknowledged
his debt to Montale for teaching him "how to manipulate lines.
How to move a line, how to move an image from one stage to
the next. How to create imaginary bridges between images and
stanzas and then to cross them, making them real, image to
image, block to block." In Montale, as in Pound and Dickinson,
he also recognized the value of compression and the power of
aphoristic compactness to suggest, rather than baldly state,
meaning and to elicit feeling. But the process of incorporating
these elements and making them his own was a long one;
indeed, Wright's idiosyncratic style—particularly the structure
of his line—has continued to evolve over the last twenty years.

After several journal and small press publications in the
Sixties, Wright presented his first major collection in 1970. *The
Grave of the Right Hand* is a competent, ambitious volume, but
not unlike others of the period; some critics have noticed re-

semblances to James Wright, for example, and Donald Justice, one of his teachers at Iowa. Today the author prefers to distance himself from that early work, and he has not reprinted it. ("One likes to say one loves all one's children, and if they're children, one does. But I don't know that one loves all one's poems.") One may note, however, that themes in the book recur throughout the collections which have followed: the importance and persistence of the past as reconstructed by memory, the relation between the human spirit and the natural world, mortality and the quest for salvation. Already apparent, too, are the richness of the poet's vocabulary and his gift for evocative imagery.

Wright's second book, *Hard Freight*, was published in 1973, and here the poet's authentic style emerged. The volume appeared a decade after his graduation from Iowa, a period he considers his apprenticeship: "I was learning for that first ten years—what meters were, how to organize poems, how to filter out what seemed unnecessary verbiage, commentary, conversations in poems—just basically how to put a poem together." Equally important, he finally discovered his true subject matter, "which was my own wonderful self." The turning point, he has said, came with "Dog Creek Mainline," a poem inspired by a place from childhood, Hiwassee Dam, North Carolina: "And from then on, everything has been different. I've been doing my autobiography in poems ever since." On the program, Wright offers a cautionary note, however: "When one starts writing about one's background and one's childhood, one writes about what one did, but basically what one didn't do and what one might've liked to have done. And most all of the stories that come out in my poems are things that not necessarily happened to me but I would like to have had happen to me."

*Hard Freight* begins with a number of "Homages" to literary mentors, Pound first of all. In the Oberlin interview, Wright explained the background of the poem, his attempts to approach the expatriate poet in Italy: "I'd follow him around for days in Venice. I'd even follow him to his restaurants. But I could never just walk up to him and say 'hello.' Anyhow, what are you going to say to a man like that, 'I like your poems'?" In the interview he also noted the influence of Venice itself upon his work: "There is a connection, a lushness, in my mind between my east Tennessee foliage and the Venetian leafage, gold leafage, that seems to have stayed with me ever since . . . the sumptuousness of Venice [has] somehow filtered in." Wright cited as an example "Dog Creek Mainline," but several other poems in *Hard Freight* display a similar imagistic richness in evoking memories and places from his past, including "Sky Valley Rider," "Blackwater Mountain," and "Northanger Ridge." Other pieces in the collection conjure states of mind or concentrate on language itself, often with uncanny effect, as in "White," "The Other Side," and "Nouns," in which the poet observes: "Nouns are precise, they wear / The boots of authority . . . they know / Whom to precede and whom to follow, / They know what dependence means. . . ."

*Hard Freight* was followed by *Bloodlines* in 1975 and *China Trace* in 1977, forming an "autobiographical" trilogy. The quotation marks are necessary, for here, as in his other work, Wright offers no ordinary exposition of his life, no straightforward accounting of fact or chronological progression; nor does he use a conventional narrator or the usual framing strategies which impose an artificial sense of order and closure. Instead, the poet makes a virtue of his abnegation, by finding fresh and ever more subtle ways for imagery and open-endedness to tell his story. On "Poets in Person," he explains:

> I'm a little suspicious of forms per se. I don't quite know why, because some of the poems that I love best in the world are written in standard forms. I feel my poems are dedicated to free verse, to proving that free verse can be just as structured, as tight, and as formally organized as any kind of received traditional form is. And I find that much more of a challenge; I find it an impetus to me that is freeing without being lawless. And I understand when people say that free verse is lawless, because most free verse is lawless. But most forms are boring. Most poetry is not good. We all know that.

In the Oberlin interview, Wright outlined in detail the several arrangements, numerical schemes, and interrelationships he devised in the books, and their rationale. One may note only a few of the major thematic and structural aspects here.

*Bloodlines* forms the center of the trilogy with two sequences, "Tattoos" and "Skins," each composed of twenty poems (the number of the "Motets" in Montale's *Le Occasioni*, 1939). Wright has explained: " 'Tattoos' hooks up with *Hard Freight* and the past, and 'Skins' hooks up with *China Trace* and the future." In "Tattoos" the poet returns to pivotal, sometimes traumatic experiences—a car accident, the death of his father, a religious snake-handling ritual—using brief notations and a montage of sharp images to depict the unerasable emotional impact of the incidents. (He appends a page with very terse notes for each poem; e. g.: "Automobile wreck; hospital; Baltimore, Maryland.") The sequence does not follow the chronology of the author's life; the object here is not to record facts so much as to register acute psychological or spiritual states arising from the physical occurrences.

By contrast, the "Skins" sequence is more abstract and concerned with concepts or attitudes. The central theme is presented directly: "There comes that moment / When what you are is what you will be / Until the end." On "Poets in Person," Wright explains the background of the perception:

> It just suddenly occurred to me that there is a moment when what you are is what you're going to be. You will not be able to alter yourself. You have already made yourself into what you are. That time comes at different ages for everyone. Mine came in the fifth grade when I realized that I was the onlooker. . . . I was the person who was always doing the observing. That has continued in my life to this day.

So, too, in "Skins": by the end of the sequence—the poet has described it as a "ladder," with ten steps up and ten down—we arrive with Wright's Pilgrim at "that moment" where we began. The descending and ascending pattern suggests a homage to Dante's elaborate architecture in the *Commedia*; in any case, the structural scheme is rather complicated, but becomes clearer with rereading. Immediately evident, however, are the contrasting formal arrangements in the two sequences. In "Tattoos," Wright uses a three-stanza format, implying an almost classical organization—exposition, development or complication, and recapitulation or conclusion—except that there is no real closure or resolution in the poems. In "Skins," as well, he employs an apparently controlling form: the 14-line stanzas suggest the structure of the sonnet (and its divisions of argument— problem/solution, question/answer); but, again, there are no "conclusions" for these meditations. Not that they are needed, or missed, in such poetry: Wright's brilliant images and cinematic "jump-cut" movements are more than enough to command attention, line after line, "block to block."

China Trace, the final volume of the trilogy, addresses philosophical and religious matters, and is often elegiac in tone. Wright has described it as "a book of Chinese poems that don't sound like Chinese poems, but are like Chinese poems in the sense that they give you an idea of one man's relationship to the endlessness, the ongoingness, the everlastingness of what's around him, and his relationship to it as he stands in the natural world." Wright's always strong visual sense (like that in Pound's imagistic poems and Chinese translations) is especially acute in these poems, and the sound is equally striking, as demonstrated in the poet's reading of "Clear Night." In form, the collection marks another phase in Wright's stylistic evolution; here he lengthens his line, which becomes his basic unit of measurement. The book also marks the poet's fortieth year, and of these sometimes eerie poems from mid-life those centered on consciousness, death, and metaphysical questions are particularly memorable: "Noon," "At Zero," "Sentences," "Snapshot," "Equation."

Wright's poems of the next decades are no more easily summarized than those in the trilogy; indeed, no true poem can be paraphrased. In Part of Nature, Part of Us, however, Helen Vendler offers a sensitive and extraordinarily insightful explication of the poet's books from the Seventies. Her general observations are even more applicable to his subsequent collections: "Because Wright's poems, on the whole, are unanchored to incident, they resist description; because they are not narrative, they defy exposition. They cluster, aggregate, radiate, add layers like pearls."

In *The Southern Cross* (1981), Wright firmly established the pattern he has continued to refine till the present. The book begins with an eight-poem "Homage to Cézanne," and it is from this artist that he has derived his mature method for structuring his complex personal vision. On the program, Wright explains the correspondences between the painter's technique and his own:

> When you look up close at a Cézanne landscape, it looks like layerings of almost mismatched coloration, and as you step farther and farther back, you see that all of these are starting to coalesce into a picture, and the farther back you get the more representational it becomes. . . . It seemed to me an interesting way of trying to put poems together. Which is to say that to make a representational, i.e., narrative poem, you did not have to do the straight, missionary narrative. You could do it in various other ways.

Several ways of layering are illustrated particularly well in Part Two of the collection, where five pieces entitled "Self-Portrait" alternate with poems depicting contrasting scenes from the past ("Mount Caribou at Night," "Holy Thursday," "Virginia Reel," "Called Back"). On the program, Wright reads the final section of the long title poem, which returns to Tennessee and the year of his birth. Other sections of "The Southern Cross" and several of the poems earlier in the volume are composed in the author's now-characteristic long lines; often (as Helen Vendler has observed) they are divided, or arranged to repeat patterns, and sound like the antiphonal responses in the Psalms.

In 1982, Wright gathered the poems from his early books into one volume, *Country Music*, which won the 1983 American Book Award. This Selected Poems was followed by two new volumes, *The Other Side of the River* (1984) and *Zone Journals* (1988). With *The Southern Cross* and the small-press edition of *Xionia* (1990), these books have been reissued as *The World of the Ten Thousand Things* (1990). The title of this large collection, embracing work from 1980 to 1990, is taken from T'sen Shen: "When the ten thousand things have been seen in their unity, we return to the beginning and remain where we have always been." Viewing all the poems of this volume together, one now sees how Wright's versions of a Cézanne landscape, with their individual "patches" of coloration and layerings, do indeed "coalesce into a picture." In the recent poems, Wright returns to his Southern childhood; remembers his life in Italy and California and imagines the China of Li Po; recalls family and friends; and ruminates on pivotal moments in his spiritual and aesthetic development. And as recollection and commentary combine, the significance of both the early and later works becomes clearer, several facets "seen in their unity."

Throughout the poems of the last decade, Wright continued to experiment, but in the long lines and discursive notations of his "Journals" he seems to have found the ideal means to express the several aspects of his art. *Zone Journals* is dedicated to Glenn Gould and Merle Travis, an acknowledgement of both his classical and country roots. This dual heritage is evident throughout the musical phrases of these poems, which blend allusions to high culture and down-home wisdom, philosophy and religious questioning, autobiography and the ephemera of everyday life. With lines that are often haunting in their imagery, "A Journal of English Days," "A Journal of True Confessions," "Chinese Journal," "Light Journal," "Night Journal"—together and in their individual sections—form a composite portrait of the artist as a mature man, complex, sympathetic, identifiable in his search for the transcendent in the natural world.

On "Poets in Person," Wright notes that juxtaposing and overlaying descriptions at first "makes a poem look, perhaps abstract in its individual parts; but by the time you've finished reading the whole poem, there is an understood story that's been going on all the time." To appreciate his work, it is necessary to read (and reread) it straight through from the beginning: Wright's art forms a continuing story that builds through the incremental gathering of its several forces. With their many pleasures, Wright's poems convey as well a spiritual intensity and seriousness of intention rare today. Asked on the program if he concurred with Montale's statement that for the ancients poetry was "the stairway to God," he replies:

> Of course, I still think poems are religious, but in a different way. They are the stairways to whatever god is for me. Poems are the only things that are going to put the coin between my teeth and to get me my ride across the river, as it were. They do tend to be constantly my argument with myself against the improbability of salvation. They tend to be my contemplation of things beyond us, yet ourselves.

# RITA DOVE

When she was awarded the Pulitzer Prize for Poetry in 1987, Rita Dove became one the youngest writers ever to receive the honor, and only the second black poet to do so, following Gwendolyn Brooks. The Prize was offered for *Thomas and Beulah*, Dove's imaginative recreation of the lives of her grandparents. But the author had already impressed the literary community with her two previous books, *The Yellow House on the Corner* and *Museum*, and her work since the Prize has confirmed critical opinion from the start that she would prove to be one of the most talented poets of her generation.

Rita Dove was born in 1951, in Akron, Ohio, where, as she recounts on "Poets in Person," her father was the first black chemist to be employed in the rubber industry. Her father's example, particularly his love of reading and discipline, had a strong influence on the future writer, as did his active participation in her education. Growing up in a strict household was not without its bittersweet moments, however, as Dove indicates in her interview and in her readings of several poems. "Flash Cards" presents a brief but vivid portrait of the young scholar being tutored in the old-fashioned rote method by her demanding father, while "My Father's Telescope" offers an amusing vignette of the perfectionist parent's frustration with his own shortcomings. Both poems demonstrate Dove's economy of means, her ability to reveal and dramatize character through carefully selected details, and her subtle technical control. (Note, for example, her ingenious but unobtrusive use of rhyme in "Telescope.")

As a pioneer in his job, his daughter relates, Mr. Dove had suffered "a lot of discrimination and humiliation," and was determined his children would not have the same experience. Rearing them in the North, Dove's parents had tried to protect them from "the harsher sides of discrimination." But in "Crab-Boil," the poet presents a crucial moment at age 10 when, visiting relatives in Ft. Myers, Florida, the child discovers the reality of segregation at "the forbidden beach." Again, the author approaches her subject through concrete particulars, rather than ready-made rhetoric. The crabs become symbols on several levels (and a focus for the girl's moral ambivalence), as the poem conveys the sense of childhood awakening with a dramatic scene of complex but understated psychological realism.

Dove notes that her parents restricted their children's television viewing, even in summer, but encouraged them to read, a liberating experience that fostered the poet-to-be's imagination. As she tells Helen Vendler, another pivotal factor in her development was her discovery of German literature through her father's collection of foreign language books. "I was reading everything I could get my hands on . . . and one of those was Schiller's long poem *Das Lied von der Glocke*, the Song of the Bell. It was a very old edition, still in Gothic script, and it was just a beautiful little book. But I couldn't read it." So in junior high school she elected to study German to be able to read the book.

At Miami University in Oxford, Ohio, Dove received a Presidential Scholarship and studied English and creative writing; she was also elected to Phi Beta Kappa and graduated *summa cum laude* in 1973. She then received a Fulbright Fellowship, which she used to study modern European literature at the University of Tübingen, in Germany. The poet's experiences in Germany—with her husband, the German novelist Fred Viebahn, she returns to Europe regularly—have offered material for several poems. One, based on a painting depicting two people who appeared in a Berlin sideshow in 1929, is called "Agosta the Winged Man and Rasha the Black Dove" and was printed in her second book, *Museum* (1983). On her first trip to Germany, Dove had been perceived as an exotic stranger, and as she relates in her program, "I was tired of being stared at . . . I just felt that that painting spoke to me."

On the program, the author reads two other poems from *Museum*, "David Walker (1785–1830)" and "Parsley." In her first book, *The Yellow House on the Corner* (1980), Dove presented poems based on slave narratives, and in "David Walker" she incorporates the black abolitionist's words and imitates his voice to tell the story of his ingenious and dangerous efforts to smuggle anti-slavery tracts into the South. "Parsley" provides a contrasting and more chilling portrait, that of a contemporary oppressor; the poem is one of Dove's best-known works, and a remarkable achievement. Taking the form of the dramatic monologue, the poem opens with the Haitian cane workers' point of view as they describe their fate, determined arbitrarily by the dictator Trujillo by a "test": their pronunciation of a single word. (Trujillo in fact massacred 20,000 Haitian blacks working in the Dominican Republic, because they could not trill the *r* in the Spanish word for parsley, *perejil*.) The second section proceeds inside El General's mind through a kind of stream of consciousness, a frightening examination of character in which prosaic memories return and are ominously transformed into perverse motives for extreme cruelty. More than any bad-man stereotype or polemic against the corruption of absolute power could, the tone of eerie calm and the very commonplaces of this twisted personality decry the dictator's barbarity, while conveying a sense of what Hannah Arendt called "the banality of evil."

Returning to the States after her Fulbright year, Dove studied in the Writers' Workshop at the University of Iowa and took her M.F.A. in 1977. Three years later she published her first book. *The Yellow House on the Corner* was well received, reviewers noting the debut volume displayed both an unusual breadth of historical knowledge and a great variety of stylistic approaches to it. Perhaps most striking, though, was her keen visual sense, her gift for precise observation expressed in concise imagery. Remarking on these qualities, Dove says on her program: "I think I do proceed by those visual moments in writing a poem. . . . I think they are in fact those anchors around which things happen and send off ripples through the poems. I think we crave that deal. One of the quickest ways to get into someone's heart with a poem, is through very specific detail."

Other poems in *The Yellow House on the Corner* indicate the range of Dove's interests and perceptions. Besides "Geometry" (also read on the program), the book includes poems on "Robert Schumann, Or: Musical Genius Begins with Affliction," "Champagne," "Beauty and the Beast," and a poignant trio on "Adolescence." In addition to a section of poems based on slave narratives, mentioned earlier, the collection presents several set in foreign locales, and a singular piece called "Ö"—a letter and the Swedish word for "island"—which concludes:

> a word is found so right it trembles
> at the slightest explanation.
> You start out with one thing, end
> up with another, and nothing's
> like it used to be, not even the future.

Dove's next book, *Museum* (1983), reveals an even greater diversity of subject matter and styles. In a poem called "Fish in Stone," a fossil, overanalyzed by scientists, wishes simply to return to the sea, but knows "to fail is / to do the living / a favor." The poet also discovers other mysteries in stone, but prefers the vital architecture of lives, like those of "Catherine of Siena" and "Catherine of Alexandria." She also returns to Boccaccio and the time of plagues, the setting of his tales. But most affecting perhaps are several lyrics set closer to home, which remember her father and a childhood nourished by "Grape Sherbet" and "Roses" and "Saturday Night at Grandfather's."

Such work earned the author the respect of her peers, but with the publication of *Thomas and Beulah* in 1986, and the Pulitzer, she now came to the attention of a larger audience. In presenting the lives of her grandparents, Dove tells their story twice, first from Thomas's perspective, in a suite of twenty-three poems, then through Beulah's eyes, in twenty-one poems. A chronology is appended to the book; but Dove's narration is elliptical, proceeding, as in a movie, through carefully selected scenes which follow quickly in sequence. The cinematic technique of crosscutting allows contrasting details and perceptions to accumulate, so that the reader gradually comes to know the protagonists and the "plot" of their lives, and times.

For *Thomas and Beulah* not only recounts the story of these individuals—their adolescence and courtship, their long marriage, with its struggles, satisfactions, and disappointments—but suggests the larger history of this country during the first seven decades of this century. The fate of Thomas when he becomes unemployed, for example, reflects the suffering of many others during the Great Depression, as well as in more recent bleak periods. Likewise, the intimate story of Thomas and Beulah retraces the experiences of many rural southern blacks who migrated to the industrial north.

In her detailed review of the book, reprinted in *The Music of What Happens*, Helen Vendler writes: "This great social movement—one of the most important for American history in the twentieth century—finds here its first extended poem." In the course of her insightful assessment of the work, Vendler also remarks on Dove's technique: "she almost always refuses editorializing, musing, and 'leading' the reader. Her brilliance lies in her arrangement of context; as the elements of meaning find their one inevitable form, juxtaposition alone takes on the work of explanation." Thus, a single scene such as that described in "Compendium," in Thomas's section, speaks volumes about Thomas's psychology and the nature of his life with Beulah—and about the "diminution of man by marriage"—following upon the incidents depicted earlier in the sequence. Again, in Beulah's interior monologue in "Wingfoot Lake" (which the author reads on the program), Dove demonstrates her dramatic ability to capture a scene and a character, and to convey a message, in spare description and brief space.

In *Grace Notes*, published in 1989, Dove returned to shorter lyrics, forms in which the poet's distinctive intelligence and technical mastery were evident from her first publications. Her title is well taken, as the four dozen poems in the volume show Dove's sure lightness of touch, her lack of straining for effect, and her ability to make her melodic lines resonate with the reader's own feelings. Several of the poems are drawn again from the author's early life, as in "Fifth Grade Autobiography," "Flash Cards," and "Crab-Boil." Others situated closer to the present convey the realities of adulthood, especially motherhood, with a sometimes unsettling psychological penetration. In "The Breathing, the Endless News," for example, the daughter in the poem acts out a primordial drama, lining up her dolls and "shooting" them. A sobering meditation on the transiency of life occurs in "Old Folk's Home, Jerusalem," where the poet projects into a possible future, beyond her present happiness and success: "Everyone waiting here was once in love." A number of poems, notably the astringent lines of "Ozone," reflect on the relation between art and life. Despite its ironic tone, perhaps Dove's most telling commentary on her own approach is contained in the closing lines of her "Ars Poetica":

> What I want is this poem to be small,
> a ghost town
> on the larger map of wills.
> Then you can pencil me in as a hawk:
> a traveling x-marks-the-spot.

From 1981 to 1989, Dove taught creative writing at Arizona State University in Tempe. Besides the Pulitzer, she has received several honors, including Guggenheim and NEA fellowships, the Peter I. B. Lavan Younger Poet Award from the Academy of American Poets (chosen by Robert Penn Warren), two honorary doctorates, and a General Electric Foundation Award. She has been active in several other areas of the literary scene. In 1985, she published a collection of short stories, called *Fifth Sunday*, and since 1986 she has been an associate editor of *Callaloo*, a journal of Afro-American and African arts and letters, as well as serving as an advisory editor for other literary magazines. She now is a professor of English at the University of Virginia in Charlottesville, where she lives with her husband and their daughter, Aviva.

# GARY SOTO

Caroline Soto

Childhood and adolescence, it has been said, provide enough material to last a writer a lifetime. Certainly stories about growing up have always fascinated American writers and readers, and they are a central focus in the work of Gary Soto. Unlike many authors, however, Soto enjoyed neither the upbringing nor evinced the early inclination and encouragement that presage a literary career. At the age of five, the poet has written, "what I knew best was at ground level." Literally and figuratively, it is this perspective—on the earth and its sounds, smells, look, and feel—that gives vitality and authenticity to Soto's poetry.

Soto's first book appeared in 1976. Since then he has made an impressive reputation with a large body of poetry and prose which is distinctive both for its technical virtuosity and deep understanding of human character, particularly evident in his accounts of the tragi-comic conflicts of growing up. His work is likewise grounded in family, friendship, neighborhood, and the shared experience of Mexican-Americans. The subjects of many of his poems are the members of the California Chicano community, whose hard lives and dignity amid poverty and often desperate circumstances are portrayed with spare diction and exact images, and without sentimentality. Throughout his writing, Soto combines realism with imagination, and his seemingly simple lines conceal the art that fashions them.

Gary Soto was born in Fresno, California, in 1952. As he relates on "Poets in Person," his grandparents immigrated from Mexico during the Great Depression and found jobs as farm laborers. Soto's parents picked fruit and harvested other crops, as well. Later his father was employed by Sun Maid Raisins and his mother peeled potatoes for a living. Like them, the Soto children worked in the fields of the San Joaquin Valley from an early age and then took factory jobs. These experiences provided the future poet with the earliest and most abiding subjects for his writing.

As he is the first to admit, Soto was only an indifferent student; his high school essays were returned "with C's and D's, never with even a B." On his program, he notes that he grew up in a household with very few books: "We had a Catholic dictionary; we had a medical dictionary; and we had Betty Crocker's cookbook. And that's about it—and some religious pamphlets from the Catholic church." Much more interesting to the schoolboy than the three R's were the two B's. Baseball has inspired his short story collection *Baseball in April* and "Black Hair," a poem he reads on the program and the title piece of his fourth book.

Although he never joined a gang, Soto did manage to get into his share of typical boyhood scrapes. "I was a playground kid," he says. "In and out of trouble, sort of good-natured trouble. . . . I'd join a baseball team, argue, get in a fight, go home with a bloody nose." At the age of 10, he recalls with amusement in the poem "Behind Grandma's House," he "wanted fame" and "to prove I was tough," and so he overturned garbage cans, harassed small animals, and spiced up his speech with four-letter words. Hearing the commotion, his grandmother came out to the alley and said: " 'Let me help you,' / And punched me between the eyes."

Other poems recall more painful, and tender, moments from his early years, as in "The Plum's Heart," where the poet remembers a joyful time picking fruit with his father. Soto's father was killed in an accident at work when the boy was five years old, and in the poem the "red globes" and the juice of the plums become ominous symbols for the tragedy to come. "The

Plum's Heart" demonstrates Soto's characteristic ability to depict a scene briefly and vividly through concrete details, while
using natural objects to convey a complex of feelings and meanings. "I think in terms of connecting ideas through image," he
notes on the program. "I think there's just a natural connection
for poets to take a thing like a plum, and they can't help but see
that it is filled with blood, the juice of life."

Dust, sunlight, rain, and ants are other frequent figures in
Soto's poetry. "In our household on Braly Street, our house was
just permeated with ants wherever you went," he observes.
Drawing upon this commonplace experience Soto has used ants
as symbols of death, as well as the struggle for existence. In
"Failing in the Presence of Ants," he describes the tireless efforts
of the insects in the face of adversity, not least attacks from
mankind, and suggests, "Perhaps they are more human than we
are." Here and elsewhere, Soto identifies with the ants and
makes them metaphors for the precariousness of life.

Insecurity, poverty, and the difficulties and dangers in
trying to make a living form a leitmotif in Soto's work. The realities of the culture of poverty were all too familiar to the Soto
family and their community, but the poet does not overdramatize
the struggles or deliver lectures. In his understated lines, precise
descriptions and acute images convey his themes more subtly
and convincingly than polemical rhetoric could. In "Field
Poem," for example, the young Chicano brothers shoulder their
hoes and return to the bus, "Speaking / In broken English, in
broken Spanish," and merely mention "The restaurant food, /
The tickets to a dance / We wouldn't buy with our pay."

On the program, Soto recalls his boyhood in Fresno in the
late Fifties and early Sixties, and his realization that society was
divided in the racially segregated town. The gulf between Mexicans and non-Mexicans, and between the haves and have-nots
generally, was underscored by comparing his experience with
the make-believe of television: "We knew where the Mexican
section of town was, and we knew the things of television, as
well. I mean, we could turn on the television [but] we saw no
brown faces." In "TV in Black and White," the poet compares
the two worlds: the familiar one of migrant laborers "In a vine-

yard / That we worked like an abacus, / A row at a time," and the imaginary middle-class scenarios of Donna Reed and Ozzie and Harriet Nelson. The poem ends with an ironic reflection on improbable role models, the persuasive power of television images in a consumer economy, and a possible effect of social inequity:

> . . . if the electricity
> Fails, in this town,
> A store front might
> Be smashed, sacks may find
> Hands, a whistle
> Point the way.
> And if someone steps out
> With a black and white TV,
> It's because we love you Donna,
> We miss you Ozzie.

Less acerbic but no less telling is the humor in "Mexicans Begin Jogging." As he relates, when he was 17 Soto ran away from home and found a job working in a tire factory, and "now and then the border patrol would come by and gather up the Mexican people." Thinking he's an illegal alien, the boss gives the teenager a dollar and tells him to run out the back door. "What could I do," the poem concludes,

> but yell *vivas*
> To baseball, milkshakes, and those sociologists
> Who would clock me
> As I jog into the next century
> On the power of a great, silly grin.

Soto presents a more sobering picture of the place in "Mission Tire Factory, 1969," in which a co-worker is injured when he falls off a machine.

Reflecting on these experiences in his interview, Soto says, "I think what influenced me in field work and any kind of manual labor was the fear of poverty. We grew up poor . . . there was a sort of deep-seated fear of poverty at a very early age. I was probably, I know my brother was anemic . . . and I'm

sure it had to do with our food—or lack of food—in the house."
Despite the fact he did not "have a lot of natural gifts in school,"
but with the prospect of making $1.65 an hour into the foresee-
able future, and with the draft on his neck, Soto developed an
interest in furthering his education.

In 1970 Soto entered Fresno City College. At first he
avoided writing classes. In high school he had read Mark Twain,
Steinbeck, and other classic American authors, but without
much enthusiasm. Still, he notes, "I always felt I was a writer."
Then, in his second year of college, he discovered a poem by
Edward Field. "It was a poem called 'Unwanted,' which is exactly how I felt at the time—unwanted. And the poem had such
a remarkable effect on me, such a pleasing effect of identity, that
I decided, Well, I'm going to try this, too."

When Soto transferred to California State University in
Fresno, he took a course in poetry writing with Philip Levine.
Levine was, and is, a charismatic teacher and highly regarded
poet whose own distinctive work depicts the lives of working
people, particularly blue-color laborers in the auto industry in
the Detroit of the Depression and Forties. The match between
master poet and pupil was ideal, and Soto credits Levine as "a
major influence." About midway through the semester, Soto
wrote what he considered his first real poem, "Field Poem": "I
felt that it was a poem that I would like to keep." A little literary
magazine wanted to keep it, too, and Soto enjoyed his first
publication by his twenty-first birthday.

After graduating *magna cum laude* from Fresno in 1974
and marrying Carolyn Oda in 1975, Soto entered graduate
school and earned his M.F.A. in poetry at the University of
California at Irvine in 1976. He became a visiting writer at San
Diego State University, and while taking other part-time jobs,
he continued to write, working on two books at once. In 1977,
he was asked to teach composition courses at Berkeley, just as
his first book was about to be published. *The Elements of San
Joaquin* (1977) was well received by the critics and won the
United States Award of the International Poetry Forum. "I knew
I wanted to write about family, I knew I wanted to write about
the valley, and I knew I wanted to write about a certain violence

that permeates the valley," the author has said of the collection. While there are some violent scenes in the book, many more poems depict the stories of family and friends, their personal struggles, disappointments, and occasional joys. Along with memorable pictures of the San Joaquin landscape, the poet leaves a striking impression of what is less well appreciated: the toil that is required in the valley to put food on the table. After describing the drudgery of hoeing onion rows, the speaker in "Daybreak" remarks: "And tears the onions raise / Do not begin in your eyes but in ours, / In the salt blown / From one blister into another . . . ."

*The Tale of Sunlight* appeared the next year and was followed by *Where Sparrows Work Hard* in 1981. Along with a number of personal lyrics about family and friends which continue Soto's explorations of life in the *barrio*, these ambitious collections include a number of imaginative narratives and more experimental poems. With support from a Guggenheim fellowship for 1979–80, Soto spent several months in Mexico, translating with a friend and studying modern poetry in Spanish, particularly the work of García Lorca and Pablo Neruda. He had read Neruda's poetry in college and "was amazed. I liked what he was writing about. He had a very imagistic line, a voice that seemed to cherish the common world." In his interview, Soto noted, "Lorca's another person that I had a kinship with. . . . I couldn't quite understand what he was getting at in his poetry, but I certainly loved the lushness in his writing. There's a line in a poem that I never understood, and to this day I don't understand, but I liked the way it sounded. The line is: 'Not even the ants know who you are.' And I thought, If the ants don't know who you are, would anyone else know who you are?" The influence of Neruda and Lorca is evident in Soto's growing sophistication in use of imagery and various surrealistic techniques.

Even more important to his development was the work of Gabriel García Marquez, whose *A Hundred Years of Solitude* Soto has termed "one of the greatest books of our time." García Marquez is principally associated with "magical realism," the philosophical and aesthetic movement in which ordinary facts and everyday images are transmuted or dislodged from their familiar contexts to create an impression of life in otherworldly terms. In *The Tale of Sunlight*, the influence of the Colombian writer and the movement is most evident in dream-poems that combine realism with fantasy, particularly in the suite "The Manuel Zaragosa Poems," which conclude the collection. In this dramatic sequence, Soto uses internal monologues and collages of imagistic fragments to depict this representative character and his world. "It's all fiction," the poet explains, "but it was a desire of mine to sort of become this man, to become a Mexican person located in the desert."

*Black Hair* was published in 1985 and shows further growth in the author's powers. Generous in size and in the range of its subjects and human sympathy, the collection contains several of the poems read on "Poets in Person" and already discussed here: "The Plum's Heart," "Behind Grandma's House," "Looking Around, Believing," and, of course, the title poem. Several other poems deserve special notice, as well: "Oranges," for its tender evocations of young love; "How to Sell Things," for its sly humor; and "Ambition," "Morning on This Street," and "How Things Work," for their rueful reflections on success, material prosperity, and adult responsibilities.

*Who Will Know Us?*, another large collection, was issued in 1990. Besides in the title poem and "The Philosophy of Dog & Man" (also read on the program), Soto's mature gifts are particularly evident in "A Red Palm," "As It Is," "Heaven," and "That Girl," which reprise the themes of his first volumes. In *Home Course in Religion* (1992), Soto likewise returns to the topics of his previous books, particularly childhood, but often with a more somber tone. He remembers the Catholic grade school that "stank of poor grades and unwashed hair" and his repressed anger for a pretentious, bullying stepfather who drank beer "to flood the hole inside." Now a husband and father himself, the poet looks back ruefully at his younger days, remembering his pious, long-suffering mother, who saw in all his scraps and pains signs of God's punishment. Here, as before, Soto has an unfailing knack for finding the precise detail or anecdote that captures the bravado, shame, and superstition that mark boyhood. And as in "The Philosophy of Dog & Man," the poet's attitude is frequently ambivalent, as he contrasts his present contentment with the less happy former life which he cannot really leave behind.

In all of Soto's poetry, there is a richness of feeling, a real warmth and engagement which mark a refreshing contrast to the emotionally thin if technically proficient writing that characterizes some contemporary verse. Soto's characteristic tone is conversational, but his use of colloquial speech is very carefully controlled and ordered in subtle rhythmic patterns. His figures and metaphors are direct, clear, even commonplace, but the poet repeatedly surprises with the several meanings and unexpected psychological connections he finds.

Soto's gift for conveying his autobiography and insights with clarity, concrete images, and understated elegance is also displayed in his several volumes of prose: the memoir *Living Up the Street* (1985), winner of the American Book Award; *Small Faces* (1986) and *Lesser Evils* (1988), essays; the short story collection *Baseball in April* (1990); and the occasional essays and reminiscences in *A Summer Life* (1990). Soto has also edited *California Childhood: Recollections and Stories of the Golden State* (1988). He now is an Associate Professor of English and Ethnic Studies at the University of California, Berkeley, and has traveled extensively throughout the state, giving poetry readings and working with school children.

# CONSULTING SCHOLARS AND INTERVIEWERS

J. D. MC CLATCHY took his Ph.D. from Yale and has taught there and at Columbia, Rutgers, Princeton, and the University of California, Los Angeles. His publications include *White Paper: On Contemporary American Poetry*, *Anne Sexton: The Artist and Her Critics*, and *Poets on Painters: Essays on the Art of Painting by Twentieth-Century Poets*. He also edited *Recitative: Prose by James Merrill* and *The Vintage Book of Contemporary American Poetry*. His poetry collections include: *Scenes from Another Life*, *Stars Principal*, and *The Rest of the Way*. He is editor of *The Yale Review* and an adviser for the Wesleyan University Press Poetry Series.

DAVID BROMWICH taught at Princeton for ten years and is now a Professor of English at Yale, where he received his Ph.D. He is the author of *Hazlitt: The Mind of a Critic* and co-editor (with Irving Howe and John Hollander) of *Literature as Experience*. His poetry and criticism have appeared in the (London) *Times Literary Supplement*, *Poetry*, *Hudson Review*, *Yale Review*, *The New Republic*, and other journals.

ALICE FULTON holds an M.F.A. from Cornell and is now an Associate Professor of English at the University of Michigan. She has also served on the faculty of the Vermont College M.F.A. program, and the Breadloaf and Wesleyan Writers' Conferences. She has published three collections of poetry: *Palladium*, *Dance Script with Electric Ballerina*, and *Powers of Congress*. She is assistant editor of *Michigan Quarterly Review*.

SANDRA M. GILBERT holds a Ph.D. in English from Columbia, and has taught at Johns Hopkins, Williams College, Indiana University, and Princeton; she is presently a Professor of English at the University of California, Davis. She is the author, with Susan Gubar, of *Shakespeare's Sisters: Feminist Essays on Women Poets* and *The Madwoman in the Attic: The Woman Writer and the 19th-Century Literary Imagination*; she also edited *The Norton Anthology of Literature by British and American Women*. The latest of her four collections of poetry are *Emily's Bread* and *Blood Pressure*.

LEWIS HYDE received an M.A. in Comparative Literature from the University of Iowa and is currently the Henry R. Luce Professor of Art & Politics at Kenyon College; he has also taught at Harvard and Tufts. He is the author of *The Gift: Imagination and the Erotic Life of Property*, and edited the critical collection *On the Work of Allen Ginsberg*. He has published two volumes of poems, *This Error Is the Sign of Love* and *Hotel with Birds*, as well as three books of translations from the work of Vicente Aleixandre.

DIANE WOOD MIDDLEBROOK received her Ph.D. from Yale and is the Watkins University Professor of English at Stanford, where she has chaired the Program in Feminist Studies. Her scholarly books include: *Walt Whitman and Wallace Stevens*, *Worlds into the Words: Understanding Modern Poems*, and *Coming to Light: American Women Poets in the Twentieth Century*, a collection of critical essays. She is the author of *Anne Sexton: A Biography* and co-editor of the *Selected Poems of Anne Sexton*.

ALICIA OSTRIKER took her Ph.D. from the University of Wisconsin and is now a Professor of English at Rutgers. Her scholarly books include *Vision and Verse in William Blake*, *Writing Like a Woman*, and *Stealing the Language: The Emergence of Women's Poetry in America*. She has also published seven poetry collections, among them: *Once More Out of Darkness*, *The Mother/Child Papers*, *A Woman Under the Surface*, *The Imaginary Lover*, and *Green Age*.

JAMES RICHARDSON received his Ph.D. from the University of Virginia and now directs the Creative Writing Program at Princeton. He has published two scholarly books, *Thomas Hardy* and *Vanishing Lives: Style and Self in Tennyson, D. G. Rossetti, Swinburne, and Yeats*, as well as three volumes of poetry: *Reservations*, *Second Guesses*, and *As If*.

HELEN VENDLER took her Ph.D. from Harvard, where she is now a Professor of English. Her several scholarly books include: *On Extended Wings: The Longer Poems of Wallace Stevens*; *The Poetry of George Herbert*; *The Odes of Keats*; *Part of Nature, Part of Us: Modern American Poets*; and *The Music of What Happens: Poems, Poets, Critics*. She has also edited *The Harvard Book of Contemporary American Poetry* and *Voices & Visions: American Poets*. Her reviews and criticism appear widely, and she is the regular poetry critic for *The New Yorker*.

JOSEPH PARISI holds a Ph.D. from the University of Chicago and taught for several years, most recently at the University of Illinois, Chicago. He co-edited *The Poetry Anthology 1912–1977*, edited *Marianne Moore: The Art of a Modernist*, and wrote the *Viewer's Guide* to the "Voices & Visions" television series; he contributes criticism regularly to a number of journals. He joined the staff of *Poetry* in 1976, and became the editor of the magazine in 1983.

# POETS
## IN PERSON

Anthology

# A. R. AMMONS

## POETICS

I look for the way
things will turn
out spiralling from a center,
the shape
things will take to come forth in

so that the birch tree white
touched black at branches
will stand out
wind-glittering
totally its apparent self:

I look for the forms
things want to come as

from what black wells of possibility,
how a thing will
unfold:

not the shape on paper—though
that too—but the
uninterfering means on paper:

not so much looking for the shape
as being available
to any shape that may be
summoning itself
through me
from the self not mine but ours.

## GRAVELLY RUN

I don't know somehow it seems sufficient
to see and hear whatever coming and going is,
losing the self to the victory
        of stones and trees,
of bending sandpit lakes, crescent
round groves of dwarf pine:

for it is not so much to know the self
as to know it as it is known
        by galaxy and cedar cone,
as if birth had never found it
and death could never end it:

the swamp's slow water comes
down Gravelly Run fanning the long
        stone-held algal
hair and narrowing roils between
the shoulders of the highway bridge:

holly grows on the banks in the woods there,
and the cedars' gothic-clustered
        spires could make
green religion in winter bones:

so I look and reflect, but the air's glass
jail seals each thing in its entity:

no use to make any philosophies here:
        I see no
god in the holly, hear no song from
the snowbroken weeds: Hegel is not the winter
yellow in the pines: the sunlight has never
heard of trees: surrendered self among
        unwelcoming forms: stranger,
hoist your burdens, get on down the road.

## EYESIGHT

It was May before my
attention came
to spring and

my word I said
to the southern slopes
I've

missed it, it
came and went before
I got right to see:

don't worry, said the mountain,
try the later northern slopes
or if

you can climb, climb
into spring: but
said the mountain

it's not that way
with all things, some
that go are gone

## HYMN

I know if I find you I will have to leave the earth
and go on out
        over the sea marshes and the brant in bays
and over the hills of tall hickory
and over the crater lakes and canyons
and on up through the spheres of diminishing air
past the blackset noctilucent clouds
            where one wants to stop and look
way past all the light diffusions and bombardments
up farther than the loss of sight
        into the unseasonal undifferentiated empty stark

And I know if I find you I will have to stay with the earth
inspecting with thin tools and ground eyes
trusting the microvilli sporangia and simplest
        coelenterates
and praying for a nerve cell
with all the soul of my chemical reactions
and going right on down where the eye sees only traces

You are everywhere partial and entire
You are on the inside of everything and on the outside

I walk down the path down the hill where the sweetgum
has begun to ooze spring sap at the cut
and I see how the bark cracks and winds like no other bark
chasmal to my ant-soul running up and down
and if I find you I must go out deep into your
        far resolutions
and if I find you I must stay here with the separate leaves

## THE DWELLING

I would as soon believe
in paradise as in
nothing: it is no great

wonder that our spiritual
energy, purified, returns
to, is, the eternal

residence: no greater
wonder than that earth is
here at all: imagine

arriving on this green
curvature and being spent!
and no great wonder that

the eternal residence is
a place nothing wants to
stay in, but only, from

the terrifying, exciting
confusions working energy
sharp, to return to:

belief's a fine cloth:
a sheen before the eyes,
it induces fabrications

ash can't get to and just
residual energy composes:
let belief down somewhere,

I say, the heart's cravings
flaring bright into near
exemplifications: this

jewelry of brick and loft,
at least!—until ready for
the greater knowledge, the

greatest, perhaps, we accede
to reason that here the plainnest
majesty gave us what it could.

# JOHN ASHBERY

## THE LONEDALE OPERATOR

The first movie I ever saw was the Walt Disney cartoon *The Three Little Pigs*. My grandmother took me to it. It was back in the days when you went "downtown." There was a second feature, with live actors, called *Bring 'Em Back Alive*, a documentary about the explorer Frank Buck. In this film you saw a python swallow a live pig. This wasn't scary. In fact, it seemed quite normal, the sort of thing you *would* see in a movie—"reality."

A little later we went downtown again to see a movie of *Alice in Wonderland*, also with live actors. This wasn't very surprising either. I think I knew something about the story; maybe it had been read to me. That wasn't why it wasn't surprising, though. The reason was that these famous movie actors, like W.C. Fields and Gary Cooper, were playing different roles, and even though I didn't know who they were, they were obviously important for doing other kinds of acting, and so it didn't seem strange that they should be acting in a special way like this, pretending to be characters that people already knew about from a book. In other words, I imagined specialties for them just from having seen this one example. And I was right, too, though not about the film, which I liked. Years later I saw it when I was grown up and thought it was awful. How could I have been wrong the first time? I knew it wasn't inexperience, because somehow I was experienced the first time I saw a movie. It was as though my taste had changed, though I had not, and I still can't help feeling that I was right the first time, when I was still relatively unencumbered by my experience.

I forget what were the next movies I saw and will skip ahead to one I saw when I was grown up, *The Lonedale Operator*, a silent short by D.W. Griffith, made in 1911 and starring Blanche Sweet. Although I was in my twenties when I saw it at the Museum of Modern Art, it seems as remote from me in time as my first viewing of *Alice in Wonderland*. I can remember almost none of it, and the little I can remember may have been in another Griffith short, *The Lonely Villa*, which may have been on the same program. It seems that Blanche Sweet was a heroic telegraph operator who managed to get through to the police and foil some gangsters who were trying to rob a railroad depot, though I also see this living room—small, though it was supposed to be in a large house—with Mary Pickford running around, and this may have been a scene in *The Lonely Villa*. At that moment the memories stop, and terror, or tedium, sets in. It's hard to tell which is which in this memory, because the boredom of living in a lonely place or having a lonely job, and even of being so far in the past and having to wear those funny uncomfortable clothes and hairstyles is terrifying, more so than the intentional scariness of the plot, the criminals, whoever they were.

Imagine that innocence (Lilian Harvey) encounters romance (Willy Fritsch) in the home of experience (Albert Basserman). From there it is only a step to terror, under the dripping boughs outside. Anything can change as fast as it wants to, and in doing so may pass through a more or less terrible phase, but the true terror is in the swiftness of changing, forward or backward, slipping always just beyond our control. The actors are like people on drugs, though they aren't doing anything unusual—as a matter of fact, they are performing brilliantly.

## SOMEONE YOU HAVE SEEN BEFORE

It was a night for listening to Corelli, Geminiani
Or Manfredini. The tables had been set with beautiful white cloths,
And bouquets of flowers. Outside the big glass windows
The rain drilled mercilessly into the rock garden, which made light
Of the whole thing. Both business and entertainment waited
With parted lips, because so much new way of being
With one's emotion and keeping track of it at the same time
Had been silently expressed. Even the waiters were happy.

It was an example of how much one can grow lustily
Without fracturing the shell of coziness that surrounds us,
And all things as well. "We spend so much time
Trying to convince ourselves we're happy that we don't recognize
The real thing when it comes along," the Disney official said.
He's got a point, you must admit. If we followed nature
More closely we'd realize that, I mean really getting your face pressed
Into the muck and indecision of it. Then it's as if
We grew out of our happiness, not the other way round, as is
Commonly supposed. We're the characters in its novel,
And anybody who doubts that need only look out of the window
Past his or her own reflection, to the bright, patterned,
Timeless unofficial truth hanging around out there,
Waiting for the signal to be galvanized into a crowd scene,
Joyful or threatening, it doesn't matter, so long as we know
It's inside, here with us.

But people do change in life,
As well as in fiction. And what happens then? Is it because we
        think nobody's
Listening that one day it comes, the urge to delete yourself,
"Take yourself out," as they say? As though this could matter
Even to the concerned ones who crowd around,
Expressions of lightness and peace on their faces,
In which you play no part perhaps, but even so
Their happiness is for you, it's your birthday, and even
When the balloons and fudge get tangled with extraneous
Good wishes from everywhere, it is, I believe, made to order
For your questioning stance and that impression
Left on the inside of your pleasure by some bivalve
With which you have been identified. Sure,

Nothing is ever perfect enough, but that's part of how it fits
The mixed bag
Of leftover character traits that used to be part of you
Before the change was performed
And of all those acquaintances bursting with vigor and
Humor, as though they wanted to call you down
Into closeness, not for being close, or snug, or whatever,
But because they believe you were made to fit this unique
And valuable situation whose lid is rising, totally
Into the morning-glory-colored future. Remember, don't throw away
The quadrant of unused situations just because they're here:
They may not always be, and you haven't finished looking
Through them all yet. So much that happens happens in small ways
That someone was going to get around to tabulate, and then never did,
Yet it all bespeaks freshness, clarity and an even motor drive
To coax us out of sleep and start us wondering what the new round
Of impressions and salutations is going to leave in its wake
This time. And the form, the precepts, are yours to dispose of as you will,
As the ocean makes grasses, and in doing so refurbishes a lighthouse
On a distant hill, or else lets the whole picture slip into foam.

# GWENDOLYN BROOKS

### kitchenette building

We are things of dry hours and the involuntary plan,
Grayed in, and gray. "Dream" makes a giddy sound, not strong
Like "rent," "feeding a wife," "satisfying a man."

But could a dream send up through onion fumes
Its white and violet, fight with fried potatoes
And yesterday's garbage ripening in the hall,
Flutter, or sing an aria down these rooms

Even if we were willing to let it in,
Had time to warm it, keep it very clean,
Anticipate a message, let it begin?

We wonder. But not well! not for a minute!
Since Number Five is out of the bathroom now,
We think of lukewarm water, hope to get in it.


### *From* the children of the poor

#### 4

First fight. Then fiddle. Ply the slipping string
With feathery sorcery; muzzle the note
With hurting love; the music that they wrote
Bewitch, bewilder. Qualify to sing
Threadwise. Devise no salt, no hempen thing
For the dear instrument to bear. Devote
The bow to silks and honey. Be remote
A while from malice and from murdering.
But first to arms, to armor. Carry hate
In front of you and harmony behind.
Be deaf to music and to beauty blind.
Win war. Rise bloody, maybe not too late
For having first to civilize a space
Wherein to play your violin with grace.

## THE BEAN EATERS

They eat beans mostly, this old yellow pair.
Dinner is a casual affair.
Plain chipware on a plain and creaking wood,
Tin flatware.

Two who are Mostly Good.
Two who have lived their day,
But keep on putting on their clothes
And putting things away.

And remembering . . .
Remembering, with twinklings and twinges,
As they lean over the beans in their rented back room that
        is full of beads and receipts and dolls and cloths,
        tobacco crumbs, vases and fringes.

## WE REAL COOL

THE POOL PLAYERS.
SEVEN AT THE GOLDEN SHOVEL.

We real cool. We
Left school. We

Lurk late. We
Strike straight. We

Sing sin. We
Thin gin. We

Jazz June. We
Die soon.

*From* THE LIFE OF LINCOLN WEST

Ugliest little boy
that everyone ever saw.
That is what everyone said.

Even to his mother it was apparent—
when the blue-aproned nurse came into the
northeast end of the maternity ward
bearing his squeals and plump bottom
looped up in a scant receiving blanket,
bending, to pass the bundle carefully
into the waiting mother-hands—that this
was no cute little ugliness, no sly baby waywardness
that was going to inch away
as would baby fat, baby curl, and
baby spot-rash. The pendulous lip, the
branching ears, the eyes so wide and wild,
the vague unvibrant brown of the skin,
and, most disturbing, the great head.
These components of That Look bespoke
the sure fibre. The deep grain.

. . .

"THERE! That's the kind I've been wanting
to show you! One of the best
examples of the specie. Not like
those diluted Negroes you see so much of on
the streets these days, but the
real thing.

Black, ugly, and odd. You
can see the savagery. The blunt
blankness. That is the real
thing."

His mother—her hair had never looked so
red around the dark brown

velvet of her face—jumped up,
shrieked "Go to—" She did not finish.
She yanked to his feet the little
Lincoln, who was sitting there
staring in fascination at his assessor. At the author of his
new idea.

All the way home he was happy. Of course,
he had not liked the word
"ugly."
But, after all, should he not
be used to that by now? What had
struck him, among words and meanings
he could little understand, was the phrase
"the real thing."
He didn't know quite why,
but he liked that.
He liked that very much.

When he was hurt, too much
stared at—
too much
left alone—he
thought about that. He told himself
"After all, I'm
the real thing."

It comforted him.

## TO THE YOUNG WHO WANT TO DIE

Sit down. Inhale. Exhale.
The gun will wait. The lake will wait.
The tall gall in the small seductive vial
will wait will wait:
will wait a week: will wait through April.
You do not have to die this certain day.
Death will abide, will pamper your postponement.
I assure you death will wait. Death has
a lot of time. Death can
attend to you tomorrow. Or next week. Death is
just down the street; is most obliging neighbor;
can meet you any moment.

You need not die today.
Stay here—through pout or pain or peskyness.
Stay here. See what the news is going to be tomorrow.

Graves grow no green that you can use.
Remember, green's your color. You are Spring.

*From* WINNIE

There are millions of words in this world.
Not necessarily may be found, all cooked,
the ones to express *my* nuances.

Yet I know
that I am Poet!
I pass you my Poem.

A poem doesn't do everything for you.
You are supposed to go *on* with your thinking.
You are supposed to enrich
the other person's poem with your extensions,
your uniquely personal understandings,
thus making the poem serve *you*.

I pass you my Poem!—to tell you
we are all vulnerable—
the midget, the Mighty,
the richest, the poor.
Men, women, children, and trees.
I am vulnerable.
Hector Petersen was vulnerable.

My Poem is life, and not finished.
It shall never be finished.
My Poem is life, and can grow.

Wherever life can grow, it will.
It will sprout out,
and do the best it can.
I give you what I have.
You don't get all your questions answered in this world.
How many answers shall be found
in the developing world of my Poem?
I don't know. Nevertheless I put my Poem,
which is my life, into your hands, where it will
do the best it can.

I am not a tight-faced Poet.

I am tired of little tight-faced poets sitting down to
shape perfect unimportant pieces.
Poems that cough lightly—catch back a sneeze.
This is the time for Big Poems,
roaring up out of sleaze,
poems from ice, from vomit, and from tainted blood.
This is the time for stiff *or* viscous poems.
Big, and Big.

# RITA DOVE

## FLASH CARDS

In math I was the whiz kid, keeper
of oranges and apples. *What you don't understand,
master,* my father said; the faster
I answered, the faster they came.

I could see one bud on the teacher's geranium,
one clear bee sputtering at the wet pane.
The tulip trees always dragged after heavy rain
so I tucked my head as my boots slapped home.

My father put up his feet after work
and relaxed with a highball and *The Life of Lincoln.*
After supper we drilled and I climbed the dark

before sleep, before a thin voice hissed
numbers as I spun on a wheel. I had to guess.
Ten, I kept saying, *I'm only ten.*

## DAVID WALKER (1785–1830)

Free to travel, he still couldn't be shown how lucky
he was: *They strip and beat and drag us about*
*like rattlesnakes.* Home on Brattle Street, he took in the sign
on the door of the slop shop. All day at the counter—
white caps, ale-stained pea coats. Compass needles,
eloquent as tuning forks, shivered, pointing north.
Evenings, the ceiling fan sputtered like a second pulse.
*Oh Heaven! I am full!! I can hardly move my pen!!!*

On the faith of an eye-wink, pamphlets were stuffed
into trouser pockets. Pamphlets transported
in the coat linings of itinerant seamen, jackets
ringwormed with salt traded drunkenly to pursers
in the Carolinas, pamphlets ripped out, read aloud:
*Men of colour, who are also of sense.*
Outrage. Incredulity. Uproar in state legislatures.

*We are the most wretched, degraded and abject set*
*of beings that ever lived since the world began.*
The jewelled canaries in the lecture halls tittered,
pressed his dark hand between their gloves.
Every half-step was no step at all.
Every morning, the man on the corner strung a fresh
bunch of boots from his shoulders. "I'm happy!" he said.
"I never want to live any better or happier than
when I can get a-plenty of boots and shoes to clean!"

A second edition. A third.
The abolitionist press is *perfectly appalled.*
*Humanity, kindness and the fear of the Lord*
*does not consist in protecting devils.* A month—
his person (is that all?) found face-down
in the doorway at Brattle Street,
his frame slighter than friends remembered.

## WINGFOOT LAKE

*(Independence Day, 1964)*

On her 36th birthday, Thomas had shown her
her first swimming pool. It had been
his favorite color, exactly—just
so much of it, the swimmers' white arms jutting
into the chevrons of high society.
She had rolled up her window
and told him to drive on, fast.

Now this *act of mercy*: four daughters
dragging her to their husbands' company picnic,
white families on one side and them
on the other, unpacking the same
squeeze bottles of Heinz, the same
waxy beef patties and Salem potato chip bags.
So he was dead for the first time
on Fourth of July—ten years ago

had been harder, waiting for something to happen,
and ten years before that, the girls
like young horses eyeing the track.
Last August she stood alone for hours
in front of the T.V. set
as a crow's wing moved slowly through
the white streets of government.
That brave swimming

scared her, like Joanna saying
*Mother, we're Afro-Americans now!*
What did she know about Africa?
Were there lakes like this one
with a rowboat pushed under the pier?
Or Thomas' Great Mississippi
with its sullen silks? (There was
the Nile but the Nile belonged

to God.) Where she came from
was the past, 12 miles into town
where nobody had locked their back door,
and Goodyear hadn't begun to dream of a park
under the company symbol, a white foot
sprouting two small wings.

## CRAB-BOIL

*(Ft. Myers, 1962)*

Why do I remember the sky
above the forbidden beach,
why only blue and the scratch,
shell on tin, of their distress?
The rest

imagination supplies:
bucket and angry pink beseeching
claws. Why does Aunt Helen
laugh before saying "Look at that—

a bunch of niggers, not
a-one get out 'fore the others pull him
back." I don't believe her—

just as I don't believe *they* won't come
and chase us back to the colored-only shore
crisp with litter and broken glass.

"When do we kill them?"
"Kill 'em? Hell, the water does *that*.
They don't feel a thing . . . no nervous system."

I decide to believe this: I'm hungry.
Dismantled, they're merely exotic,
a blushing meat. After all, she *has*
grown old in the South. If
we're kicked out now, I'm ready.

# PARSLEY

### 1. *The Cane Fields*

There is a parrot imitating spring
in the palace, its feathers parsley green.
Out of the swamp the cane appears

to haunt us, and we cut it down. El General
searches for a word; he is all the world
there is. Like a parrot imitating spring,

we lie down screaming as rain punches through
and we come up green. We cannot speak an R—
out of the swamp, the cane appears

and then the mountain we call in whispers *Katalina*.
The children gnaw their teeth to arrowheads.
There is a parrot imitating spring.

El General has found his word: *perejil*.
Who says it, lives. He laughs, teeth shining
out of the swamp. The cane appears

in our dreams, lashed by wind and streaming.
And we lie down. For every drop of blood
there is a parrot imitating spring.
Out of the swamp the cane appears.

### 2. *The Palace*

The word the general's chosen is parsley.
It is fall, when thoughts turn
to love and death; the general thinks
of his mother, how she died in the fall
and he planted her walking cane at the grave
and it flowered, each spring stolidly forming
four-star blossoms. The general

pulls on his boots, he stomps to
her room in the palace, the one without
curtains, the one with a parrot
in a brass ring. As he paces he wonders
Who can I kill today. And for a moment
the little knot of screams
is still. The parrot, who has traveled

all the way from Australia in an ivory
cage, is, coy as a widow, practising
spring. Ever since the morning
his mother collapsed in the kitchen
while baking skull-shaped candies
for the Day of the Dead, the general
has hated sweets. He orders pastries
brought up for the bird; they arrive

dusted with sugar on a bed of lace.
The knot in his throat starts to twitch;
he sees his boots the first day in battle
splashed with mud and urine
as a soldier falls at his feet amazed—
how stupid he looked!—at the sound
of artillery. *I never thought it would sing*
the soldier said, and died. Now

the general sees the fields of sugar
cane, lashed by rain and streaming.
He sees his mother's smile, the teeth
gnawed to arrowheads. He hears
the Haitians sing without R's
as they swing the great machetes:
*Katalina*, they sing, *Katalina*,

*mi madle, mi amol en muelte.* God knows
his mother was no stupid woman; she
could roll an R like a queen. Even
a parrot can roll an R! In the bare room

the bright feathers arch in a parody
of greenery, as the last pale crumbs
disappear under the blackened tongue. Someone

calls out his name in a voice
so like his mother's, a startled tear
splashes the tip of his right boot.
*My mother, my love in death.*
The general remembers the tiny green sprigs
men of his village wore in their capes
to honor the birth of a son. He will
order many, this time, to be killed

for a single, beautiful word.

## GEOMETRY

I prove a theorem and the house expands:
the windows jerk free to hover near the ceiling,
the ceiling floats away with a sigh.

As the walls clear themselves of everything
but transparency, the scent of carnations
leaves with them. I am out in the open

and above the windows have hinged into butterflies,
sunlight glinting where they've intersected.
They are going to some point true and unproven.

# ALLEN GINSBERG

## From HOWL

II

What sphinx of cement and aluminum bashed open their skulls
and ate up their brains and imagination?
Moloch! Solitude! Filth! Ugliness! Ashcans and unobtainable
dollars! Children screaming under the stairways! Boys
sobbing in armies! Old men weeping in the parks!
Moloch! Moloch! Nightmare of Moloch! Moloch the loveless!
Mental Moloch! Moloch the heavy judger of men!
Moloch the incomprehensible prison! Moloch the crossbone
soulless jailhouse and Congress of sorrows! Moloch
whose buildings are judgment! Moloch the vast stone
of war! Moloch the stunned governments!
Moloch whose mind is pure machinery! Moloch whose blood is
running money! Moloch whose fingers are ten armies!
Moloch whose breast is a cannibal dynamo! Moloch
whose ear is a smoking tomb!
Moloch whose eyes are a thousand blind windows! Moloch
whose skyscrapers stand in the long streets like endless Jehovahs! Moloch whose factories dream and
croak in the fog! Moloch whose smokestacks and an-
tennae crown the cities!
Moloch whose love is endless oil and stone! Moloch whose soul
is electricity and banks! Moloch whose poverty is the
specter of genius! Moloch whose fate is a cloud of
sexless hydrogen! Moloch whose name is the Mind!
Moloch in whom I sit lonely! Moloch in whom I dream Angels!
Crazy in Moloch! Cocksucker in Moloch! Lacklove
and manless in Moloch!
Moloch who entered my soul early! Moloch in whom I am a
consciousness without a body! Moloch who frightened me out of my natural ecstasy! Moloch whom I
abandon! Wake up in Moloch! Light streaming out of
the sky!
Moloch! Moloch! Robot apartments! invisible suburbs! skeleton
treasuries! blind capitals! demonic industries! spectral
nations! invincible madhouses! granite cocks! mon-
strous bombs!

They broke their backs lifting Moloch to Heaven! Pavements, trees, radios, tons! lifting the city to Heaven which exists and is everywhere about us!

Visions! omens! hallucinations! miracles! ecstasies! gone down the American river!

Dreams! adorations! illuminations! religions! the whole boatload of sensitive bullshit!

Breakthroughs! over the river! flips and crucifixions! gone down the flood! Highs! Epiphanies! Despairs! Ten years' animal screams and suicides! Minds! New loves! Mad generation! down on the rocks of Time!

Real holy laughter in the river! They saw it all! the wild eyes! the holy yells! They bade farewell! They jumped off the roof! to solitude! waving! carrying flowers! Down to the river! into the street!

*From* WICHITA VORTEX SUTRA

I lift my voice aloud,
    make Mantra of American language now,
        I here declare the end of the War!
            Ancient days' Illusion!—
      and pronounce words beginning my own millennium.
Let the States tremble,
    let the Nation weep,
        let Congress legislate its own delight
            let the President execute his own desire—
this Act done by my own voice,
              nameless Mystery—
published to my own senses,
        blissfully received by my own form
      approved with pleasure by my sensations
      manifestation of my very thought
      accomplished in my own imagination
        all realms within my consciousness fulfilled
    60 miles from Wichita
          near El Dorado,
            The Golden One,
in chill earthly mist
    houseless brown farmland plains rolling heavenward
                in every direction
one midwinter afternoon Sunday called the day of the Lord—
    Pure Spring Water gathered in one tower
      where Florence is
        set on a hill,
      stop for tea & gas

## "YOU MIGHT GET IN TROUBLE"

Opening a bus window in N.Y.
      with the left hand in front of
      Bellevue you might get a
            hernia.
Walking across First avenue
      you might stumble into a
            pothole
& get your head run over by a
            taxicab
Plowing the field by Cherry
      Creek your trailer might
      turn over & fall on your ear
you might get your ear cut off
      arresting a junkie
or having an angry conversation with
      a speedfreak on E. 10 street
or arguing your case before the
      supreme court
someone might shoot you in
      the brain
There's nothing you can do to
      keep your nose clean
taking baths plunging in the
      ice & snow
you might catch cold, the
      flu Swine epidemic's
      "in" this year
according to the Authorities.

*September 18, 1976*

# AFTER WHITMAN & REZNIKOFF

## 1
### *What Relief*

If my pen hand were snapped by a Broadway truck
—What relief from writing letters to the *Nation*
disputing tyrants, war gossip, FBI—
My poems'll gather dust in Kansas libraries,
adolescent farmboys opening book covers with ruddy hands.

## 2
### *Lower East Side*

That round faced woman, she owns the street with her three big dogs,
screeches at me, waddling with her shopping bag across Avenue B
Grabbing my crotch, "Why don't you talk to me?"
baring her teeth in a smile, voice loud like a taxi horn,
"Big Jerk . . . you think you're famous?"—reminds me of my mother.

*April 29, 1980*

# MAXINE KUMIN

## OUR GROUND TIME HERE WILL BE BRIEF

Blue landing lights make
nail holes in the dark.
A fine snow falls. We sit
on the tarmac taking on
the mail, quick freight,
trays of laboratory mice,
coffee and Danish for
the passengers.

Wherever we're going
is Monday morning.
Wherever we're coming from
is Mother's lap.
On the cloud-pack above, strewn
as loosely as parsnip
or celery seeds, lie
the souls of the unborn:

my children's children's
children and their father.
We gather speed for the last run
and lift off into the weather.

## HOW IT IS

Shall I say how it is in your clothes?
A month after your death I wear your blue jacket.
The dog at the center of my life recognizes
you've come to visit, he's ecstatic.
In the left pocket, a hole.
In the right, a parking ticket
delivered up last August on Bay State Road.
In my heart, a scatter like milkweed,
a flinging from the pods of the soul.
My skin presses your old outline.
It is hot and dry inside.

I think of the last day of your life,
old friend, how I would unwind it, paste
it together in a different collage,
back from the death car idling in the garage,
back up the stairs, your praying hands unlaced,
reassembling the bites of bread and tuna fish
into a ceremony of sandwich,
running the home movie backward to a space
we could be easy in, a kitchen place
with vodka and ice, our words like living meat.

Dear friend, you have excited crowds
with your example. They swell
like wine bags, straining at your seams.
I will be years gathering up our words,
fishing out letters, snapshots, stains,
leaning my ribs against this durable cloth
to put on the dumb blue blazer of your death.

## LIFE'S WORK

Mother my good girl
I remember this old story:
you fresh out of the Conservatory
at eighteen a Bach specialist
in a starched shirtwaist
begging permission to go on tour
with the nimble violinist you were
never to accompany and he
flinging his music down
the rosin from his bow
flaking line by line
like grace notes on the treble clef
and my grandfather
that estimable man I never met
scrubbing your mouth with a handkerchief
saying no daughter of mine
tearing loose the gold locket
you wore with no one's picture in it
and the whole German house on 15th Street
at righteous whiteheat. . . .

At eighteen I chose to be a swimmer.
My long hair dripped through dinner
onto the china plate.
My fingers wrinkled like Sunsweet
yellow raisins from the afternoon workout.
My mouth chewed but I was doing laps.
I entered the water like a knife.
I was all muscle and seven doors.
A frog on the turning board.
King of the Eels and the Eel's wife.
I swallowed and prayed
to be allowed to join the Aquacade
and my perfect daddy
who carried you off to elope
after the fingerboard snapped
and the violinist lost his case
my daddy wearing gravy on his face

swore on the carrots and the boiled beef
that I would come to nothing
that I would come to grief. . . .

Well, the firm old fathers are dead
and I didn't come to grief.
I came to words instead
to tell the little tale that's left:
the midnights of my childhood still go on
the stairs speak again under your foot
the heavy parlor door folds shut
and "Au Clair de la Lune"
puckers from the obedient keys
plain as a schoolroom clock ticking
and what I hear more clearly than Debussy's
lovesong is the dry aftersound
of your long nails clicking.


## HOW IT GOES ON

Today I trade my last unwise
ewe lamb, the one who won't leave home,
for two cords of stove-length oak
and wait on the old enclosed
front porch to make the swap.
November sun revives the thick
trapped buzz of horseflies. The siren
for noon and forest fires blows
a sliding scale. The lamb of woe
looks in at me through glass
on the last day of her life.

Geranium scraps from the window box
trail from her mouth, burdock burrs
are stickered to her fleece like chicken pox,
under her tail stub, permanent smears.

I think of how it goes on,
this dark particular bent of our hungers:
the way wire eats into a tree
year after year on the pasture's perimeter,
keeping the milk cows penned
until they grow too old to freshen;
of how the last wild horses were scoured
from canyons in Idaho, roped, thrown,
their nostrils twisted shut with wire
to keep them down, the mares aborting,
days later, all of them carted to town.

I think of how it will be
in January, nights so cold
the pond ice cracks like target practice,
daylight glue-colored, sleet falling,
my yellow horse slick with the ball-bearing
sleet, raising up from his dingy browse
out of boredom and habit
to strip bark from the fenced-in trees;
of February, month of the hard palate,
the split wood running out,
worms working in the flour bin.

The lamb, whose time has come, goes off
in the cab of the dump truck, tied to the seat
with baling twine, durable enough
to bear her to the knife and rafter.

O lambs! The whole wolf-world sits down to eat
and cleans its muzzle after.

## THE ENVELOPE

It is true, Martin Heidegger, as you have written,
*I fear to cease*, even knowing that at the hour
of my death my daughters will absorb me, even
knowing they will carry me about forever
inside them, an arrested fetus, even as I carry
the ghost of my mother under my navel, a nervy
little androgynous person, a miracle
folded in lotus position.

Like those old pear-shaped Russian dolls that open
at the middle to reveal another and another, down
to the pea-sized, irreducible minim,
may we carry our mothers forth in our bellies.
May we, borne onward by our daughters, ride
in the Envelope of Almost-Infinity,
that chain letter good for the next twenty-five
thousand days of their lives.

# JAMES MERRILL

## THE BROKEN HOME

Crossing the street,
I saw the parents and the child
At their window, gleaming like fruit
With evening's mild gold leaf.

In a room on the floor below,
Sunless, cooler—a brimming
Saucer of wax, marbly and dim—
I have lit what's left of my life.

I have thrown out yesterday's milk
And opened a book of maxims.
The flame quickens. The word stirs.

Tell me, tongue of fire,
That you and I are as real
At least as the people upstairs.


My father, who had flown in World War I,
Might have continued to invest his life
In cloud banks well above Wall Street and wife.
But the race was run below, and the point was to win.

Too late now, I make out in his blue gaze
(Through the smoked glass of being thirty-six)
The soul eclipsed by twin black pupils, sex
And business; time was money in those days.

Each thirteenth year he married. When he died
There were already several chilled wives
In sable orbit—rings, cars, permanent waves.
We'd felt him warming up for a green bride.

He could afford it. He was "in his prime"
At three score ten. But money was not time.

When my parents were younger this was a popular act:
A veiled woman would leap from an electric, wine-dark car
To the steps of no matter what—the Senate or the Ritz Bar—
And bodily, at newsreel speed, attack

No matter whom—Al Smith or José Maria Sert
Or Clemenceau—veins standing out on her throat
As she yelled *War mongerer! Pig! Give us the vote!*,
And would have to be hauled away in her hobble skirt.

What had the man done? Oh, made history.
Her business (he had implied) was giving birth,
Tending the house, mending the socks.

Always that same old story—
Father Time and Mother Earth,
A marriage on the rocks.


One afternoon, red, satyr-thighed
Michael, the Irish setter, head
Passionately lowered, led
The child I was to a shut door. Inside,

Blinds beat sun from the bed.
The green-gold room throbbed like a bruise.
Under a sheet, clad in taboos
Lay whom we sought, her hair undone, outspread,

And of a blackness found, if ever now, in old
Engravings where the acid bit.
I must have needed to touch it
Or the whiteness—was she dead?
Her eyes flew open, startled strange and cold.
The dog slumped to the floor. She reached for me. I fled.

Tonight they have stepped out onto the gravel.
The party is over. It's the fall
Of 1931. They love each other still.

She: Charlie, I can't stand the pace.
He: Come on, honey—why, you'll bury us all!

A lead soldier guards my windowsill:
Khaki rifle, uniform, and face.
Something in me grows heavy, silvery, pliable.

How intensely people used to feel!
Like metal poured at the close of a proletarian novel,
Refined and glowing from the crucible,
I see those two hearts, I'm afraid,
Still. Cool here in the graveyard of good and evil,
They are even so to be honored and obeyed.


. . . Obeyed, at least, inversely. Thus
I rarely buy a newspaper, or vote.
To do so, I have learned, is to invite
The tread of a stone guest within my house.

Shooting this rusted bolt, though, against him,
I trust I am no less time's child than some
Who on the heath impersonate Poor Tom
Or on the barricades risk life and limb.

Nor do I try to keep a garden, only
An avocado in a glass of water—
Roots pallid, gemmed with air. And later,

When the small gilt leaves have grown
Fleshy and green, I let them die, yes, yes,
And start another. I am earth's no less.

A child, a red dog roam the corridors,
Still, of the broken home. No sound. The brilliant
Rag runners halt before wide-open doors.
My old room! Its wallpaper—cream, medallioned
With pink and brown—brings back the first nightmares,
Long summer colds, and Emma, sepia-faced,
Perspiring over broth carried upstairs
Aswim with golden fats I could not taste.

The real house became a boarding-school.
Under the ballroom ceiling's allegory
Someone at last may actually be allowed
To learn something; or, from my window, cool
With the unstiflement of the entire story,
Watch a red setter stretch and sink in cloud.


## CHANNEL 13

It came down to this: that merely naming the creatures
        Spelt their doom.
Three quick moves translated camelopard, dik-dik, and
        Ostrich from
Grassland to circus to Roman floor mosaic to
        TV room.

Here self-excusing voices attended (and music,
        Also canned)
The lark's aerobatics, the great white shark's blue shadow
        Making sand
Crawl fleshwise. Our ultimate "breakthrough" lenses took it
        In unmanned.

Now the vast shine of appearances shrinks to a tiny
        Sun, the screen
Goes black. Anaconda, tree toad, alpaca, clown-face
        Capuchin—
Launched at hour's end in the snug electronic ark of
        What has been.

## MANOS KARASTEFANÍS

Death took my father.
The same year (I was twelve)
Thanási's mother taught me
Heaven and hell.

None of my army buddies
Called me by name—
Just "Styles" or "Fashion Plate."
One friend I had, my body,

And, evenings at the gym
Contending with another,
Used it to isolate
Myself from him.

The doctor saved my knee.
You came to the clinic
Bringing *War and Peace*,
Better than any movie.

Why are you smiling?
I fought fair, I fought well,
Not hurting my opponent,
To win this black belt.

Why are you silent?
I've brought you a white cheese
From my island, and the sea's
Voice in a shell.

### From THE BALLROOM AT SANDOVER

Empty perfection, as I take you in
My heart pounds. Not the shock of elegance,
High ceiling where a faun-Pythagoras
Loses his calipers to barefoot, faintly
Goitrous nymphs, nor pier-glasses between
Floral panels of the palest green,
Nor chandeliers—indulgent chaperones—
Aclick, their crystal charges one by one
Accenting the donnée sun-beamed through tall
French window, silver leaf and waxing bud;
All a felicity—that does not, however,
Fully account for mine. Great room, I know you!
Somewhere on Earth I've met you in disguise,
Scouted your dark English woods and blood-red
Hangings, and glared down the bison head
Above a hearth of stony heraldry—
How many years before your "restoration"
Brought to light this foreign, youthful grace.
Ah, but styles. They are the new friend's face
To whom we sacrifice the tried and true,
And are betrayed—or not—by. For affection's
Poorest object, set in perfect light
By happenstance, grows irreplaceable,
And whether in time a room, or a romance,
Fails us or redeems us will have followed
As an extension of our "feel" for call them
Immaterials, the real right angle,
The golden section—grave proportions here,
Here at the heart of structure, and alone
Surviving now to tell me where I am:
In the old ballroom of the Broken Home.

# W. S. MERWIN

## BERRYMAN

I will tell you what he told me
in the years just after the war
as we then called
the second world war

don't lose your arrogance yet he said
you can do that when you're older
lose it too soon and you may
merely replace it with vanity

just one time he suggested
changing the usual order
of the same words in a line of verse
why point out a thing twice

he suggested I pray to the Muse
get down on my knees and pray
right there in the corner and he
said he meant it literally

it was in the days before the beard
and the drink but he was deep
in tides of his own through which he sailed
chin sideways and head tilted like a tacking sloop

he was far older than the dates allowed for
much older than I was he was in his thirties
he snapped down his nose with an accent
I think he had affected in England

as for publishing he advised me
to paper my wall with rejection slips
his lips and the bones of his long fingers trembled
with the vehemence of his views about poetry

he said the great presence
that permitted everything and transmuted it
in poetry was passion
passion was genius and he praised movement and invention

I had hardly begun to read
I asked how can you ever be sure
that what you write is really
any good at all and he said you can't

you can't you can never be sure
you die without knowing
whether anything you wrote was any good
if you have to be sure don't write


## FOR THE ANNIVERSARY OF MY DEATH

Every year without knowing it I have passed the day
When the last fires will wave to me
And the silence will set out
Tireless traveller
Like the beam of a lightless star

Then I will no longer
Find myself in life as in a strange garment
Surprised at the earth
And the love of one woman
And the shamelessness of men
As today writing after three days of rain
Hearing the wren sing and the falling cease
And bowing not knowing to what

# BREAD

Each face in the street is a slice of bread
wandering on
searching

somewhere in the light the true hunger
appears to be passing them by
they clutch

have they forgotten the pale caves
they dreamed of hiding in
their own caves
full of the waiting of their footprints
hung with the hollow marks of their groping
full of their sleep and their hiding

have they forgotten the ragged tunnels
they dreamed of following in out of the light
to hear step after step
the heart of bread
to be sustained by its dark breath
and emerge

to find themselves alone
before a wheat field
raising its radiance to the moon

## ST VINCENT'S

Thinking of rain clouds that rose over the city
on the first day of the year

in the same month
I consider that I have lived daily and with
eyes open and ears to hear
these years across from St Vincent's Hospital
above whose roof those clouds rose

its bricks by day a French red under
cross facing south
blown-up neo-classic facades the tall
dark openings between columns at
the dawn of history
exploded into many windows
in a mortised face

inside it the ambulances have unloaded
after sirens' howling nearer through traffic on
Seventh Avenue long
ago I learned not to hear them
even when the sirens stop

they turn to back in
few passers-by stay to look
and neither do I

at night two long blue
windows and one short one on the top floor
burn all night
many nights when most of the others are out
on what floor do they have
anything

I have seen the building drift moonlit through geraniums
late at night when trucks were few
moon just past the full

upper windows parts of the sky
as long as I looked
I watched it at Christmas and New Year
early in the morning I have seen the nurses ray out through
arterial streets
in the evening have noticed internes blocks away
on doorsteps one foot in the door

I have come upon the men in gloves taking out
the garbage at all hours
piling up mountains of
plastic bags white strata with green intermingled and
black
I have seen one pile
catch fire and studied the cloud
at the ends of the jets of the hoses
the fire engines as near as that
red beacons and
machine-throb heard by the whole body
I have noticed molded containers stacked outside
a delivery entrance on Twelfth Street
whether meals from a meal factory made up with those
mummified for long journeys by plane
or specimens for laboratory
examination sealed at the prescribed temperatures
either way closed delivery

and approached faces staring from above
crutches or tubular clamps
out for tentative walks
have paused for turtling wheel-chairs
heard visitors talking in wind on each corner
while the lights changed and
hot dogs were handed over at the curb
in the middle of afternoon
mustard ketchup onions and relish

and police smelling of ether and laundry
were going back

and I have known them all less than the papers of our days
smoke rises from the chimneys do they have an incinerator
what for
how warm do they believe they have to maintain the air
in there
several of the windows appear
to be made of tin
but it may be the light reflected
I have imagined bees coming and going
on those sills though I have never seen them

who was St Vincent


## THE REMOVAL

*To the endless tribe*

### I *The Procession*

When we see
the houses again
we will know that we are asleep at last

when we see
tears on the road
and they are ourselves
we are awake
the tree has been cut
on which we were leaves
the day does not know us
the river where we cross does not taste salt

the soles of our feet are black stars
but ours is the theme
of the light

II *The Homeless*

A clock keeps striking
and the echoes move in files
their faces
have been lost
flowers of salt
tongues from lost languages
doorways closed with pieces of night

III *A Survivor*

The dust never settles
but through it tongue tongue comes walking
shuffling like breath
but the old speech
is still in its country
dead

IV *The Crossing of the Removed*

At the bottom of the river
black ribbons cross under
and the water tries to soothe them
the mud tries to soothe them
the stones turn over and over trying
to comfort them
but they will not be healed
where the rims cut
and the shadows
sawed carrying
mourners
and some that had used horses
and had the harness
dropped it in half way over
on the far side the ribbons come out
invisible

V *A Widow Is Taken*

I call leave me here
the smoke on the black path
was my children
I will not walk
from the house I warmed
but they carry me through the light
my blackening face
my red eyes
everywhere I leave
one white footprint
the trackers will follow us into the cold
the water is high
the boats have been stolen away
there are no shoes
and they pretend that I am a bride
on the way to a new house

VI *The Reflection*

Passing a broken window
they see
into each of them the wedge of blackness
pounded
it is nothing
it splits them
loose hair
bare heels
at last they are gone
filing on in vacant rooms

THE NIGHT OF THE SHIRTS

Oh pile of white shirts who is coming
to breathe in your shapes to carry your numbers
to appear
what hearts
are moving toward their garments here
their days
what troubles beating between arms

you look upward through
each other saying nothing has happened
and it has gone away and is sleeping
having told the same story
and we exist from within
eyes of the gods

you lie on your backs
and the wounds are not made
the blood has not heard
the boat has not turned to stone
and the dark wires to the bulb
are full of the voice of the unborn


## TO THE INSECTS

Elders

we have been here so short a time
and we pretend that we have invented memory

we have forgotten what it is like to be you
who do not remember us

we remember imagining that what survived us
would be like us

and would remember the world as it appears to us
but it will be your eyes that will fill with light

we kill you again and again
and we turn into you

eating the forests
eating the earth and the water

and dying of them
departing from ourselves

leaving you the morning
in its antiquity

## GIFT

I have to trust what was given to me
if I am to trust anything
it led the stars over the shadowless mountain
what does it not remember in its night and silence
what does it not hope knowing itself no child of time

what did it not begin what will it not end
I have to hold it up in my hands as my ribs hold up my heart
I have to let it open its wings and fly among the gifts of the unknown
again in the mountain I have to turn
to the morning

I must be led by what was given to me
as streams are led by it
and braiding flights of birds
the gropings of veins the learning of plants
the thankful days
breath by breath

I call to it Nameless One O Invisible
Untouchable Free
I am nameless I am divided
I am invisible I am untouchable
and empty
nomad live with me
be my eyes
my tongue and my hands
my sleep and my rising
out of chaos
come and be given

# SHARON OLDS

## THE LANGUAGE OF THE BRAG

I have wanted excellence in the knife-throw,
I have wanted to use my exceptionally strong and accurate arms
and my straight posture and quick electric muscles
to achieve something at the center of a crowd,
the blade piercing the bark deep,
the haft slowly and heavily vibrating like the cock.

I have wanted some epic use for my excellent body,
some heroism, some American achievement
beyond the ordinary for my extraordinary self,
magnetic and tensile, I have stood by the sandlot
and watched the boys play.

I have wanted courage, I have thought about fire
and the crossing of waterfalls, I have dragged around

my belly big with cowardice and safety,
my stool black with iron pills,
my huge breasts oozing mucus,
my legs swelling, my hands swelling,
my face swelling and darkening, my hair
falling out, my inner sex
stabbed again and again with terrible pain like a knife.
I have lain down.

I have lain down and sweated and shaken
and passed blood and feces and water and
slowly alone in the center of a circle I have
passed the new person out
and they have lifted the new person free of the act
and wiped the new person free of that
language of blood like praise all over the body.

I have done what you wanted to do, Walt Whitman,
Allen Ginsberg, I have done this thing,
I and the other women this exceptional
act with the exceptional heroic body,
this giving birth, this glistening verb,
and I am putting my proud American boast
right here with the others.

## THE MOTHER

In the dreamy silence after bath,
hot in the milk-white towel, my son
announces that I will not love him when I'm dead
because people can't think when they're dead. I can't
think at first—not love him? The air outside the
window is very black, the old locust
beginning to lose its leaves already . . .
I hold him tight, he is white as a buoy
and my death like dark water is rising
swiftly in the room. I tell him I loved him
before he was born. I do not tell him
I'm damned if I won't love him after I'm
dead, necessity after all being
the mother of invention.

## YOUNG MOTHERS I

That look of attention
on the face of the young mother
like an animal,

bending over the carriage, looking up,
ears erect, eyes showing
the whites all around.

Startled as a newborn, she glances from side to side.
She has pushed, lying alone on a bed,
sweating, isolated by pain,
splitting slowly. She has pressed out
the child in her. It lies, separate,
opening and closing its mouth, its hands
wrinkled with long immersion in salt water.

Now the mother is the other one,
breasts hard bags of rock salt,
the bluish milk seeping out, her soul
there in the small carriage, the child in her
risen to the top, like cream,
and skimmed off.

Now she is alert for violation,
hearing acute as a deer's, her pupils
quick, her body bent in a curve,
wet rope which has dried and tightened,
a torture in some cultures.
She dreams of death by fire, death
by falling, death by disembowelling,
death by drowning, death by removal
of the head. Someone starts to scream
and it wakes her up, the hungry baby
wakes and saves her.

## THE UNJUSTLY PUNISHED CHILD

The child screams in his room. Rage
heats his head.
He is going through changes like metal under deep
pressure at high temperatures.

When he cools off and comes out of that door
he will not be the same child who ran in
and slammed it. An alloy has been added. Now he will
crack along different lines when tapped.

He is stronger. The long impurification
has begun this morning.

## THE GUILD

Every night, as my grandfather sat
in the darkened room in front of the fire,
the liquor like fire in his hand, his eye
glittering meaninglessly in the light
from the flames, his glass eye baleful and stony,
a young man sat with him
in silence and darkness, a college boy with
white skin, unlined, a narrow
beautiful face, a broad domed
forehead, and eyes amber as the resin from
trees too young to be cut yet.
This was his son, who sat, an apprentice,
night after night, his glass of coals
next to the old man's glass of coals,
and he drank when the old man drank, and he learned
the craft of oblivion—that young man
not yet cruel, his hair dark as the
soil that feeds the tree's roots,
that son who would come to be in his turn
better at this than the teacher, the apprentice
who would pass his master in cruelty and oblivion,
drinking steadily by the flames in the blackness,
that young man my father.

## SUMMER SOLSTICE, NEW YORK CITY

By the end of the longest day of the year he could not stand it,
he went up the iron stairs through the roof of the building
and over the soft, tarry surface,
to the edge, put one leg over the complex green tin cornice
and said if they came a step closer that was it.
Then the huge machinery of the earth began to work for his life,
the cops came in their suits blue-grey as the sky on a cloudy evening,
and one put on a bullet-proof vest, a
black shell around his own life,
life of his children's father, in case
the man was armed, and one, slung with a
rope like the sign of his bounden duty,
came up out of a hole in the top of the neighboring building
like the gold hole they say is in the top of the head,
and began to lurk toward the man who wanted to die.
The tallest cop approached him directly,
softly, slowly, talking to him, talking, talking,
while the man's leg hung over the lip of the next world
and the crowd gathered in the street, silent, and the
hairy net with its implacable grid was
unfolded near the curb and spread out and
stretched as the sheet is prepared to receive at a birth.
Then they all came a little closer
where he squatted next to his death, his shirt
glowing its milky glow like something
growing in a dish at night in the dark in a lab and then
everything stopped
as his body jerked and he
stepped down from the parapet and went toward them
and they closed on him, I thought they were going to
beat him up, as a mother whose child has been
lost will scream at the child when it's found, they
took him by the arms and held him up and
leaned him against the wall of the chimney and the
tall cop lit a cigarette
in his own mouth, and gave it to him, and
then they all lit cigarettes, and the
red, glowing ends burned like the
tiny campfires we lit at night
back at the beginning of the world.

## TOPOGRAPHY

After we flew across the country we
got in bed, laid our bodies
delicately together, like maps laid
face to face, East to West, my
San Francisco against your New York, your
Fire Island against my Sonoma, my
New Orleans deep in your Texas, your Idaho
bright on my Great Lakes, my Kansas
burning against your Kansas your Kansas
burning against my Kansas, your Eastern
Standard Time pressing into my
Pacific Time, my Mountain Time
beating against your Central Time, your
sun rising swiftly from the right my
sun rising swiftly from the left your
moon rising slowly from the left my
moon rising slowly from the right until
all four bodies of the sky
burn above us, sealing us together,
all our cities twin cities,
all our states united, one
nation, indivisible, with liberty and justice for all.

# ADRIENNE RICH

## STORM WARNINGS

The glass has been falling all the afternoon,
And knowing better than the instrument
What winds are walking overhead, what zone
Of gray unrest is moving across the land,
I leave the book upon a pillowed chair
And walk from window to closed window, watching
Boughs strain against the sky

And think again, as often when the air
Moves inward toward a silent core of waiting,
How with a single purpose time has traveled
By secret currents of the undiscerned
Into this polar realm. Weather abroad
And weather in the heart alike come on
Regardless of prediction.

Between foreseeing and averting change
Lies all the mastery of elements
Which clocks and weatherglasses cannot alter.
Time in the hand is not control of time,
Nor shattered fragments of an instrument
A proof against the wind; the wind will rise,
We can only close the shutters.

I draw the curtains as the sky goes black
And set a match to candles sheathed in glass
Against the keyhole draught, the insistent whine
Of weather through the unsealed aperture.
This is our sole defense against the season;
These are the things that we have learned to do
Who live in troubled regions.

## BALTIMORE: A FRAGMENT FROM THE THIRTIES

Medical textbooks propped in a dusty window.
Outside, it's summer. Heat
swamping stretched awnings, battering dark-green shades.
The Depression, Monument Street,
ice-wagons trailing melt, the Hospital
with its segregated morgues . . .
I'm five years old and trying to be perfect
walking hand-in-hand with my father.
A Black man halts beside us
croaks in a terrible voice, *I'm hungry* . . .
I'm a lucky child but I've read about beggars—
how the good give, the evil turn away.
But I want to turn away. My father gives.
We walk in silence. Why did he sound like that?
Is it evil to be frightened? I want to ask.
*He has no roof in his mouth,*
                              my father says at last.

*1985*

## PLANETARIUM

*Thinking of Caroline Herschel, 1750–1848,*
*astronomer, sister of William; and others.*

A woman in the shape of a monster
a monster in the shape of a woman
the skies are full of them

a woman          'in the snow
among the Clocks and instruments
or measuring the ground with poles'

in her 98 years to discover
8 comets

she whom the moon ruled
like us
levitating into the night sky
riding the polished lenses

Galaxies of women, there
doing penance for impetuousness
ribs chilled
in those spaces          of the mind

An eye,
          'virile, precise and absolutely certain'
          from the mad webs of Uranisborg

                              encountering the NOVA

every impulse of light exploding
from the core
as life flies out of us

Tycho whispering at last
'Let me not seem to have lived in vain'

What we see, we see
and seeing is changing

the light that shrivels a mountain
and leaves a man alive

Heartbeat of the pulsar
heart sweating through my body

The radio impulse
pouring in from Taurus

       I am bombarded       yet I stand

I have been standing all my life in the
direct path of a battery of signals
the most accurately transmitted most
untranslateable language in the universe
I am a galactic cloud so deep       so invo-
luted that a light wave could take 15
years to travel through me       And has
taken       I am an instrument in the shape
of a woman trying to translate pulsations
into images       for the relief of the body
and the reconstruction of the mind.

*1968*

## CARTOGRAPHIES OF SILENCE

1.
A conversation begins
with a lie. And each

speaker of the so-called common language feels
the ice-floe split, the drift apart

as if powerless, as if up against
a force of nature

A poem can begin
with a lie. And be torn up.

A conversation has other laws
recharges itself with its own

false energy. Cannot be torn
up. Infiltrates our blood. Repeats itself.

Inscribes with its unreturning stylus
the isolation it denies.

2.
The classical music station
playing hour upon hour in the apartment

the picking up and picking up
and again picking up the telephone

The syllables uttering
the old script over and over

The loneliness of the liar
living in the formal network of the lie

twisting the dials to drown the terror
beneath the unsaid word

3.
The technology of silence
The rituals, etiquette

the blurring of terms
silence not absence

of words or music or even
raw sounds

Silence can be a plan
rigorously executed

the blueprint to a life

It is a presence
it has a history        a form

Do not confuse it
with any kind of absence

4.
How calm, how inoffensive these words
begin to seem to me

though begun in grief and anger
Can I break through this film of the abstract

without wounding myself or you

there is enough pain here

This is why the classical or the jazz music station plays?
to give a ground of meaning to our pain?

5.

The silence that strips bare:
In Dreyer's *Passion of Joan*

Falconetti's face, hair shorn, a great geography
mutely surveyed by the camera

If there were a poetry where this could happen
not as blank spaces or as words

stretched like a skin over meanings
but as silence falls at the end

of a night through which two people
have talked till dawn

6.

The scream
of an illegitimate voice

It has ceased to hear itself, therefore
it asks itself

How do I exist?

This was the silence I wanted to break in you
I had questions but you would not answer

I had answers but you could not use them
This is useless to you and perhaps to others

7.
It was an old theme even for me:
Language cannot do everything—

chalk it on the walls where the dead poets
lie in their mausoleums

If at the will of the poet the poem
could turn into a thing

a granite flank laid bare, a lifted head
alight with dew

If it could simply look you in the face
with naked eyeballs, not letting you turn

till you, and I who long to make this thing,
were finally clarified together in its stare

8.
No. Let me have this dust,
these pale clouds dourly lingering, these words

moving with ferocious accuracy
like the blind child's fingers

or the newborn infant's mouth
violent with hunger

No one can give me, I have long ago
taken this method

whether of bran pouring from the loose-woven sack

or of the bunsen-flame turned low and blue

If from time to time I envy
the pure annunciations to the eye

the *visio beatifica*
if from time to time I long to turn

like the Eleusinian hierophant
holding up a simple ear of grain

for return to the concrete and everlasting world
what in fact I keep choosing

are these words, these whispers, conversations
from which time after time the truth breaks moist and green.

*1975*


## DELTA

If you have taken this rubble for my past
raking through it for fragments you could sell
know that I long ago moved on
deeper into the heart of the matter

If you think you can grasp me, think again:
my story flows in more than one direction
a delta springing from the riverbed
with its five fingers spread

*1987*

# KARL SHAPIRO

## UNIVERSITY

To hurt the Negro and avoid the Jew
Is the curriculum. In mid-September
The entering boys, identified by hats,
Wander in a maze of mannered brick
    Where boxwood and magnolia brood
    And columns with imperious stance
    Like rows of ante-bellum girls
        Eye them, outlanders.

In whited cells, on lawns equipped for peace,
Under the arch, and lofty banister,
Equals shake hands, unequals blankly pass;
The exemplary weather whispers, "Quiet, quiet"
    And visitors on tiptoe leave
    For the raw North, the unfinished West,
    As the young, detecting an advantage,
        Practice a face.

Where, on their separate hill, the colleges,
Like manor houses of an older law,
Gaze down embankments on a land in fee,
The Deans, dry spinsters over family plate,
    Ring out the English name like coin,
    Humor the snob and lure the lout.
    Within the precincts of this world
        Poise is a club.

But on the neighboring range, misty and high,
The past is absolute: some luckless race
Dull with inbreeding and conformity
Wears out its heart, and comes barefoot and bad
    For charity or jail. The scholar
    Sanctions their obsolete disease;
    The gentleman revolts with shame
        At his ancestor.

And the true nobleman, once a democrat,
Sleeps on his private mountain. He was one
Whose thought was shapely and whose dream was broad;
This school he held his art and epitaph.
    But now it takes from him his name,
    Falls open like a dishonest look,
    And shows us, rotted and endowed,
        Its senile pleasure.

## FULL MOON: NEW GUINEA

These nights we fear the aspects of the moon,
Sleep lightly in the radiance falling clear
On palms and ferns and hills and us; for soon
The small burr of the bombers in our ear
Tickles our rest; we rise as from a nap
And take our helmets absently and meet,
Prepared for any spectacle or mishap,
At trenches fresh and narrow at our feet.

Look up, look up, and wait and breathe. These nights
We fear Orion and the Cross. The crowd
Of deadly insects caught in our long lights
Glitter and seek to burrow in a cloud
Soft-minded with high explosive. Breathe and wait,
The bombs are falling darkly for our fate.

## THE PROGRESS OF FAUST

He was born in Deutschland, as you would suspect,
And graduated in magic from Cracow
In Fifteen Five. His portraits show a brow
Heightened by science. The eye is indirect,
As of bent light upon a crooked soul,
And that he bargained with the Prince of Shame
For pleasures intellectually foul
Is known by every court that lists his name.

His frequent disappearances are put down
To visits in the regions of the damned
And to the periodic deaths he shammed,
But, unregenerate and in Doctor's gown,
He would turn up to lecture at the fair
And do a minor miracle for a fee.
Many a life he whispered up the stair
To teach the black art of anatomy.

He was as deaf to angels as an oak
When, in the fall of Fifteen Ninety-four,
He went to London and crashed through the floor
In mock damnation of the playgoing folk.
Weekending with the scientific crowd,
He met Sir Francis Bacon and helped draft
"Colours of Good and Evil" and read aloud
An obscene sermon at which no one laughed.

He toured the Continent for a hundred years
And subsidized among the peasantry
The puppet play, his tragic history;
With a white glove he boxed the devil's ears
And with a black his own. Tired of this,
He published penny poems about his sins,
In which he placed the heavy emphasis
On the white glove which, for a penny, wins.

Some time before the hemorrhage of the Kings
Of France, he turned respectable and taught;
Quite suddenly everything that he had thought
Seemed to grow scholars' beards and angels' wings.
It was the Overthrow. On Reason's throne
He sat with the fair Phrygian on his knees
And called all universities his own,
As plausible a figure as you please.

Then back to Germany as the sages' sage
To preach comparative science to the young
Who came from every land in a great throng
And knew they heard the master of the age.
When for a secret formula he paid
The Devil another fragment of his soul,
His scholars wept, and several even prayed
That Satan would restore him to them whole.

Backwardly tolerant, Faustus was expelled
From the Third Reich in Nineteen Thirty-nine.
His exit caused the breaching of the Rhine,
Except for which the frontier might have held.
Five years unknown to enemy and friend
He hid, appearing on the sixth to pose
In an American desert at war's end
Where, at his back, a dome of atoms rose.

# NEBRASKA

I love Nowhere where the factories die of malnutrition.

I love Nowhere where there are no roads, no rivers, no interesting
Indians,

Where history is invented in the History Department and there are no
centennials of anything,

Where every tree is planted by hand and has a private tutor.

Where the "parts" have to be ordered and the sky settles all questions,

Where travelers from California bitch at the backwardness and
New Yorkers step on the gas in a panic,

Where the grass in winter is gray not brown,

Where the population diminishes.

Here on the boundary of the hired West, equidistant from every
tourist office, and the air is washed by distance, here
at last there is nothing to recommend.

May no one ever attempt a recommendation; Chicago be as far as
Karachi.

Though the warriors come with rockets, may they fall off the trucks.

May the voting he light and the clouds like a cruise and the criminal
boredom enter the district of hogs.

I love Nowhere where the human brag is a brag of neither time nor
place,

But an elephant house of Smithsonian bones and the white cathedrals
of grain,

The feeding-lots in the snow with the steers huddled in
symmetrical misery, backs to the sleet,

To beef us up in the Beef State plains, something to look at.

## THE ALPHABET

The letters of the Jews as strict as flames
Or little terrible flowers lean
Stubbornly upwards through the perfect ages,
Singing through solid stone the sacred names.
The letters of the Jews are black and clean
And lie in chain-line over Christian pages.
The chosen letters bristle like barbed wire
That hedge the flesh of man,
Twisting and tightening the book that warns.
These words, this burning bush, this flickering pyre
Unsacrifices the bled son of man
Yet plaits his crown of thorns.

Where go the tipsy idols of the Roman
Past synagogues of patient time,
Where go the sisters of the Gothic rose,
Where go the blue eyes of the Polish women
Past the almost natural crime,
Past the still speaking embers of ghettos,
There rise the tinder flowers of the Jews.
The letters of the Jews are dancing knives
That carve the heart of darkness seven ways.
These are the letters that all men refuse
And will refuse until the king arrives
And will refuse until the death of time
And all is rolled back in the book of days.

# GARY SOTO

## LOOKING AROUND, BELIEVING

How strange that we can begin at anytime.
With two feet we get down the street.
With a hand we undo the rose.
With an eye we lift up the peach tree
And hold it up to the wind—white blossoms
At our feet. Like today. I started
In the yard with my daughter,
With my wife poking at a potted geranium,
And now I am walking down the street,
Amazed that the sun is only so high,
Just over the roof, and a child
Is singing through a rolled newspaper
And a terrier is leaping like a flea
And at the bakery I pass, a palm
Like a suctioning starfish, is pressed
To the window. We're keeping busy—
This way, that way, we're making shadows
Where sunlight was, making words
Where there was only noise in the trees.


## FIELD POEM

When the foreman whistled
My brother and I
Shouldered our hoes,
Leaving the field.
We returned to the bus
Speaking
In broken English, in broken Spanish
The restaurant food,
The tickets to a dance
We wouldn't buy with our pay.

From the smashed bus window,
I saw the leaves of cotton plants
Like small hands
Waving good-bye.

## BLACK HAIR

At eight I was brilliant with my body.
In July, that ring of heat
We all jumped through, I sat in the bleachers
Of Romain Playground, in the lengthening
Shade that rose from our dirty feet.
The game before us was more than baseball.
It was a figure—Hector Moreno
Quick and hard with turned muscles,
His crouch the one I assumed before an altar
Of worn baseball cards, in my room.

I came here because I was Mexican, a stick
Of brown light in love with those
Who could do it—the triple and hard slide,
The gloves eating balls into double plays.
What could I do with 50 pounds, my shyness,
My black torch of hair, about to go out?
Father was dead, his face no longer
Hanging over the table or our sleep,
And mother was the terror of mouths
Twisting hurt by butter knives.

In the bleachers I was brilliant with my body,
Waving players in and stomping my feet,
Growing sweaty in the presence of white shirts.
I chewed sunflower seeds. I drank water
And bit my arm through the late innings.
When Hector lined balls into deep
Center, in my mind I rounded the bases
With him, my face flared, my hair lifting
Beautifully, because we were coming home
To the arms of brown people.

## MEXICANS BEGIN JOGGING

At the factory I worked
In the fleck of rubber, under the press
Of an oven yellow with flame,
Until the border patrol opened
Their vans and my boss waved for us to run.
"Over the fence, Soto," he shouted,
And I shouted that I was American.
"No time for lies," he said, and pressed
A dollar in my palm, hurrying me
Through the back door.

Since I was on his time, I ran
And became the wag to a short tail of Mexicans—
Ran past the amazed crowds that lined
The street and blurred like photographs, in rain.
I ran from that industrial road to the soft
Houses where people paled at the turn of an autumn sky.
What could I do but yell *vivas*
To baseball, milkshakes, and those sociologists
Who would clock me
As I jog into the next century
On the power of a great, silly grin.

## TV IN BLACK AND WHITE

In the mid sixties
We were sentenced to watch
The rich on TV—Donna Reed
High-heeled in the kitchen,
Ozzie Nelson bending
In his eighth season, over golf.
While he swung, we hoed
Fields flagged with cotton
Because we understood a sock
Should have a foot,
A cuff a wrist,
And a cup was always
Smaller than the thirst.
When Donna turned
The steak and onions,
We turned grape trays
In a vineyard
That we worked like an abacus,
A row at a time.

And today the world
Still plots, unravels with
Piano lessons for this child,
Braces for that one—
Gin in the afternoon,
Ice from the bucket . . .
But if the electricity
Fails, in this town,
A store front might
Be smashed, sacks may find
Hands, a whistle
Point the way.

And if someone steps out
With a black and white TV,
It's because we love you Donna,
We miss you Ozzie.

## THE PLUM'S HEART

I've climbed in trees
To eat, and climbed
Down to look about
This world, mouth red
From plums that were
Once clouds in March
—rain I mean, that
Pitiless noise against
Leaves and branches.
Father once lifted me
Into one, and from
A distance I might
Have been a limb,
Moving a little heavier
Than most but a limb
All the same. My hands
Opened like mouths,
The juice running
Without course down
My arms, as I stabbed
For plums, bunched
Or half-hidden behind
Leaves. A bird fluttered
From there, a single
Leaf cutting loose,
And gnats like smoke
Around a bruised plum.
I climbed searching
For those red globes,
And with a sack filled,
I called for father
To catch—father
Who would disappear
Like fruit at the end
Of summer, from a neck
Wound some say—blood

Running like the juice
Of these arms. I
Twisted the throat
Of the sack, tossed
It, and started down
To father, his mouth
Already red and grinning
Like the dead on their
Rack of blackness.
When I jumped, he was
Calling, arms open,
The sack at his feet
For us, the half-bitten,
Who bring on the flies.

## FAILING IN THE PRESENCE OF ANTS

We live to some purpose, daughter.
Across the park, among
The trees that give the eye
Something to do, let's spread
A blanket on the ground
˙And examine the ants, loose
Thread to an old coat.
Perhaps they are more human than we are.
They live for the female,
Rescue their hurt, and fall earthward
For their small cause. And
Us? We live for our bellies,
The big O of our mouths.
*Give me, give me,* they say,
And many people, whole countries,
May go under because we desire TV
And chilled drinks, clothes
That hang well on our bodies—
Desire sofas and angled lamps,
Hair the sea may envy
On a slow day.
It is hurtful to sweep
Ants into a frenzy, blow
Chemicals into their eyes—
Those austere marchers who will lift
Their heads to rumor—seed,
Wafer of leaf, dropped apple—
And start off, over this
And that, between sloppy feet
And staggered chairs, for no
Purpose other than it might be good.

## THE PHILOSOPHY OF DOG & MAN

Stray dogs come with the rain,
Two hours before the garbage men
And their elephant noise of truck
Crushing eggshell and tuna can,
Light bulbs with their bleak rattle.
Or so I hear. I struggle into slippers,
Part the curtain: a tall dog,
Paws up on the heap, is
Working on a sour casserole,
The noodles marching into his mouth,
And a moist nose sniffing
For chicken bone and week-old stew,
For pie tins with buttery crust.
I've never seen happiness
Over a bone with little meat,
Happiness in rain. This
Is what I want, to be up before light,
To be in rain with garbage men
On the back porch, I snap
A finger, call, "Here boy,"
And the dog throws down its ears,
Ashamed to be caught eating.
I show him the pink emptiness of my palm,
But what am I to him? He doesn't know me.
I'm a man in a robe, not a friend
Of green alleys and poor days,
A man in slippers clomping
Pathetically down wet stairs.
Hurried love trots away on three legs,
The hurt paw touching ground
Only when he looks back.

# CHARLES WRIGHT

## REUNION

Already one day has detached itself from all the rest up ahead.
It has my photograph in its soft pocket.
It wants to carry my breath into the past in its bag of wind.

I write poems to untie myself, to do penance and disappear
Through the upper right-hand corner of things, to say grace.

## *From* THE SOUTHERN CROSS

The life of this world is wind.
Wind-blown we come, and wind-blown we go away.
All that we look on is windfall.
All we remember is wind.

———

Pickwick was never the wind . . .

It's what we forget that defines us, and stays in the same place,
And waits to be rediscovered.
Somewhere in all that network of rivers and roads and silt hills,
A city I'll never remember,
                      its walls the color of pure light,
Lies in the August heat of 1935,
In Tennessee, the bottom land slowly becoming a lake.
It lies in a landscape that keeps my imprint
Forever,
             and stays unchanged, and waits to be filled back in.
Someday I'll find it out
And enter my old outline as though for the 1st time,

And lie down, and tell no one.

*From* TATTOOS

12.

Oval oval oval oval push pull push pull . . .
Words unroll from our fingers.
A splash of leaves through the windowpanes,
A smell of tar from the streets:
Apple, arrival, the railroad, shoe.

The words, like bees in a sweet ink, cluster and drone,
Indifferent, indelible,
A hum and a hum:
Back stairsteps to God, ropes to the glass eye:
Vineyard, informer, the chair, the throne.

Mojo and numberless, breaths
From the wet mountains and green mouths; rustlings,
Sure sleights of hand,
The news that arrives from nowhere:
Angel, omega, silence, silence . . .

1945

## CLEAR NIGHT

Clear night, thumb-top of a moon, a back-lit sky.
Moon-fingers lay down their same routine
On the side deck and the threshold, the white keys and the
    black keys.
Bird hush and bird song. A cassia flower falls.

I want to be bruised by God.
I want to be strung up in a strong light and singled out.
I want to be stretched, like music wrung from a dropped seed.
I want to be entered and picked clean.

And the wind says "What?" to me.
And the castor beans, with their little earrings of death, say
    "What?" to me.
And the stars start out on their cold slide through the dark.
And the gears notch and the engines wheel.

## *From* HOMAGE TO PAUL CÉZANNE

At night, in the fish-light of the moon, the dead wear our white
    shirts
To stay warm, and litter the fields.
We pick them up in the mornings, dewy pieces of paper and
    scraps of cloth.
Like us, they refract themselves. Like us,
They keep on saying the same thing, trying to get it right.
Like us, the water unsettles their names.

Sometimes they lie like leaves in their little arks, and curl up at the
    edges.
Sometimes they come inside, wearing our shoes, and walk
From mirror to mirror.
Or lie in our beds with their gloves off
And touch our bodies. Or talk
In a corner. Or wait like envelopes on a desk.

They reach up from the ice plant.
They shuttle their messengers through the oat grass.
Their answers rise like rust on the stalks and the spidery leaves.

We rub them off our hands.

### From A JOURNAL OF TRUE CONFESSIONS

The stars are fastening their big buckles
                                    and flashy night shoes,
Thunder chases its own tail down the sky,
My forty-ninth year, and all my Southern senses called to horn,
August night hanging like cobwebs around my shoulders:
How existential it all is, really,
                            the starting point always the starting point
And what's-to-come still being the What's-to-Come.
Some friends, like George, lurk in the memory like locusts,
                                while others, flat one-sided fish
Looking up, handle themselves like sweet stuff:
                        look out for them, look out for them.
                                            —25 August 1984


—Cicadas wind up their one note to a breaking point.
The sunlight, like fine thread, opens and closes us.
The wind, its voice like grasshoppers' wings,
                                rises and falls.
Sadness is truer than happiness.

Walking tonight through the dwarf orchard,
The fruit trees seem etched like a Durer woodcut against the sky,
The odd fruit
            burined in bas-relief,
The moon with its one foot out of the clouds,
All twenty-one trees growing darker in a deepening dark.

When the right words are found I will take them in and be filled
through with joy.
My mouth will be precious then,
                        as your mouth is precious.
If you want to hear me, you'll have to listen again.
You'll have to listen to what the wind says,
                                whatever its next direction.
                                        —9 September 1984

—It's all such a matter of abstracts—
                              love with its mouth wide open,
Affection holding its hand out,
Impalpable to the impalpable—
No one can separate the light from the light.

They say that he comes with clouds,
The faithful witness,
                    the first-begotten of the dead.
And his feet are like fine brass,
His voice the perpetual sound of many waters.

The night sky is darker than the world below the world,
The stars medieval cathedral slits from a long way.
This is the dark of the *Metamorphoses*
When sparks from the horses' hooves
                              showed us Persephone
And the Prince's car in its slash and plunge toward Hell.

Seventy-four years ago today,
                    Dino Campana, on the way back
From his pilgrimage on foot
To the holy chill of La Verna inside the Apennines
To kiss the rock where St. Francis received the stigmata,

Stopped in a small inn at Monte Filetto
And sat on a balcony all day
                              staring out at the countryside,
The hawks circling like lost angels against the painted paradise of the
     sky,
The slope below him
                    a golden painting hung from the walnut tree:

The new line will be like the first line,
                              spacial and self-contained,
Firm to the touch
But intimate, carved, as though whispered into the ear.
                                        —*25 September 1984*

# BIBLIOGRAPHY

## ANTHOLOGIES

*The Norton Anthology of Modern Poetry, Second Edition*, ed. by Richard Ellmann and Robert O'Clair. New York: W. W. Norton, 1988.

*The Vintage Book of Contemporary American Poetry*, ed. by J. D. McClatchy. New York: Vintage, 1990.

*New American Poets of the '90s*, ed. by Jack Myers and Roger Weingarten. Boston: David R. Godine, Publisher, 1991.

*The Morrow Anthology of Younger American Poets*, ed. by Dave Smith and David Bottoms. New York: William Morrow and Company, 1985.

## HISTORY AND CRITICISM

*The Post Moderns*, by Donald Allen and George Butterick. New York: Grove Press, 1982.

*The Psycho-Political Muse: American Poetry Since the Fifties*, by Paul Breslin. Chicago: University of Chicago Press, 1987.

*Shakespeare's Sisters: Feminist Essays on Women Poets*, ed. by Sandra M. Gilbert and Susan Gubar. Bloomington: Indiana University Press, 1979.

"Poetry: After Modernism," "Poetry: Schools of Dissidents," "Poetry: Dissidents from Schools," by Daniel Hoffman. Chapters 10, 11, 12 of *Harvard Guide to Contemporary American Writing*, ed. by Daniel Hoffman. Cambridge, MA: The Belknap Press, 1979.

*The Fate of American Poetry*, by Jonathan Holden. Athens: University of Georgia Press, 1991.

*Rhyme's Reason* (enlarged edition), by John Hollander. New Haven, CT: Yale University Press, 1989.

*White Paper: On Contemporary American Poetry*, by J. D. McClatchy. New York: Columbia University Press, 1989.

*Coming to Light: American Women Poets in the 20th Century*, ed. by Diane Wood Middlebrook and Marilyn Yalom. Ann Arbor: University of Michigan Press, 1985.

*Writing Like a Woman*, by Alicia Ostriker. Ann Arbor: University of Michigan Press, 1983.

*Stealing the Language: The Emergence of Women's Poetry in America*, by Alicia Ostriker. Boston: Beacon Press, 1986.

*A History of Modern Poetry: Modernism and After*, by David Perkins. Cambridge: Harvard University Press, 1987.

*Missing Measures: Modern Poetry and the Revolt Against Meter*, by Timothy Steele. Fayetteville: University of Arkansas Press, 1990.

*Five Temperaments: Elizabeth Bishop, Robert Lowell, James Merrill, Adrienne Rich, John Ashbery*, by David Kalstone. New York: W. W. Norton, 1977.

*The Music of What Happens: Essays on Poetry and Criticism*, by Helen Vendler. Cambridge, MA: Harvard University Press, 1988.
*Part of Nature, Part of Us: Modern American Poets*, by Helen Vendler. Cambridge, MA: Harvard University Press, 1980.
*Contemporary Poets: Fourth Edition*, ed. by James Vinson and D. L. Kirkpatrick. New York: St. Martin's Press, 1985.


### A. R. AMMONS

*The Selected Poems, Expanded Edition.* New York: W. W. Norton, 1987.
*Sumerian Vistas: Poems.* New York: W. W. Norton, 1987.
*The Really Short Poems of A. R. Ammons.* New York: W. W. Norton, 1990.

*A. R. Ammons: Modern Critical Views*, ed. by Harold Bloom. New York: Chelsea House, 1988.
*A. R. Ammons*, by Alan Holder. Boston: Twayne Publishers, 1978.


### JOHN ASHBERY

*Selected Poems.* New York: Penguin Books, 1985
*April Galleons.* New York, Viking Press, 1987.
*Flow Chart.* New York: Alfred A. Knopf, 1991.

*Reported Sightings: Art Chronicles 1957–1987.* Ed. by David Bergman. Cambridge: Harvard University Press, 1991.

*John Ashbery: A Comprehensive Bibliography*, by David K. Kermani. New York: Garland Publishing, 1976.
*Beyond Amazement: New Essays on John Ashbery*, ed. by David Lehman. Ithaca: Cornell University Press, 1980.
*John Ashbery: An Introduction to the Poetry*, by David Shapiro. New York: Columbia University Press, 1979.


### GWENDOLYN BROOKS

*Selected Poems.* New York: Harper & Row, 1963.
*In the Mecca.* New York: Harper & Row, 1968.
*Blacks.* Chicago: Third World Press, 1991.
*The Near-Johannesburg Boy.* Chicago: Third World Press, 1991.
*Winnie.* Chicago: Third World Press, 1991.

*Report from Part One: An Autobiography.* Detroit: Broadside Press, 1972.
*Primer for Blacks.* Chicago: Third World Press, 1991.

*Gwendolyn Brooks*, by Harry B. Shaw. Boston: Twayne Publishers, 1980.
*Langston Hughes and Gwendolyn Brooks: A Reference Guide*, by R. Baxter
Miller. Boston: G. K. Hall, 1978.
*A Life Distilled: Gwendolyn Brooks, Her Poetry and Fiction*, ed. by Maria K.
Mootry and Gary Smith. Champaign: University of Illinois Press,
1987.
*Gwendolyn Brooks: Poetry and the Heroic Voice*, by D. H. Melhem. Lex-
ington: University of Kentucky Press, 1987.
*A Life of Gwendolyn Brooks*, by George E. Kent. Lexington: University
Press of Kentucky, 1990.


RITA DOVE

*Museum*. Pittsburgh: Carnegie-Mellon University Press, 1983.
*Thomas and Beulah*. Pittsburgh: Carnegie-Mellon University Press,
1986.
*The Yellow House on the Corner*. Pittsburgh: Carnegie-Mellon University
Press, 1989.
*Grace Notes*. New York: W. W. Norton, 1989.

*Fifth Sunday* (short stories). Charlottesville, VA: Callaloo Fiction Series,
1985.


ALLEN GINSBERG

*Collected Poems 1947–1980*. New York: Harper & Row, 1984.
*White Shroud: Poems 1980–1985*. New York: Harper & Row, 1986.

*Off the Road: My Years with Cassady, Kerouac & Ginsberg*, by Carolyn
Cassady. New York: Viking Penguin, 1991.
*A Bibliography of Works by Allen Ginsberg, October 1943 to July 1967*, by
George Dowden. San Francisco: City Lights, 1971.
*On the Poetry of Allen Ginsberg*, ed. by Lewis Hyde. Ann Arbor: Univer-
sity of Michigan Press, 1984.
*Allen Ginsberg: An Annotated Bibliography, 1969–1977*, by Michelle
Kraus. Metuchen, NJ: Scarecrow Press, 1980.
*Allen Ginsberg*, by Thomas F. Merrill. New York: Twayne, 1969.
*Ginsberg: A Biography*, by Barry Miles. New York: Simon & Schuster,
1989.


MAXINE KUMIN

*House, Bridge, Fountain, Gate*. New York: Viking, 1975.
*The Retrieval System*. New York: Viking, 1978.

*Our Ground Time Here Will Be Brief.* New York: Viking, 1982.
*The Long Approach.* New York: Viking, 1985.
*Nurture.* New York: Viking, 1989.
*Looking for Luck: Poems.* New York: W. W. Norton, 1992.

*To Make a Prairie: Essays on Poets, Poetry, and Country Living.* Ann Arbor: University of Michigan Press, 1980.
*In Deep: Country Essays.* New York: Viking, 1987.


JAMES MERRILL

*The Changing Light at Sandover.* New York: Atheneum, 1982.
*From the First Nine: Poems 1946–1976.* New York: Atheneum, 1982.
*Late Settings.* New York: Atheneum, 1985.
*The Inner Room.* New York: Alfred A. Knopf, 1988.

*Recitative: Prose by James Merrill.* Ed. by J. D. McClatchy. San Francisco: North Point Press, 1986.

*James Merrill: Modern Critical Views,* ed. by Harold Bloom. New York: Chelsea House, 1985.
*James Merrill: Essays in Criticism,* ed. by David Lehman and Charles Berger. Ithaca: Cornell University Press, 1983.
*James Merrill: An Introduction to the Poetry,* by Judith Moffett. New York: Columbia University Press, 1984.
*The Consuming Myth: The Work of James Merrill,* by Stephen Yenser. Cambridge: Harvard University Press, 1987.


W. S. MERWIN

*Selected Poems.* New York: Alfred A. Knopf, 1988.
*The Rain in the Trees.* New York: Alfred A. Knopf, 1988.

*Unframed Originals: Recollections.* New York: Atheneum, 1982.
*Regions of Memory: Uncollected Prose 1949–1982.* Ed. by Ed Folsom and Cary Nelson. Champaign: University of Illinois Press, 1987.

*Selected Translations 1968–1978.* New York: Atheneum, 1979.
*From the Spanish Morning.* New York: Atheneum, 1985.

*Poetry as Labor and Privilege: The Writings of W. S. Merwin,* ed. by Edward J. Brunner. University of Illinois Press, 1991.

*W. S. Merwin the Mythmaker*, by Mark Christhilf. Columbia: University of Missouri Press, 1986.
*W. S. Merwin: Essays on the Poetry*, ed. by Cary Nelson and Ed Folsom. Champaign: University of Illinois Press, 1987.


### SHARON OLDS

*Satan Says*. Pittsburgh: University of Pittsburgh Press, 1980.
*The Dead and the Living*. New York: Alfred A. Knopf, 1984.
*The Gold Cell*. New York: Alfred A. Knopf, 1987
*The Father*. New York: Alfred A. Knopf, 1992.


### ADRIENNE RICH

*The Fact of a Doorframe: Poems Selected and New 1950–1984*. New York: W. W. Norton, 1984.
*Time's Power: Poems 1985–1988*. New York: W. W. Norton, 1989.
*An Atlas of the Difficult World*. New York: W. W. Norton, 1991.

*Of Woman Born: Motherhood as Experience and Institution*. New York: W. W. Norton, 1976.
*Of Lies, Secrets, and Silence: Selected Prose 1966–1978*. New York, W. W. Norton, 1979.
*Blood, Bread & Poetry: Selected Prose 1979–1985*. New York: W. W. Norton, 1986.

*Reading Adrienne Rich: Reviews and Re-Visions, 1951–81*, ed. by Jane Roberta Cooper. Ann Arbor: University of Michigan Press, 1984.
*Adrienne Rich's Poetry*, ed. by Barbara Charlesworth Gelpi and Albert Gelpi. New York: W. W. Norton, 1975.
*The Aesthetics of Power: The Poetry of Adrienne Rich*, by Claire Keyes. Athens: University of Georgia Press, 1986.
*American Triptych: Anne Bradstreet, Emily Dickinson, Adrienne Rich*, by Wendy Martin. Chapel Hill: University of North Carolina Press, 1984.
*Adrienne Rich: The Poet and Her Critics*, by Craig Werner. Chicago: American Library Association, 1988.


### KARL SHAPIRO

*Collected Poems 1940–1978*. New York: Random House, 1976.
*New & Selected Poems*. Chicago: University of Chicago Press, 1987.

*In Defense of Ignorance.* New York: Random House, 1960.
*To Abolish Children and Other Essays.* Chicago: Quadrangle, 1968.
*The Poetry Wreck: Selected Essays 1950–1970.* New York: Random House, 1975.
*The Younger Son: An Autobiography in Three Parts, Volume 1.* Chapel Hill, NC: Algonquin Books, 1988.
*Reports of My Death: An Autobiography, Volume 2.* Chapel Hill, NC: Algonquin Books, 1990.

*Karl Shapiro: A Descriptive Bibliography 1933–1977,* by Lee Bartlett. New York: Garland, 1979.
*Karl Shapiro,* by Joseph Reino. Boston: Twayne, 1981.


GARY SOTO

*The Elements of San Joaquin.* Pittsburgh: University of Pittsburgh Press, 1977.
*The Tale of Sunlight.* Pittsburgh: University of Pittsburgh Press, 1978.
*Where Sparrows Work Hard.* Pittsburgh: University of Pittsburgh Press, 1981.
*Black Hair.* Pittsburgh: University of Pittsburgh Press, 1985.
*A Fire in My Hands.* New York: Scholastic. 1990.
*Who Will Know Us?* San Francisco: Chronicle Books, 1990.
*Home Course in Religion.* San Francisco: Chronicle Books, 1991.

*Living Up the Street.* San Francisco: Strawberry Hill Press, 1985.
*Small Faces.* Houston: Arte Publico/University of Houston, 1986.
*Lesser Evils: Ten Quartets.* Houston: Arte Publico/University of Houston, 1988.
*A Summer Life.* Hanover, NH: University Press of New England, 1990.
*Baseball in April and Other Stories.* New York: Harcourt Brace Jovanovich, 1990.


CHARLES WRIGHT

*The Grave of the Right Hand.* Middletown, CT: Wesleyan University Press, 1970.
*Hard Freight.* Middletown, CT: Wesleyan University Press, 1973.
*Bloodlines.* Middletown, CT: Wesleyan University Press, 1975.
*China Trace.* Middletown, CT: Wesleyan University Press, 1977.
*The Southern Cross.* New York: Random House, 1981.
*Country Music: Selected Early Poems.* Middletown, CT: Wesleyan University Press, 1982.

*Zone Journals*. New York: Farrar, Straus & Giroux, 1988.
*The World of the Ten Thousand Things: Poems 1980–1990*. New York: Farrar, Straus & Giroux, 1990.

*Halflife: Improvisations and Interviews, 1977–87*. Ann Arbor: University of Michigan Press, 1988.

*The Storm and Other Things*, by Eugenio Montale. Tr. by Charles Wright. Oberlin, OH: Field Editions, 1978.
*Orphic Songs*, by Dino Campana. Tr. by Charles Wright. Oberlin, OH: Field Editions, 1984.

# AUDIOGRAPHY

## BACKGROUND

*The Poet's Voice.* Readings by 13 modern poets at Harvard from 1933 to 1970: Ezra Pound, T. S. Eliot, Marianne Moore, William Carlos Williams, Wallace Stevens, Robert Frost, W. H. Auden, Robinson Jeffers, Theodore Roethke, Randall Jarrell, John Berryman, Robert Lowell, Sylvia Plath. Poets reading aloud and commenting upon their works. Cambridge: Harvard University Press, 1978. Six cassettes.

*The Jack Kerouac Collection.* Produced by James Austin. Baker & Taylor (501 S. Gladiolus, Momence, IL 60954), 1990. Forty page booklet. Three cassettes, 143 minutes, #6730173193X, or three compact discs, #6301730275.

*Poetic Forms.* Ten conversational programs for students (age 14 or so) about Free Verse, Haiku, The Ode, The List, The Sonnet, The Prose Poem, The Villanelle, The Ballad, The Acrostic, and The Blues Poems. Teachers & Writers Collaborative (5 Union Square West, New York, NY 10003), 1988. Five cassettes, 60 minutes each, #0-915924-25-0.

## A. R. AMMONS

*A.R. Ammons.* New Letters Award Series. New Letters on Air, 1984. Cassette, 29 minutes, #022484.

## JOHN ASHBERY

*John Ashbery.* New Letters Award Series. New Letters on Air, 1986. Cassette, 29 minutes, #092686.

*John Ashbery: What Is Poetry?* John Ashbery is interviewed by Liz Dribben. He answers her questions about the New York School of Poetry and reads his poem, "What Is Poetry." Vital History Cassettes. New York: Encyclopedia Americana/CBS News Audio Resource Library, 1978. Cassette, 18 minute segment.

*The Poetry of John Ashbery.* Read by author. YM-YWHA Poetry Center Series. Audio-Forum, 1967. Cassette, 39 minutes, #23157.

*Songs We Know Best.* Selected poems read by author. Watershed Tapes, 1989. Cassette, 60 minutes.

in *The Spoken Arts Treasury of 100 Modern American Poets Reading Their Poems, Volume 17.* Four poems: "Thoughts of a Young Girl," "A Last World," "They Dream Only of America," and "Some Trees." Spoken Arts, 1985. Cassette, 8 minute segment.

## GWENDOLYN BROOKS

*Gwendolyn Brooks I.* New Letters Award Series. New Letters on Air, 1980. Cassette, 29 minutes, #110488.

*Gwendolyn Brooks II.* New Letters Award Series. New Letters on Air, 1990. Cassette, 29 minutes, #020689.

*Gwendolyn Brooks Reading Her Poetry.* Harper Audio, 1969. Cassette, 60 minutes, (SWC 1244, Caedmon).

## RITA DOVE

*Rita Dove.* New Letters Award Series. New Letters on Air, 1985. Cassette, 29 minutes, #080985.

## ALLEN GINSBERG

*Allen Ginsberg.* New Letters Award Series. New Letters on Air, 1988. Cassette, 29 minutes, #040188.

*Allen Ginsberg and Anne Waldman: Beauty and the Beast.* Allen Ginsberg reads his poem "Howl" on side one and Anne Waldman reads "Fast Talking Woman" and other poems on side two—from their 1975 public performance at the Naropa Institute in Boulder, Colorado. Encore Series. Watershed Tapes, 1990. Cassette, 53 minutes.

in *The Spoken Arts Treasury of American Jewish Poets, Volume 6.* Spoken Arts, 1981. #SAC1150.

## MAXINE KUMIN

*Maxine Kumin I.* New Letters Award Series. New Letters on Air, 1980. Cassette, 29 minutes, #050580.

*Maxine Kumin II.* New Letters Award Series. New Letters on Air, 1987. Cassette, 29 minutes, #122587.

*Progress Report.* Selected poems read by author. Signature Series. Watershed Tapes, 1977. Cassette, 42 minutes.

## JAMES MERRILL

*Reflected Houses.* Selected poems read by author. Watershed Tapes, 1988. Cassette, 60 minutes.

## W. S. MERWIN

*W. S. Merwin.* New Letters Award Series. New Letters on Air, 1979. Cassette, 29 minutes, #051279.

*W. S. Merwin Reading His Poetry.* Harper Audio, 1970. Cassette, 60 minutes (SWC 1295, Caedmon).

## SHARON OLDS

*Coming Back to Life.* Selected poems read by author. Signature Series. Watershed Tapes, 1985. Cassette, 60 minutes.

## ADRIENNE RICH

*Planetarium: A Retrospective 1950–1980.* Signature Series. Watershed Tapes, 1986. Cassette, 63 minutes.

*The Poetry of Adrienne Rich.* Read by author. YM-YWHA Poetry Center Series. Audio-Forum, 1968. Cassette, 36 minutes, #23203.

*Tracking the Contradictions: Poems 1981–1985.* Signature Series. Watershed Tapes, 1986. Cassette, 55 minutes.

in *The Spoken Arts Treasury of 100 Modern American Poets Reading Their Poems, Volume 17.* Five poems: "Peeling Onions," Ghost of a Chance," The Roof Walker," "Mourning Picture," and "In the Woods." Spoken Arts, 1985. Cassette, 8 minute segment.

## KARL SHAPIRO

in *The Spoken Arts Treasury of 100 Modern American Poets Reading Their Poems, Volume 11.* Three poems: "The Figurehead," "Love for a Hand," and "Adam and Eve." Spoken Arts, 1985. Cassette, 9 minute segment.

in *The Spoken Arts Treasury of American Jewish Poets, Volume 2.* Spoken Arts, 1981. #SAC1145.

## GARY SOTO

No recordings, other than those made for "Poets in Person," are known to be available at this time.

## CHARLES WRIGHT

*The Tongue Is a White Water.* Selected poems read by author. Signature Series. Watershed Tapes, 1985. Cassette, 62 minutes.

## TAPES ARE AVAILABLE FROM

Audio-Forum, 96 Broad St., Guilford, CT 06437.

Harper Audio, Keystone Industrial Park, Scranton, PA 18512.

New Letters Award Series is a collection of radio programs with winners of National Book or Pulitzer Prize Awards. Authors talk about and read their work. Produced by New Letters on Air, 5100 Rockhill, Kansas City, MO 64110.

Spoken Arts, Inc., 310 North Avenue, New Rochelle, NY 10801.

Watershed Tapes, 6925 Willow St. N.W., Washington, DC 20012.

*List compiled by Joseph F. Keppler*

# ACKNOWLEDGEMENTS

A. R. Ammons: "Poetics," "Gravelly Run," "Eyesight," "Hymn," from *The Selected Poems: 1951–1977*. Copyright © 1977, 1975, 1974, 1972, 1971, 1970, 1966, 1965, 1964, 1955 by A. R. Ammons. "The Dwelling" from *Sumerian Vistas: Poems*. Copyright © 1987 by A. R. Ammons. Reprinted by permission of the author and W. W. Norton & Company, Inc.

John Ashbery: "Someone You Have Seen Before, " from *April Galleons*, by John Ashbery. Copyright © 1984, 1985, 1986, 1987 by John Ashbery. Used by permission of Viking Penguin, a division of Penguin Books USA Inc. "The Lonedale Operator" from *A Wave*, by John Ashbery (New York: Viking, 1984). Copyright © 1980, 1981, 1982, 1983, 1984 by John Ashbery. Reprinted by permission of Georges Borchardt, Inc. and the author.

Gwendolyn Brooks: "kitchenette building," "The Bean Eaters," "We Real Cool," "To the Young Who Want To Die," and sections from "The Children of the Poor," "The Life of Lincoln West," and "Winnie," © by author Gwendolyn Brooks. © copyright by The David Company, Chicago. Used by permission of the author.

Rita Dove: "Flash Cards" and "Crab Boil" from *Grace Notes*, poems by Rita Dove, W. W. Norton, New York; copyright 1989 by Rita Dove. "David Walker (1785–1830)" and "Geometry" from *The Yellow House on the Corner*, poems by Rita Dove, Carnegie-Mellon University Press, Pittsburgh; copyright 1980 by Rita Dove. "Wingfoot Lake" from *Thomas and Beulah*, poems by Rita Dove, Carnegie-Mellon University Press, Pittsburgh; copyright 1986 by Rita Dove. "Parsley" from *Museum*, poems by Rita Dove, Carnegie-Mellon University Press, Pittsburgh; copyright 1983 by Rita Dove. All poems used by permission of the author.

Allen Ginsberg: " 'You Might Get in Trouble,' " "After Whitman & Reznikoff," and sections from "Howl" and "Wichita Vortex Sutra" from *Collected Poems 1947–1980*, by Allen Ginsberg. Copyright © 1984 by Allen Ginsberg. Used by permission of HarperCollins Publishers.

Maxine Kumin: "Our Ground Time Here Will Be Brief," copyright © 1979 by Maxine Kumin, from *Our Ground Time Here Will Be Brief*, by Maxine Kumin. "How It Is," copyright © 1975 Maxine Kumin; "How It Goes On," copyright © 1978 by Maxine Kumin; and "The Envelope," copyright © 1978 by Maxine Kumin, from *The Retrieval System*, by Maxine Kumin. "Life's Work," copyright © 1972 by Maxine Kumin, from *House, Bridge, Fountain, Gate*, by Maxine Kumin. All used by permission of Viking Penguin, a division of Penguin Books USA Inc.

James Merrill: "Manos Karastefanís" from *Divine Comedies*. Copyright © 1976 by James Merrill. "The Broken Home" from *Nights and Days*. Copyright © 1960,

1961, 1962, 1963, 1964, 1965, 1966 by James Merrill. "Channel 13" from *Late Settings*. Copyright © 1985 by James Merrill. From "The Ballroom at Sandover" from *The Changing Light at Sandover*. Copyright © 1960, 1961, 1962, 1963, 1964, 1965, 1966, 1976, 1980, 1981, 1982 by James Merrill. Used by permission of the author.

W. S. Merwin: "Berryman" from *Opening the Hand*. © 1983 by W. S. Merwin. "The Gods," "For the Anniversary of My Death" from *The Lice*. © 1963, 1964, 1965, 1966, 1967 by W. S. Merwin. "St Vincent's" from *The Compass Flower*. © 1977 by W. S. Merwin. "The Removal," "The Night of the Shirts" from *The Carrier of Ladders*. © 1967, 1968, 1969, 1970 by W. S. Merwin. "Bread" from *Writings to an Unfinished Accompaniment*. © 1969, 1970, 1971, 1972, 1973 by W. S. Merwin. Used by permission of Georges Borchardt, Inc.

Sharon Olds: "The Language of the Brag," "The Mother, " "Young Mothers I" from *Satan Says*. Copyright © 1980, Sharon Olds. "The Guild" from *The Dead and the Living*. Copyright © 1975, 1978, 1979, 1980, 1981, 1982, 1983 by Sharon Olds. "Summer Solstice, New York City," "Topography" from *The Gold Cell*. Copyright 1987 by Sharon Olds. All used by permission of the author.

Adrienne Rich: "Storm Warnings" from *Poems Selected and New, 1950–1974*. Copyright © 1975, 1973, 1971, 1969, 1966 by W. W. Norton & Company, Inc. Copyright © 1967, 1963, 1962, 1961, 1960, 1959, 1958, 1957, 1956, 1955, 1954, 1953, 1952, 1951 by Adrienne Rich. "Baltimore: a fragment from the Thirties" from *Your Native Land, Your Life*. Copyright © 1986 by Adrienne Rich. "Planetarium" from *The Will To Change*. Copyright © 1971 by W. W. Norton. "Cartographies of Silence" from *The Dream of a Common Language*. Copyright © 1978 by W. W. Norton. "Delta" from *Time's Power*. Copyright © 1989 by Adrienne Rich. Used by permission of the author.

Karl Shapiro: "University," "Full Moon in New Guinea," "The Progress of Faust," "Nebraska," and "The Alphabet" from *Collected Poems*. Copyright 1940, 1941, 1942, 1943, 1944, 1945, 1946, 1947, 1948, 1949, 1950, 1951, 1952, 1953, 1954, © 1956, 1957, 1958, 1961, 1962, 1963, 1964, 1966, 1967, 1968, 1969, 1970, 1972, 1973, 1974, 1975, 1976, 1978 by Karl Shapiro. Copyright renewed 1968, 1969, 1970, 1971, 1972, 1973, 1974, 1975 by Karl Shapiro. Used by permission of the author.

Gary Soto: "Black Hair" reprinted from *Black Hair*, by Gary Soto, by permission of the University of Pittsburgh Press. © 1985 by Gary Soto. "Field Poem" reprinted from *The Elements of San Joaquin*, by Gary Soto, by permission of the University of Pittsburgh Press. © 1977 by Gary Soto. "The Philosophy of Dog and Man," from *Who Will Know Us?* by Gary Soto. Copyright © 1990. Published by Chronicle Books. "Looking Around, Believing," "The Plum's Heart," "Failing in the Presence of Ants" from *Black Hair*. Copyright 1982, 1983, 1984 by the Modern Poetry Association. "Mexicans Begin Jogging," "TV in Black and White" from *Where Sparrows Work Hard*. Copyright 1981, Gary Soto. Reprinted by permission of the author. "TV in Black and White" first appeared in *The Missouri Review*.

Charles Wright: "Reunion" © 1976 by Charles Wright. "Clear Night" © 1977 by Charles Wright, originally printed in *The New Yorker*. "Tattoos" © 1975 by Charles Wright. All used by permission of Wesleyan University Press. Selections from *The World of the Ten Thousand Things*, by Charles Wright. Copyright © 1990 by Charles Wright. Reprinted by permission of Farrar, Straus & Giroux, Inc.